Praise for
Riding the Outlaw Trail

"A record of a courageous quest – absolutely gripping"
Daily Mail

"The account of duplicating Butch Cassidy and the Sundance Kid
makes a bumptious and entertaining adventure story. Not Paul
Newman and Robert Redford but wonderful chroniclers of the
sights, sounds and feelings of that grand, harsh country."
Time Magazine

"A fast read, a compelling story"
The New Mexico Magazine (USA)

"A glorious story, part adventure, part history, full of marvellous
characters and amusing episodes. An outstanding book.
Highly recommended."
Douglas Preston, author of *Cities of Gold*

"An interesting read. One heck of a ride, an accomplishment – it
made me think more of what Butch went through."
Bill Betenson, great-great nephew of Butch Cassidy

"An intriguing adventure that Butch and Sundance
fans will surely enjoy."
Richard Patterson, author of *Butch Cassidy – A Biography*

"A fast-paced read into the history of Butch and Sundance.
Experience unforgiving wilderness, along with the challenges
of mounting such an epic."
Richard Dunwoody MBE

"A delightfully revealing mix of candour and humour – a first-rate
read of a frequently treacherous trek."
Journal of the Western Outlaw-Lawman Association (USA)

"A highly enjoyable read"
Kirkus Reviews UK

RIDING THE OUTLAW TRAIL

IN THE FOOTSTEPS OF BUTCH CASSIDY & THE SUNDANCE KID

by SIMON CASSON & RICHARD ADAMSON

eye books

Challenging the way we see things

This Eye Classics edition first published in Great Britain in 2011, by:
Eye Books
7 Peacock Yard
Iliffe Street
London
SE17 3LH
www.eye-books.com

First published in Great Britain in 2004

Cover design by Emily Atkins/Jim Shannon
Text layout by Helen Steer

British Library Cataloguing in Publication Data
A catalogue record for this book is available from the British Library.

The paperback edition of this book is printed in Poland.

ISBN: 978-1-903070-65-9

To Butch & Sundance for existing, Richard Adamson for his excellent leadership, A.C. Ekker for starting this grand adventure and Gene Vieh for making THE connection…

RICHARD ADAMSON

Sadly, whilst heading operations for security company ArmorGroup, Richard was murdered in a robbery in Kabul, Afghanistan on August 16, 2007. Richard's CV would make James Bond envious. Tasked by Margaret Thatcher to lead secret teams training Afghans in the use of stinger missiles, (credited in turning the course of the war against the Russians), he returned to Kabul in 2001. Richard opened ex-pat bar Elbow Room and took a partnership in Samarkand, a club. His working knowledge of the people, culture and languages was vital. He was recognized as a true friend of Afghanistan.

A.C. EKKER

A.C. personified the American cowboy. He knew the Robbers Roost country like the back of his hand. His grandparents homesteaded the famous ranch over a century ago – great grandfather was Charlie Gibbons, friend and employer of Butch Cassidy, who hid out at the Roost and did business with Gibbons at his store in Hanksville. Tragically, on November 17, 2000, A.C. died crashing his plane searching for stray cattle on the final round-up. In the toughest tradition of the Old West, he died with his boots on.

GENE VIEH

A big 'tip of the hat' to Gene, who passed in April 2008, he was instrumental in connecting me to his cousin Dr Joe Armstrong, who assisted the Swedes in the attempt to ride the trail. Without that connection and knowledge brought, our quest would have been higher risk, with stronger likelihood of failure. Gene introduced me to many ranchers, land-owners and families that were supportive of our challenge.

Contents

"Riders who passed along that trail were men of iron, accustomed to the roughest sort of life, able to ride all day and night without rest over dry deserts and through dangerous canyons. When required, endurance and courage were paramount – those who lacked either were quickly eliminated."

Charles Kelly
The Outlaw Trail: A History of Butch Cassidy and His Wild Bunch. New York, 1959

FOREWORD

To ride the length of America on horseback is a reasonably serious business. But why do it the hard way: across vast deserts, mountains, and high plains wilderness, at the height of a hot, dry Western summer and without back-up?

A century ago it could only have been to evade the law, remain at liberty and enjoy ill-gotten gains, which is presumably what motivated the outlaws of the Old West.

But to face all the same hazards and hardships when you don't have to, as Simon Casson and Richard Adamson did, can only be because – despite being men in their middle years – they were driven by an irresistible spirit of adventure, a laudable condition in a material age.

They had a tough trip, and they write with candour and humour about their moments of frustration, fear, exhaustion, self-indulgence and deep satisfaction. They learned a lot about horseback expeditions, but even more about themselves.

After reading their gripping account you may well find yourself digging out and dusting off your own long-forgotten dream of adventure. If so I hope you will go for it, as they did.

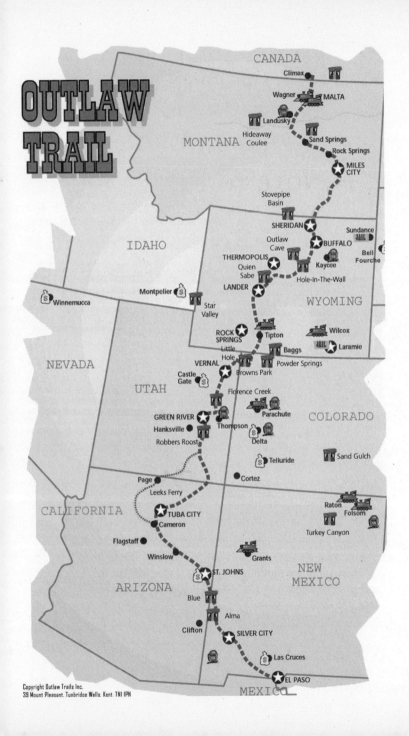

OUTLAW TRAIL

CANADA

Climax

Wagner MALTA

Landusky

MONTANA Hideaway
Coulee Sand Springs

Rock Springs

MILES
CITY

Stovepipe
Basin

IDAHO SHERIDAN Sundance

Outlaw BUFFALO
Cave Bell
THERMOPOLIS Fourche
Quien Kaycee
Sabe Hole-In-The-Wall
LANDER

Montpelier WYOMING

Winnemucca Star
Valley

ROCK Tipton Wilcox
SPRINGS Laramie
Little Baggs
Hole Powder Springs
VERNAL Browns Park
Castle
Gate Florence Creek
UTAH Parachute COLORADO
GREEN RIVER
Hanksville Thompson
Robbers Roost Delta
Sand Gulch
Telluride

Page Cortez
Leeks Ferry
CALIFORNIA Raton
Folsom
TUBA CITY
Cameron Turkey Canyon
Flagstaff
Winslow Grants
ST. JOHNS NEW
MEXICO
Blue
ARIZONA
Alma
Clifton SILVER CITY
Las Cruces
EL PASO
MEXICO

A NOTE TO THE READER

No one who relished every second of George Roy Hill's brilliant and now cult 1969 movie *Butch Cassidy and the Sundance Kid* can be surprised to learn that the real life Butch and Sundance made a lasting impression on everyone they met. Leaving no diaries or personal accounts, they wrote few letters, but managed to write themselves handsomely into the history books and the legends – and they are still writing.

We know that Robert LeRoy Parker, alias Butch Cassidy, and Harry Alonzo Longabaugh, the Sundance Kid, were something special. Both were respected by most who knew them, and had been born to caring families in the West and East respectively.

Both were restless youths who left home early, eventually meeting to discover a shared love of adventure and a cheerful disregard for the law.

All written and oral records confirm that talented screenwriter William Goldman and megastar actors Paul Newman and Robert Redford got the basic characters just about right: Butch was affable, good-humoured and intelligent while Sundance, warier but still friendly, was the quieter of the two – though he liked sharp suits and monogrammed clothing. Both were criminals rather than killers. Indeed some historians believe that right up to the final shoot-out in Bolivia neither Butch nor Sundance had blood on their hands. If true this is likely to have been a matter of sheer efficiency rather than conscience – for years they were clearly happy to ride and rob with some very desperate and bloody men.

What is certainly true is that Butch and Sundance were

consummate professionals at their craft, undoubtedly the best in their business in every way: longer active careers, more sophisticated planning, higher success rates, less prison time and greater financial returns for a given investment of risk. However, as law enforcement entered the telegraph age and the frontier finally closed in 1900, they were smart enough to know the game was up. They moved to South America and tried to go straight. Sadly, their best-laid plans didn't quite work out.

But this book concentrates on their travels and exploits in the American West. It describes a daunting – maybe insane would be a better word – journey by two Englishmen who followed the Outlaw Trail on horseback across two thousand miles of desert, mountain, canyon and high plains wilderness, from Mexico to Canada via New Mexico, Arizona, Utah, Colorado, Wyoming and Montana.

With 20-20 hindsight it is remarkable if not ridiculous that we undertook this demanding trip with no previous experience of long distance riding or horse-packing. We were absolutely determined to study at first hand the most physically challenging – and in research terms the most neglected – aspects of a hard, violent but heroic, action-packed era. We would ride, as nearly as possible exactly as they did, the almost inaccessible trails that linked the robberies, escapes and hideouts of the two most elusive and successful outlaws of the Wild West.

Where we went and what we experienced we have recorded faithfully and placed in their proper (and sometimes improper) historical context, which in turn is as accurate as five years careful prior research could make it. As well as our adventures and the many colourful characters we met, we have described baldly the life-threatening hazards, hopes and fears, tensions and often angry dissentions and confrontations of riding the Outlaw Trail, whether then or now.

Enjoy the read.

Simon Casson
&
Richard Adamson

A Hundred Years Too Late

"I got vision and the rest of the world wears bifocals."
BUTCH CASSIDY

SIMON:

The classic blockbuster 'buddy' movie almost certainly ensured that Butch Cassidy and the Sundance Kid will remain immortal. Remember the second train-robbing sequence which opens with Sundance moving cat-like along the tops of the swaying carriages just prior to the holdup? At its climax is a cataclysmic dynamite explosion when half the railroad car is blown sky high and thousands of dollar bills come fluttering down out of the sky through the still quivering air. The gang's instinctive reaction to this unplanned development is to dart about, greedily gathering up the falling greenbacks like manna from heaven.

Then we see another, much shorter train approach and stop very close by. A brief pause for surprise and speculation, then a whistle blows, a huge wooden ramp crashes down and out of the sinister train rides the handpicked 'Super-Posse', armed to the teeth and led by legendary lawman Joe Lefors in his trademark straw boater. Newman, as Butch, says urgently:

"Whatever they're selling, I don't want it."

But I did.

Family history gave me the perfect excuse to pursue my love affair with the West. My father's family is connected with Stonewall Jackson, the famous Civil War Confederate General. My mother's is connected with James Wolfe, hero of Quebec – of whom King George II famously said, "If Wolfe is mad, I wish he would bite some other of my Generals." When I was young, this somehow didn't seem quite as glamorous as Butch and Sundance's bloodlines, but it was close.

From the age of six I did, of course, possess a cowboy outfit complete with hat, chaps, boots, neckerchief and six-guns, and I ran wild in the neighbourhood chasing imaginary Indians and pop-popping my guns.

But the story of our ride really began quite unconsciously in a secondhand bookshop when I first laid hands on a copy of Robert Redford's *Outlaw Trail*. Glossy pictures and a fast-reading script sold me on the quest of one of Hollywood's finest to seek the Outlaw Trail and learn about the Sundance Kid. I forked out my last seven quid and departed. It was a great read, but the subject matter then remained dormant until the summer of 1994.

We were vacationing in Arizona. The Grand Canyon was awesome and Monument Valley spellbinding. Tombstone, billed as 'the town too tough to die,' ignited the real flame of interest. Whose imagination would not run wild on the stomping ground of the legendary Wyatt Earp, his brothers and their deadly dentist friend Doc Holliday? As we walked through the OK Corral, my partner Julie suddenly announced her ideal holiday for next year: a Western dude ranch experience. A deal was struck there and then.

There was one problem. All the ranching brochures were offering soft adventure – I badly wanted risk, blended with history. That winter, on impulse, I tracked down the same people who had outfitted Robert Redford and *National Geographic* all those years before. In minutes, I was speaking to Glori Ekker, the wife of a highly regarded outfitter. I put the vital question:

"Do you still outfit horse trips in the Canyonlands?"

"Sure. AC operates maybe two a year. We'll mail you information."

Their brochure promised a fascinating trip, and I made arrangements for a five-day ride in mid-September. It was as easy as that.

So September found us driving deep into southeast Utah to a remote outpost called Hanksville, little changed from Redford's descriptions.

The gas station still functioned in the town centre. Opposite, a restaurant-campsite was the jump-off for tourists heading for Lake Powell. Our hotel, The Whispering Sands, even had a pet bison.

I rang the Ekkers, left a message and sat back to wait for the rendezvous. The phone woke us from slumber at six the next morning, and AC announced he would collect us within the hour. Sure enough, a huge truck, all V8 muscle, drove up and shut down, and out stepped AC. Medium height, swarthy, late forties, decked out in rodeo Wranglers and the mandatory weather-beaten black Stetson, he wore a toothpick in the corner of his mouth. The quintessential cowboy. Grinning, he shook hands firmly.

There were just the three of us. We trailer-hauled the horses sixty-five miles across remote country. There were no signposts or phone boxes, no anything, just a red, dusty track leading to the infamous Robbers Roost. If you broke down here, you were dead. Two hours later, the old stucco ranch hove into view. I recognised the tack store and weathered corrals shown in Redford's book. It was heartening to find little had altered. The ancient bunkhouse was still there too. Gnarled cedars were split and twisted by the brutal elements. Time seemed to have stood still around here since 1909.

We saddled up and headed off into Utah's forbidding canyon country to find the West that was. It was challenging riding. We rode our horses into places you would never think possible. Butch and Sundance had undoubtedly been the boldest (and smartest) of outlaws to ride into this beautiful but broken and hostile country, with its untamed myriad of interlocking red rock canyons, pinnacles, spires and mesas shrouding secret caverns, watering holes and grazing pastures.

AC generously shared his vast range of knowledge, history and anecdotes of the Roost whilst my camera struggled to capture the stunning scenery. It was awesome. Fabulously hot blue-sky days merged into bitterly cold nights, and the five days flew past. When it was time to leave, I was sad, but I had enjoyed my first taste of riding the trail, and I felt the early stirrings of an idea which was not yet fully formed.

Once home, I found myself becoming obsessed with those remarkable outlaw riders. I returned to America five times, travelling and researching Butch and Sundance just for fun, eventually clocking up an incredible 15,000 miles. During autumn 1996, I learned that two Swedes had ridden much of the Outlaw Trail, from Las Cruces, New Mexico to Miles City, Montana. It was a tough ride, but it didn't go all the way. Rancher Gene Vieh informed me that his cousin Dr Joe Armstrong, an equine and agriculture professor from Las Cruces, had outfitted the Swedish duo four years earlier – a casual comment which later proved highly significant.

In between my American trips I consulted everyone I could think of in the UK who might be willing to give me the benefit of some straight talking from their own firsthand experience. I talked to blonde, blunt Ruth Taggart and her partner Nigel Harvey of British riding specialists Ride World Wide in London. I telephoned Robin Hanbury-Tenison OBE, FRGS, a renowned British explorer and long rider of four major equine expeditions. Robin said he had no useful contacts in America, but advised me to ring Dylan Winter, who had ridden the Oregon Trail. Later, I had a really valuable session with Dylan at his Buckinghamshire base. I contacted equine explorer James Greenwood, recently back from completing the arduous Argentina to Peru section of AF Tschiffely's famous ride. I rang to congratulate him, and to glean advice.

To each of these experts, I outlined what somewhere along the line had crystallised into a firm objective: to be the first man to ride Butch Cassidy's Outlaw Trail from Mexico to Canada on horseback. Without exception, they were friendly and helpful. Basically, however, they were all singing from the same hymn sheet, and between them they made me face up to some unwelcome realities.

First, they scared the shit out of me with their rough cost estimates for what I had in mind – they were talking telephone numbers, way beyond my reach. Then they pointed out politely but brutally that I had neither the expertise nor the resources to tackle the projected trip on my own. They also severely disillusioned me about the prospects for some easy sponsorship money. Finally, they urged me to find someone else who was also planning a horseback expedition, and try to persuade them to join forces. Bloody but unbowed, I continued to develop my plans; though I was no longer sure they would ever come to fruition.

I joined the English Westerners Society and the Outlaw Trail History Association through which I made contact with respected former Spokane journalist Jim Dullenty, responsible for monumental research on Butch Cassidy and now an Americana book dealer. He was a founding member of the Western Outlaw-Lawman History Association (WOLA) in America, which comprises key historians and writers, including leading authorities on Butch, Sundance and the Wild Bunch. This association also led me to the outlaws' families and living descendants

I bought literally dozens of history books, whilst Jim provided added inspiration and contacts. He confirmed that nobody had authentically ridden the full length of the Outlaw Trail on horseback from Mexico to Canada. It would be a first – if I made it. I set about planning how to ride the trail, keeping one eye always on the possibility of spinning off a new business venture from all this present and projected effort.

To have real value, the project would have to replicate Butch and Sundance's travels with precise historical accuracy. I spent hours poring over maps pinpointing the Outlaw Trail's ghostly traces. It would be a massive task. I was no explorer or long distance rider, and certainly not a horse-packer, but I believed in myself. Others had misgivings, which I ignored. Riding a horse was like riding a bike, I told myself. Once done, you never forget how. The doubters and pessimists bluntly informed me I was out of shape, out of order and out of my mind. We would see.

I was getting more apprehensive by the day but continued to throw myself into the planning. Prudently, I wrote to ranchers and landowners for permission to cross their private land, so that my route could follow faithfully the faded trail from Mexico to Canada. I was greatly encouraged to receive a thumbs-up every time. These were kind folks, proud of their heritage, and it was clear that they really cared. They did, however, add to the mounting chorus of cautionary verses: did I *really* know what I was letting myself in for?

Oh yeah, of course I did. Well, sort of.

The fact is that Butch and Sundance had made some of the most demanding rides ever known, with the added pressure to outpace pursuit, avoid ambush and evade capture. The only way truly to understand their experiences and some of their risks was to share them, to travel the same barren desert and mountain country in exactly the same way: on horseback, with packhorses, carrying bare essentials only, finding grazing and water where and when I could and with no motorised back-up.

In those thinly populated regions, the Code of The West was important. It was the Westerner's offer of assistance to anyone in need without denial or question. A civil traveller weary or lost might expect the offer of a meal and rest. In exchange, the traveller might offer to do ranch chores or contribute financially. In Butch and Sundance's time, ranches were never locked and riders were welcome, provided they remained polite and respectful. If nobody was home, a long distance rider might well help himself, taking only what was needed for immediate use. If a man was afoot, he could procure a horse – later, he was expected to return it.

The spirit of that Code held true today, with the important addition that in an age of phones and emails, you were supposed to use them – or, better still, get your hosts to use them. Thus, a well-endorsed traveller can be passed like a parcel from household to household across the nation. So the outlaws and I would be riding the same trails in much the same conditions – apart from the fact that I was starting a hundred years too late.

I constantly debated with myself whether to continue or quit. Was it possible that so many respected authorities could be overly pessimistic? Or was it conceivable that, like Butch, I had vision and the rest of the world was wearing bifocals? Each time I confronted it (not more than ten times a day), the decision felt like twisting on nineteen when your option is to pay twenty-ones. Each time, I assessed the unattractive odds realistically. Then I twisted anyway.

Russian Ride was interesting. It told the story of a woman's 2,500 mile trek across Russia with Cossack horses. I wrote to Barbara Whittome's publisher seeking her ideas and help. Well, why not? So far these explorers had all proved to be both approachable and helpful. Weeks later, a reply indicated that Barbara was planning to ride across Europe.

On the phone she sounded bright, ever-so-English, confident, even slightly bossy – just a hint, perhaps, of the voice that lost us the Empire.

"Join me for a couple of weeks in Hungary. See what you're in for. I'm selling places to help fund the ride. My Russian trip cost a fortune."

Shrewd lady! I admired her approach, but I wasn't buying.

"I'm interested, so let's talk horses," I replied.

We met, and discussions were fruitful. Barbara hoped that I might join and subsidise her trip. Similar thoughts were crossing my mind. We agreed to correspond. As time passed, zilch happened. My major concern was not to be pre-empted on the Butch and Sundance project. Barbara eventually rang to tell me her journey was off. I cheekily suggested that we should team up for my trip, and after some more chat she accepted. Success! I maybe couldn't ride like these horseback explorers, but I hadn't entirely lost my touch – my plan was gradually coming together.

In 1998, I spent a glorious three weeks in Texas, then snuck into La Mesa, New Mexico to meet the Armstrongs. Joe and Rusty confirmed their willingness to help, advise and outfit the expedition. Timing was set for spring 1999.

One snag: Barbara seemed to know her stuff, and I certainly knew mine, but neither of us was checked out on mountain and desert survival. Barbara suggested we invite Richard Adamson to join us. Richard was described as an ex-Royal Marine Commando with impeccable credentials, presently in East Africa. Despite being nervous about someone else coming on board, it sounded logical. Besides, the three of us would neatly replicate the movie trio: the new Butch Cassidy, Sundance Kid and Etta Place. I record it a bit red-faced, but that unbelievably soppy reasoning was probably the clincher. I agreed.

No hint came from Richard about whether or not he would accept our offer. The sands of time were dribbling away, and I got mighty nervous. I was committed, and I continued methodically with arrangements. I also wrote endless letters in search of sponsorship. As predicted, I failed, and we were forced to self-fund. Groan! I even invited Robert Redford to join us. Politely, or wisely, he declined the offer.

Redford had waxed lyrical: "The Outlaw Trail fascinated me – a geographical anchor in Western folklore. Whether real or imagined, it was a phrase that for me held a kind of magic, a freedom, a mystery."

I knew it was real and I was ready to endure, a century after Butch and Sundance were at their peak and thirty years since the runaway success of the Hill and Goldman movie. And I would complete the mission playing strictly by my self-imposed rules. My main reward would be to get a unique gut-feel for the outlaw way of life, but I would also be retaking control of my own life. Freed of petty restrictions, I would become an accomplished horseman and I would ride back into the past, Winchester strapped to my saddle, determining the distinction between right and wrong and making my choices. Heady stuff.

Meanwhile, for months Richard had ignored all letters, emails, phone calls and messages. It seemed he would not be joining us. Then, at the eleventh hour, Barbara rang to tell me Richard had arrived unannounced for formalities and dinner in London. So I finally shook hands with a raw-boned, silver-haired, tanned and supremely fit ex-Marine Commando who had been permanently delayed in Somalia since October 1998.

RICHARD:

I had been working in Nairobi helping to set up an aviation service for the European Community Humanitarian Office. After establishing outstations in Kenya, Somalia and Djibouti I moved my base to Hargeysa in northern Somalia, as General Manager of Airbridge. This was a small regional airline, which we set up in partnership with Candy Logistics, and in which quite a lot of Somali money was invested.

I was aboard our plane minding my own business (which at that precise moment was to get the aircraft back to its native Ukraine for re-certification). Just prior to take-off, armed Somalis came on board, and the plane was commandeered and grounded. Along with the Ukrainian crew I was abruptly taken hostage at gunpoint.

It was fairly dramatic, and I had visions of a Keenan/McCarthy type incarceration in a dungeon, but within twenty-four hours I was allowed to take up residence in a Government hotel, albeit still under house arrest. It turned out that the Somali investors, dissatisfied with the progress made, were demanding the immediate return of their substantial investment. They had me snatched just in case I was doing a flit with all their loot. Chance would be a fine thing.

They then attempted to give their entirely improper behaviour some slight whiff of legality by bringing a civil action against Airbridge and *me* in the Courts, claiming that the contracts signed by both parties were not in fact contracts.

Farcical court procedures ensued which went on for two months. First the Regional Court found in our favour, then the Court of Appeal found against us, then the High Court of Appeal ruled. During this time Barbara persuaded me to join the Outlaw Trail expedition. I had no idea if and when I was going to be released.

Whilst Simon was trying to contact me, I was requesting meetings with the President of Somalia. We had met on many occasions, and he knew of my plight. He asked what he could do, since court procedure was slow, biased and expensive. I requested arbitration.

A committee was formed, but mysteriously all the members turned out to be related in some way to the plaintiffs, so it was no surprise whatsoever when they ruled our contract null and void. Airbridge was required to return 50% of the funding, plus six months running costs of the complete operation. Thus, my freedom cost $600,000. I left Hargeysa rapidly and spent Christmas and part of January in Zanzibar scuba diving with my sons Ben and Jamie.

I met Simon in London a month later and we had four hours together. I wasn't that impressed, and had reservations about our compatibility, but I was already committed. Ours was not a partnership based on prior knowledge and shared experience – it was a completely unknown quantity. On paper, we possessed the relevant and complementary skills for such an expedition, but we were very different people.

I'd spent many years in the Royal Marines, Barbara had been a lecturer and Simon was a dodgy ex-used car salesman with a bee in his bonnet. Barbara would manage the horses, Simon would be responsible for contacts, PR, photography and the historical side, and I would handle the logistics and assume ground leadership.

After dinner, I wanted to map out the expedition in detail. I provided six state maps. Decent topographical US Government Survey maps, I was assured, could easily be procured on arrival. Next, we discussed the trail. We were to traverse a strip of land nearly two-thirds the length of Chile and seemingly less than three-tenths of a mile wide. The first thousand miles were a vast desert. Water sources were scarce: springs, streams and cattle troughs. Depending how deep we rode into the Gila and Blue Wildernesses, there was also tricky mountain country to negotiate.

What concerned me most was the Canyonlands district in southeast Utah. The section we would be riding through was 527 square miles of pure wilderness. In the time of Butch and Sundance, it was inaccessible and seldom visited by the law; nothing much had changed. Beyond that, we had to negotiate the San Rafael Desert and the little-known Book Cliffs country. I predicted the maps would be devoid of markings, which always denotes a harsh, arid and trackless landscape. And we were thinking of riding horses through it.

Over coffee, we calculated the distance. Two thousand miles. Barbara estimated we could cover an easy twenty miles a day and the trip would take just over three months. Simon agreed. I was more cautious and measured the trail again. Then I suggested we think of scouting the lower end of the trail from Silver City south to the Mexican border. Simon protested there was no time.

"No. We'll have to ride like the outlaws and make out," he said, adding that, "this was no truck-and trailer-backed expedition."

"What about pre-dumping feed and supplies?" I asked.

Simon shook his head again.

"No way. This has to be *unsupported*. If we do it any other way, it's cheating. We've got to do it just as Butch and Sundance did – with packhorses, and whatever impromptu help is forthcoming from sympathetic locals."

The planned route Simon showed me would take us across six States, six Indian reservations, three National Forests, two Wildlife Refuges, a Primitive Wilderness area, a National Recreation area and a National Park. Not forgetting the deserts, of which I counted five. At least Simon had already written to friendly ranchers and outfitters checking on permission to access land.

"Now what about the authorities?" I asked. Simon deftly brushed the question aside:

"Joe's looked into all that. My contacts should be able to negotiate and advise on permits. If refused access we're in trouble, but we've still got to ride through whatever."

Simon seemed very positive, or was he just intending to wing it? We discussed private land issues. Again, it was impossible to discover who owned what. We would ride through regardless. If and when problems arose, I had already decided to rely on Simon's silver-tongued bullshit to extricate us.

Simon:

My last day in the rat race was 6 April 1999. I wondered if I would disappear permanently into the jaws of obscurity, or only momentarily. Commissioned to write a report for the *Travel Trade Gazette*, I hoped to be successful and have some interesting tales to tell.

One difficult duty remained: saying goodbye to my mother who was valiantly losing a seven year battle against cancer. Our hopes were to reunite on my return. Before leaving, I fought the demons, and during the goodbyes my sixth sense told me it might be the last time. I momentarily froze when Mum bade me good luck and instructed me to finish the ride whatever. That was the last time we saw one another. I stepped into the clear night. Our party was departing tomorrow – early.

My farewell to my father was again very difficult. We bear-hugged. Ill with worry, I fought back the tears. It was also to be the last evening with my patient, loving girlfriend Sharon for over five months.

Richard:

Simon seemed unusually quiet at the airport, while I found I had no worries. I had brightened at the prospect of the challenge. After the kidnap episode, I was off on another exploit and eager for it.

There was little luggage when we met at London Gatwick as I had kept an open mind on our requirements for the ride, intending to purchase most of the equipment in New Mexico. Obtaining goods on the dollar-to-pound ratio was advantageous, and also avoided paying enormous amounts in excess baggage, which would impinge on our slim budget.

As I sat back to quaff a coffee, the airport's tannoy system blared my name, calling me back to the check-in. British Airways wanted to remove an item from my baggage. They were unhappy with my stove – it showed remnants of fuel and was immediately deemed hazardous cargo. I was forced to leave it behind and actually never saw it again. Bugger! *And* it had interrupted my Burger King breakfast. The world's favourite airline lost some of its popularity. We had a few precious moments to say our last goodbyes, and then we lit out for a supreme adventure.

WILD BUNCH VERSUS SUPER-POSSE

"Who are those guys?"
BUTCH CASSIDY

SIMON:

The Wild Bunch was the largest, most dangerous, successful and organised outlaw gang in the history of the American West. They rode and robbed right up till 1912, when the last survivor Ben Kilpatrick was killed at Dryden, Texas in the last train hold-up conducted from horseback. When they died, the Old West died with them.

Today, Butch Cassidy and the Sundance Kid are renowned as a part of Western lore, but in their time, they were not noticeably romantic. Though they had many sympathizers, they were bad men who were badly wanted. Sheriffs, posses, US Marshals, the Union Pacific Railroad, the Pinkerton Detective Agency, freelance bounty hunters – literally scores of people were desperate to find them. That included the popular writers, whose colourful reports of their doings right up to the present day have seldom been understated.

Though Butch and Sundance are long dead and buried, the historians, researchers, authors and filmmakers are still actively chasing their last known whereabouts. If they are looking down at us today, apart from deploring the lack of progress – still too much corporate power and too many customer-unfriendly railways – they will surely be amused and gratified to be the objects of such interest. Painstaking research by dedicated historians has (mostly) separated myth from reality in the events of their lives, but many important questions still remain open.

What actually happened to Butch and Sundance? Did they really die in a shootout with the Bolivian cavalry, as depicted in the movie? Where are they buried? Did they return to America and assume new identities, as some relatives have claimed? Renowned historians continue to debate – sometimes hotly. Faint hopes still survive of some day unearthing their bones, thus providing the final solution to a great Western mystery.

And who named Butch and Sundance's "Wild Bunch?" Various outlaw gangs operated in the southwest during the late nineteenth century. Perhaps the survivors, the "best of the rest," evolved into a super-gang known as the Wild Bunch whose members came and went?

The "inner circle" were later labelled the Fort Worth Five. A famous picture taken in Fort Worth, Texas, in November 1900 by photographer John Swartz is now legendary. It shows Sundance, Ben Kilpatrick (the "Tall Texan") and Butch Cassidy seated, while standing behind are Will Carver and Harvey (Kid Curry) Logan.

Swartz was impressed with these five handsome dudes in their Sunday best when they came to visit him. They had gone mob-handed into expensive local stores and purchased entire new outfits, down to spats and derbies (or as we would say, bowlers). Apparently, the outlaws were headquartering locally in a rooming house – said to be a brothel – in Fort Worth's sporting district, where by day they rode bicycles and by night spent their gold recklessly on the resident "soiled doves."

The finished picture was prominently displayed in Swartz's studio window as a good advert for the business. It became the most famous photograph he took. It was also the gang's biggest mistake. Before long, the major law enforcement agencies were fighting for copies of what was the first really reliable guide to the visual identification of the gallant but vain band. It was almost certainly the direct cause of their splitting up and going to meet their destinies by different routes.

Butch Cassidy is born Robert LeRoy Parker on April 13, 1866, in the town of Beaver, Utah, of Mormon parents. He is the eldest of thirteen children to Maximilian and Ann Gillies Parker. Butch's origins are British. His namesake, his grandfather Robert Parker, born in Accrington, had been a weaver in Lancashire's textile industry.

The Parker family emigrates, walks (pushing a handcart) west and south to Salt Lake City, Utah and eventually settles at Beaver. Butch's parents meet and marry there in 1865. His father acquires a 160 acre property and a two-room cabin in Circleville, a small town comprising a few stores and a schoolhouse.

He first carries mail on horseback from Beaver to Panguitch through the rough, unsettled Circle Valley where Indians are a constant source of trouble. He also takes temporary employment with mining companies, and eventually buys a few head of cattle. It is a tough existence, and the winter of 1879 virtually wipes out the Parker herd, leading to legal disputes and an unjust settlement which impoverishes (and enrages!) the elder Parker.

Perhaps this unsuccessful family brush with authority has a lasting effect on young Robert. Now called Bob, he works for neighbouring farmer Jim Marshall, where he forms a solid friendship with a skilled livestock handler and horse wrangler named Mike Cassidy. Mike is everything Bob wants to be: tough, self-reliant, free as a bird, with itchy feet and sticky fingers. He uses the Marshall ranch as a cover for discreet rustling and mavericking, and it is virtually certain that Bob Parker drifts into crime under the Cassidy tutelage, perhaps leaving home (to his mother's anguish) initially to deliver a bunch of stolen horses to the infamous and remote Robbers Roost in southeast Utah.

Butch, still known as Bob Parker, surfaces next at Telluride, Colorado; a staging post on the pipeline for stolen livestock. There he makes a new friend who has exactly the same background as himself: raised in Utah by a Mormon family, ran away from home, cowboy turned part-time petty rustler. Matt Warner (real name Willard Christianson) has a fine mare named Betsy, which he races on the Colorado circuit. Their paths cross, Bob matches his horse against Matt's mare and loses, then the pair join forces and became partners in the horse business.

Later, Matt introduces Bob to his brother-in-law Tom McCarty.

Tom and his own brother Bill operate near Nephi and Manti, Utah, stealing horses, cutting cattle out of herds and selling to whoever will overlook doctored brands in Telluride. Now the McCartys have a cabin near Cortez, Colorado, only a mile from where Harry Longabaugh (later the Sundance Kid) lives for a spell with his cousin. Through the Warner-McCarty family connection, the future Butch Cassidy and the Sundance Kid may well meet as early as 1885.

Bob pulls his first bank job on June 24, 1889. The San Miguel Valley Bank is robbed of $20,750 – a huge sum of money, enough to retire on. The culprits are listed as Bob Parker, Matt Warner and Tom McCarty. Newspaper reports suggest the three robbers are assisted by another unidentified accomplice:

"The robbery of the San Miguel Valley Bank of Telluride, on Monday by four daring cowboys… the four rode over to the bank, and leaving their horses in the charge of one of their number, two remained on the side walk and the fourth entered the bank." Who was the fourth man? Some say it was the Sundance Kid.

The future Kid is born Harry Alonzo Longabaugh to Josiah and Annie Longabaugh in the spring of 1867, at Mont Clare, Philadelphia. Harry is the youngest of five children of a Baptist family which originated in Germany. Harry's father Josiah marries Annie G. Place on August 11, 1855 in Phoenixville, Pennsylvania. Josiah is a farm laborer who is drafted for the Civil War and moves frequently. By early 1880, Harry is not living with his family but is listed as a servant boarding with Wilmer Ralston in West Vincent, Pennsylvania. Ralston farms just ten miles from Harry's parents.

Harry reads the dime novels that take him West in search of adventure and joins his cousin George Longenbaugh (sic) with pregnant wife Mary at a homestead in Durango, Colorado. George raises horses with Harry and in 1884 moves his family to Cortez. Harry stays with them but works as a wrangler for Henry Goodman, foreman for the LC Ranch. Other families stake their claims in the nearby La Sal Mountain area – one is McCarty's. Close by at Mancos are the Maddens – Harry and Bill, who figure in a train robbery with Sundance in 1892. Many key outlaw partnerships blossom from southwestern Colorado.

Will Carver (aka GW Franks) is born on September 12, 1868

in Wilson County, Texas. Youngest of two, his parents George and Martha Jane Carver are originally from Missouri and move to Texas in 1863. Will leaves the family home in 1880 in search of adventure. Riding out with his uncle Dick Carver, a man whose standing with the law is questionable, he begins his career on the Sixes Ranch (later the T Half Circle) near Sonora, Texas. Will builds a reputation there, meeting the Kilpatrick and Ketchum brothers who will play an important part in his later outlaw life.

In 1892, Will marries Viana Byler, but sadly, she dies of pregnancy complications within a year – the loss may well influence his subsequent behaviour. He joins Sam Ketchum in a saloon and gambling venture in San Angelo, Texas but a disagreement over debts with a John Powers results in Powers being found shot dead close to his home. Suspicion points to Will and Sam, who decamp hastily rather than face a trial.

Will becomes a full-time member of the Black Jack Ketchum Gang operating out of New Mexico. Along for the ride is Ben Kilpatrick (aka "the Tall Texan") of Eden, Texas. The Ketchum Gang start their spree of train and bank robberies around 1896. The first is an ill-fated attempt to relieve the International Bank of Nogales, Arizona but they flee empty handed. In another, the gang is credited with netting a staggering $100,000 from the Santa Fe Railroad at Grants Station in November, 1897. A young, educated and highly intelligent cowboy named Elzy Lay joins Will, Tom Ketchum and Ben for that robbery. They escape to Alma, New Mexico and possibly there meet Bob Parker, who now calls himself Butch Cassidy.

The Tall Texan is born Benjamin Arnold Kilpatrick on January 5, 1874, in Coleman County, Texas, his owlhoot nickname coming from his formidable six-foot-one frame. His father George serves in the Confederate Army then moves post-war to Bosque County, Texas and marries Mary Davis in 1869. They live in Hillsboro before settling in Concho County and by 1885, George is ranching, assisted by Ben, aged ten. Ben meets Harvey Logan (alias Kid Curry) working as a cowboy, and the two youngsters strike up a friendship which lasts until the final days of the Wild Bunch.

Ben, Sam Ketchum, Will Carver and Dave Atkins all work for the T Half Circle Ranch near Knickerbocker, Texas between 1881 and 1891. Later, Ben drifts to New Mexico and works in the Erie Cattle Company alongside Will Carver and the Ketchums. He then appears at the Victoria Land Company, later known as the Diamond A Ranch, before arriving at the WS Ranch in Alma under the alias of Slim Catlow. These ranches all play an important part in the Outlaw Trail.

Harvey Alexander Logan is the fifth man. Harvey, better known as the infamous "Kid Curry," has no official birthday, as nobody agrees on a date or place. Estimates group around 1870, the most likely being Richland, Iowa in 1867. Harvey has three brothers and possibly a sister. Orphaned at an early age, he grows up without parents on the farm of his aunt Liz Lee, learning the cowboy trade before departing for work in the stockyards and on the trail drives of Dodge City, Kansas. Excitement draws Harvey west – by 1885, he has met Ben Kilpatrick at Big Springs, Texas.

Aliases are commonplace amongst the outlaws of the period, and prove invaluable for nearly all of them in an age when identification is always uncertain. Harvey's principle alias, Kid Curry, is used throughout his adulthood absolutely interchangeably with his real name, and subsequent records invariably cite both names. Circa 1890, Harvey, together with his brothers Lonnie and Johnny, buys a run-down ranch on the headwaters of Rock Creek, south of the Little Rocky Mountains. They soon fall foul of the town's founder, Pike Landusky. A feud ensues, and the conflict finally results in Pike's death during the Christmas festivities of 1894.

Despite acting in self-defence, shortly after the shooting Harvey rapidly leaves Montana – possibly to stay at Hole-in-the-Wall, Wyoming. Here, Harvey meets with old friends, probably Butch Cassidy, and becomes a member of the blossoming "Train Robbers Syndicate."

SIMON:

Butch led the outlaw band known variously as the Hole-in-the-Wall Gang, the Train Robbers Syndicate and the Wild Bunch. He perfected a strategy that in North America remained undefeated for eleven years. The gang cased prospective hold-up sites carefully, noted the best getaway routes, cached food and ammunition and placed high-quality horses at strategic intervals across the West. Their robberies were successful because Butch researched so thoroughly, and his excellent planning netted big gains. The gang hauled impressive amounts of cash, and well-planned escapes across difficult country ensured that local law enforcement and part-time posses were easily outrun.

By 1899, Butch's Wild Bunch was beginning to feel the heat. Big money was put up by the Union Pacific Railroad to catch the bandits who had been robbing trains with impunity. There was much more communication and cooperation between different States and law enforcement agencies, and Butch and Sundance's adversaries were now real man-hunters – seasoned, cunning trackers, fearless and very well paid. Butch and Sundance were exceptionally good at what they did, but so was this group of ex-lawmen and bounty hunters publicised as the Super-Posse.

EH Harriman of the Union Pacific Railroad was an extremely wealthy entrepreneur who acquired the rolling stock of the railway in the early 1890s. By 1898, train robbery in Wyoming was an embarrassing problem. The Union Pacific was being relieved regularly of considerable bank and payroll funds, and something urgently needed to be done to stem the flow.

Hence the handpicked Super-Posse, heavily armed and superbly mounted, assembled into a highly organised mobile troop and conveyed to likely holdup points in modified baggage cars drawn by specially built fast locomotives. Ruthless (and some say unscrupulous) Joe Lefors is usually credited with leading this posse, though some sources suggest Big Tim Kelliher actually headed the new division under Harriman's authority.

The renowned Pinkerton Detective Agency also allocated two of its best operatives to the manhunt. Charlie Siringo and WO Sayles were both courageous men and expert trackers. Siringo in particular was absolutely tireless. He spent four years pursuing the Wild Bunch and claimed to have ridden in excess of 25,000 miles in search of the bandit riders.

Other railroad companies retained or encouraged freelance bounty hunters to join in the hunt, men with fearsome reputations like Frank

Canton, Fred M. Hans, William H. Reno, and George Scarborough.

The message was clear and simple: Butch, Sundance and the Wild Bunch must be hunted down, and expense, time and distance were no object.

Eventually and inevitably, the long-run criminal success of the Wild Bunch brought national notoriety. Ever larger rewards were posted for their capture, and, tempted by fame as much as finance, numerous public and private man-hunters joined the search. Between 1889 and 1901, Butch and his pals had made off with some $200,000 – the equivalent of $4 million today. But you don't survive twenty years in the bandit trade unless you are very smart indeed. No way could Butch and Sundance not have been aware that it was only a matter of time before they were all hunted down, captured or killed.

OUTFITTING THE OUTFIT

"Everything's harder than it used to be – you got to be damn sure what you're doing or you're dead."
BUTCH CASSIDY

RICHARD:

From the air, Texas west of the Pecos looked a little bit like parts of the Ogaden region of Ethiopia – real badlands, a yellow and brown sun-baked landscape of sand and scrub, with enough rocks and hidden canyons to hide an army. We were crossing the *Llano Estacado*, the Staked Plain, when a voice came over the intercom warning us of turbulence. Minutes later, the sky disappeared. We were flying through a sandstorm. The plane was buffeted mercilessly and plummeted twice as it hit big air pockets. It was as bad as anything I'd experienced, and Simon and Barbara were both looking decidedly green. I hoped neither of them would lose their lunch. It was a relief all round when we touched down. Stepping out of the plane, the heat hit you like a furnace.

Rusty Armstrong, our hostess and outfitter, arrived in a huge black GMC pickup truck. We headed north to the horse ranch in La Mesa, a small Spanish settlement south of Las Cruces. At Vado, we bumped over the Atchison, Topeka and Santa Fe Railroad line and followed the back road for nearly four miles. Then we swung into the driveway, our preliminary journey over and the important one just about to begin.

Plans were to spend a week buying equipment. We would be riding and trial-packing the horses Joe Armstrong had already bought on our behalf. Joe, in his fifties, is a very successful equine and agricultural professor teaching locally at the Las Cruces, New Mexico Student Union. He is a bear of a man and a true southern gentleman. When his wife Rusty isn't running the daily business of the ranch, she organizes endurance races throughout Western America. Together with their bright sons, they make up a very impressive family, and Simon did well to find them.

Buying horses is never easy. During the spring and summer sales, you pay more for the privilege since the ranches always increase their herd to be ready for the international holiday season. We would appraise our mounts next day. Over dinner in a very good local Mexican restaurant, we discussed short-term plans. The choice was whether to scout the country near the border ahead of departure or to start buying equipment and working the horses straight away.

We would take five horses: two to pack and three to ride. The *remuda* comprised a ten-year-old, sixteen-hand black gelding, a seven-eighths thoroughbred quarter-horse (and an ex-racehorse to boot). I named him Yossarian after the character in Catch 22. We shortened it to Yazz. The other black gelding was an ex-ranch horse aged seventeen. He stood fifteen and three-tenths hands and was the "horse with no name." Dube (Doobie) was a twelve-year-old sorrel, sixth-eighths thoroughbred quarter-horse around fifteen and three-tenths hands. A mean looking twelve-year-old chestnut cowpony was the smallest, standing at fourteen and three-tenths hands. Joe named him Outlaw.

Finally, there was an Appaloosa mare. She stood at fifteen hands, and at six was the youngest of the bunch. We re-named her Miss-Ap. She was almost a pure grey, but was of course sprinkled with the small reddish-brown spots that distinguish the breed. We agreed Barbara would rotate the smaller three, leaving Dube as Simon's saddle horse and Yazz as mine.

Our equipment comprised:

~ three Western riding saddles, including a heavy roping saddle (two centerfire and one rimfire)

~ two sawbuck packsaddles, with two pairs of heavy-duty brown-coloured carbon fibre panniers

~ tack, including lead ropes, halters and bridles, morales (nosebags), leather hobbles

~ neatsfoot oil, spare leather tie strings

~ two axes and one military folding shovel

 three canteens, three military water bags and a canvas bucket

~ horseshoes, nails, hammer and file

~ fencing pliers and baling wire

~ three Silva compasses and a Magellan Global Positioning System (GPS)

~ a pair of binoculars

~ a complete medical kit, including needles, snakebite kit, painkillers, antibiotics, bandages

~ a comprehensive horse medical kit, including gall salve, sprays, antiseptic and bandages

~ stove, fuel, lighters, lantern and matches

~ two Dutch ovens, two pots, a frying pan, three plates, three mugs and cutlery

~ a three-man tent

~ bedrolls and military Gore-Tex bivvy bags

~ three "four season" sleeping bags

~ plastic groundsheets (large and small)

~ spare ropes

~ yellow slickers

~ two cameras, a video camera, numerous films, a charger and a fax modem

~ .30-30 Winchester rifle, and Smith & Wesson .38 Special handgun, with shells for each

~ notebook, pens and diary

In addition, we bought supplies of cooking oil, spices, candy, herbs, flour, coffee, pasta, biscuit mix, sugar, nuts, beef jerky, powdered milk plus 100 pounds of sweet feed (two bags).

SIMON:

How much riding preparation did we embark on before leaving England? Barbara kept a beautiful Russian stallion in Suffolk and rode most weekends. Her riding experience extended over more than forty years. Richard had recently joined her to get the feel of being with horses again. He had not been in the saddle for five years. Nor had I for over a year. Months earlier, Dylan Winter had informed me he rode in excess of thirty hours per week in preparation for the Oregon Trail expedition. I was shocked and panicked. But it was already far too late to start worrying.

I knew I was facing a stiff challenge. Never considering myself a real horseman, I would have to learn the hard way. If the average rider for pleasure hacked out for two hours a week, and assuming we would spend around eight hours a day in the saddle, I calculated that just two weeks would give me the equivalent of a year's experience!

After breakfast, we drifted over to an enormous white barn. Adjacent was a sandy arena split by a tree-lined drive, holding pens and two lush pastures. Behind were more pens full of brood mares, colts and fillies. The studs were safely housed in the horse barn, part of an impressive breeding programme.

The ranch house nestled securely amongst the cooling cottonwoods. Green, irrigated pastures were home to horses contentedly grazing. Beyond, through hazy sunshine, lay the foothills of the San Andres Mountains and San Andres Peak towering at an impressive 8,241 feet. The customary New Mexico spring wind blew frequently. It was hot and dusty.

With generous assistance from Joe's Mexican hands, we tacked up for the first time. Richard had no idea how to saddle with Western tack, but my time with AC had left me with a good working knowledge of the equipment used and the riding style. Like most things in life, it's simple when you know how and it's no black art, but even so, one of the hands managed to over-tighten the cinch on Dube, which cold-backed him.

This is an immediate reaction to cinching too fast and too tight without letting the horse acclimatize to saddle pressure. To our alarm Dube suddenly collapsed to his knees and flipped onto his side. The situation was compounded, as the lead rope had been secured to the hitch rail a little too short, and the horse was head-locked. Dube panicked, but luckily Joe Armstrong was on hand to free him. Dube suffered no ill effects, and we got busy.

On ranches, it is still considered good sport to put the new pilgrim up on a spirited horse, like Gregory Peck in William Wyler's *The Big Country*. So naturally, neither of the black geldings had been exercised in advance. I discreetly decided to let the more experienced Barbara and Richard take the edge off their friskiness. All went well until Joe politely insisted I fork the saddle.

Getting comfortable whilst thinking about adjusting my stirrups, the "horse with no name" barrelled into a fast lope and caught me off guard. Whoa! As we galloped round the arena, no amount of reining slowed us down. Again we circuited blindly. I started desperately to look for an escape, but everything was a blur. Then I noticed Joe's Mexican hands quietly slinking into view from the barn to watch. They, like Dobbin, had quickly sized me up as a greenhorn.

At a gallop we charged towards a closed gate in the corner of the corral.

"Shit!" I thought, "Here comes trouble."

I pulled and turned to no avail. With no chance of a sliding stop, I speculated where I might end up: into the gate, over it or slam-dunked onto the floor? Whichever it was, I knew it was going to hurt like hell.

"Turn him," Richard shouted. Already dismounting with my left foot in the stirrup, clutching the pommel, the horse stopped on a dime. At what felt like thirty miles an hour, I continued my journey airborne and solo, hitting the iron fencing with tremendous force. Wham! My mount stood still, snorted and shook his head. Job done.

Amazingly, in mid-air I had remembered the cowboy's golden rule: hang on to your reins so your horse can't back over you or piss off into the desert and leave you for dead. Fazed, choking dirt but still attached, I clawed back onto my feet. Barbara, watching with interest, asked the horse's name. I didn't hear Joe's answer. I was busy calling the beast a few names of my own, of which "son-of-a-bitch" was the most friendly.

"You okay?" Richard asked, genuinely concerned for my welfare.

"Yeah, yeah," I replied dismissively while noting that I'd shredded my shirt and could feel the warm trickle of blood on my back. I dusted myself off.

"Shorten your reins next time," Richard advised and walked off.

I avoided further participation in the rodeo business and retired, satisfied that I had provided the requisite entertainment for the hopeful onlookers, and that already the smart money was going on our not making it out of New Mexico, never mind to Canada.

RICHARD:

The following morning, Simon was bruised black and blue. His pride survived, but not his favourite shirt. We laughed the episode off, but we counted our lucky stars that no ribs were broken in the fall. It would have been a hell of a way to start a two thousand mile ride.

Joe quickly explained the rudiments of packing as Simon and I unwrapped our shiny new gear from the Denver Colorado Saddle Company. When using packhorses, balance and weight distribution are everything.

Joe showed us how. Blanketing first, he placed a wooden sawbuck on top then firmly cinched up. Panniers were hooked over the buck and the "H" pack (a canvas bag literally shaped like an H) was placed across the frame. Next, roping the gear securely on the horse's back was essential. It looked straightforward as Joe threw the rope around Miss-Ap, looping, twisting and turning to make a neat job. We followed instructions to the letter, and our efforts were deemed acceptable. The process took us fifteen minutes per pack. On the trail, timings had to shorten dramatically without compromising safety, otherwise we would spend large portions of each day packing and unpacking.

Joe advised us to use the Diamond hitch. Ideal for top packing, it is standard procedure. Obviously, too much weight on top means the centre of gravity gets too high, but the Diamond acts like a net. It ties the entire load to the horse or mule via the cinch, not just to the packsaddle. The contoured carbon fibre panniers were an excellent choice and easy to use, only requiring correct weight distribution.

We spent a good deal of time searching locally for maps. I procured just three US Government Survey maps and planned stops at twenty mile intervals for the first two hundred and fifty miles. Allowing one rest day every seven for 2,000 miles, this would be very serious riding.

SIMON:

An Armstrong friend in his early seventies, Herb Greathouse, wished us well and put us straight about travelling in the Gila Wilderness. He advised extreme caution. The wilderness demanded great respect, and we did not know the region or the packing drill, and the horses (not to mention ourselves) were untested as a bunch. It was therefore suggested that we make a short trial trip before setting off, just to shake things down. In the light of subsequent experience, that might have been a smart idea, but I was impatient to get started on the real mission. Summer was a-coming in, bringing with it dramatic temperatures.

Joe also advised branding our horses. It provided identification and, along with a bill of sale, would enable us to prove ownership of a stolen or strayed animal on recovery. Another thoughtful suggestion, and this time we went for it.

Back at the table, I checked the final route. Starting from downtown El Paso in the midst of noise and traffic seemed risky. Anapra, Mexico, only a few miles outside El Paso, was technically the most accurate, despite the Outlaw Trail having no definitive line further south of Silver City. A major concern for me was the risk of incurring disapproval from Wild Bunch historians who might claim we rode the wrong line of departure. The problem was simple. Neither Butch nor Sundance had written anything down, and they were hardly likely to. We had to think like the outlaws, and I didn't believe they would ride north from El Paso along the Rio Grande.

Richard and I drove to the Border Patrol located near Sunland Park Racetrack. We met Don Lucero, head of the horse unit. Don suggested where to ride for water and also confirmed much drug running activity near Columbus. We would be safer to ride from Anapra trailing northwest along the railroad. Advising us to keep clear of the boundary, Don told us helicopters flew daily across the 'boot-heel' and would keep an eye out. For us, or for the drug-runners, we wondered.

Riding with firearms had barely been discussed. We were told they were essential equipment in the admittedly unlikely event of an attack by a bear or a mountain lion or (less improbably) should it be our unenviable duty to destroy a badly injured horse on the trail. The alternative of using rocks to crush its skull was even less appealing. So we agreed to pack iron.

RICHARD:

Whilst Simon spent many (for him) engrossing hours checking and double-checking the historical aspects, I selected a scale of lightweight equipment from my personal store. I chose three hooped Gore-Tex bivvy bags, a sleeping mat and an inflatable mat. I was still missing my holdall thanks to the world's favourite airline. All my important gear, including three Silva compasses, Magellan GPS, map case (an invaluable veteran of many journeys), a four-season sleeping bag and a clip torch, were inside.

For clothing, I worked on the old service rule of three of each item: one on, one clean and one in the wash. I chose loose-fitting trousers to ride in, granddad shirts, cotton jocks and a "holds the kitchen sink" waistcoat (another old friend) for all my in-the-saddle and emergency needs. A baseball cap sufficed to keep the sun off my balding pate when working off the horses. I bought thermal underwear, gloves, an Australian slouch hat, riding boots and an SLR camera. Barbara wore a versatile skirt and cowgirl shirt, fishing jacket, roper boots and cowboy hat. As for Simon, complete with Stetson, tooled leather boots, waistcoat and kerchief, he looked more like a cowboy than cowboys do.

I obtained maps to complete the first section of the ride and Simon had a good Bureau of Land Management map for the Gila Wilderness. I hoped to procure the next batch showing relief and lines of latitude and longitude close to Arizona. I was surprised at their scarcity, but on reflection, there must have been zero demand. There was not one good reason to ride through this zone unless you were on the Outlaw Trail.

Emergency procedures were my biggest headache. The land we were about to cover was vast and remote. Although we would never be further than a day's ride from any possible assistance, the thought of a seriously incapacitating injury was chilling.

I wanted a means of radio or telephone communication to summon help if needed. To our amazement, Iridium, the global satellite phone, cost $600 a month, which was prohibitive. A mobile phone was no use outside certain areas, and so it was with grave reservations, against all my training and experience, that the decision was taken to travel *without* any means of emergency communications. I made sure we packed a set of pilgrim splints for ground-to-air communication. These are made of high-density fabric with Velcro ties and day-glo panels, highly visible to passing pilots – if there are any.

Another worry was horses going lame. No foot, no horse and no finish, so I packed bute, liniment, vet wrap and easy boots, but was unable to buy Stockholm Tar. Horseshoes were a major consideration. To include a full set for each horse was out of the question, so I packed two spares for each mount, along with nails and a farrier's hammer.

Unlike in the UK, American horses are cold shod, usually by their owners. It was essential I acquire some competence as a farrier. I apprenticed myself to Joe's farrier for a day and learned how to remove and tack on a shoe, trim and fit. My only worry was that I must not pierce the quick and damage the tender white line that lames a horse instantly.

Consideration turned to packing and weight. Joe taught well and complimented us on our new skills. It was critical to have the weight evenly distributed, because if packs slipped, they could instigate a horse wreck. I was particularly fearful of losing an animal in the high country; a horse whose pannier slid under its belly could easily panic and bolt. We were told the maximum weight a packhorse could take was 200 pounds. However, none of our advisors had packed on a trip lasting more than a fortnight, and in the early stages this lack of expedition riding was a weakness in our packhorse management.

The saddle horses had a heavy burden too. The average weight of a Western saddle is forty pounds. Full pommel bags came in at ten, saddlebags close to twenty, a rifle eight and water canteens twelve. Simon noted he was 285 pounds all up. His outfit alone weighed a hundred pounds – a huge weight difference compared to riding English. Though the least capable rider, Simon understood the Western system well. Barbara discovered she cared little for Western tack and methods, but it was the only game in town.

Weight was a continual worry. Less weight carried per horse meant more horses in the string. Not an option. More horses automatically meant greatly magnified feeding and grazing problems. Personally, I found the Western saddle enormously comfortable, and I was anyway extremely grateful not to be using English tack. Quite apart from its unsuitability for the task, where on earth could we obtain replacement parts along the trail?

Food needed to be nourishing, varied and light in weight. We could procure fresh provisions in larger towns but must carry a minimum of seven days' rations. I set about planning daily menus with sufficient calories to sustain us. The mainstays were rice, pasta, potato powder, dehydrated vegetables, beef and chicken flavoured soya, oil, oatmeal, porridge, sugar, along with tea, coffee, lemonade and milk powder.

For lunch I made up a trail mix of nuts, raisins and dried fruit with cereal, and also energy bars with Jolly Rancher boiled sweets. I acquired some strongly recommended beef jerky, basically dried and smoked beef strips from "the best butcher in Las Cruces." I requested eleven pounds of the stuff until told it would fill two panniers. We settled for five pounds.

Then, just two days before departure, death and disaster.

SIMON:

We had decided to pack Outlaw. I thought he was a cunning brute, but Joe packed him carefully, saddled and mounted Dube and began his cautious appraisal. Immediately, Outlaw erupted into a bucking frenzy, jerked the lead rope out of Joe's hand, dashed round the corral and hurtled through the other horses standing quietly tied to the rails, en route snapping their lead ropes off at the halters. Panic ensued and horses broke free to escape.

Outlaw continued running recklessly. Joe, seeing the danger in a confined space, yelled for us to vacate the arena. It was pandemonium. With Yazz cornered nearby against the corral fence Outlaw decided to buck the panniers from his own back. Yazz spooked, laid his ears back and struck out, delivering a devastating hammer blow with both hind hooves. We heard the telltale sound of an awful, expensive, cracking noise, and immediately feared one of the new panniers had been destroyed.

Outlaw stopped in his tracks and stood still, his flanks heaving. We quickly caught the other horses and let them out into an adjacent field, relieved that there had been no injuries. Then Joe noticed Outlaw had a deep, ugly cut on his shoulder, which was pumping blood copiously. Yazz had missed the pannier and kicked a chunk out of Outlaw. This was trouble of mammoth proportions. Local vet Skip Pritchard was on site, heard the commotion and immediately raced over. We described the dangerous mêlée whilst Skip closely inspected the wounded horse. Outlaw trembled – and I confess, so did I.

I stood helplessly, adrenaline still pumping. Nobody moved a muscle.

"What have we, Skip?" Joe asked quietly.

"Bone fragments."

Skip poked, prodded and rooted inside the horse's chest as the wound poured blood.

"He's over – I don't think he'll mend. You'll have to destroy him immediately."

We were stunned. Joe looked, nodded to approve the action, and then retreated to ranch HQ to try and get a replacement horse. Barbara vanished too, leaving Richard and me to assist Skip with the grisly task. Skip quickly produced the necessary drugs from his truck and concocted a light pinkish potion. In silence, I led Outlaw out of the corrals into a field. He hobbled pitifully – even I could see that nothing could save this horse. I felt nauseous and a bit light-headed.

Skip stuck the needle in and administered the lethal mixture. Within moments, Outlaw stiffened and crashed sideways to the floor, dust billowing over him. After a few snorts his eyes glazed over and he was out forever. I stood over the body of the chestnut cowpony thinking that Hollywood always skips this chapter – the death and destruction of animals. Death under your nose deals a devastating blow. I had assumed that an accident like this might take place if at all in the dangerous high country – not in the yard. It was over and done with, but I think we were all a little bit in shock.

Over dinner, nobody said a word about the demise of Outlaw. We were supposed to be leaving Mexico on Saturday, but the situation was further compounded because none of our horses was insured. We were getting round to that. Barbara called an underwriter at Lloyd's of London and arranged immediate cover.

Joe felt sorry for our predicament. Knowing we were unable to buy another horse at such short notice, he lent us a fine bay mare aged three years. Pistolera was fifteen hands and a beauty. Eternally grateful for such a generous gesture, we now had the added worry of maintaining a very valuable horse. And we hadn't even begun.

BREAK FROM THE BORDER

"It was your great ideas got us here…"
THE SUNDANCE KID

SIMON:

Rusty Armstrong and Joby Priest dropped us off at Sierra de Cristo Rey, Mexico. We were seven miles west from downtown El Paso where the state lines of Texas, New Mexico and Chihuahua converge, and exactly where historians, scholars and Wild Bunch *aficionados* reckon the southern end of the Outlaw Trail commenced.

It was April 17, 1999, just a century after Butch and Sundance had last ridden across the border. Our beginning was very different to theirs. They could pack their horses in their sleep, while we could just about complete the task, albeit slowly. They knew exactly what the desert held in store, we didn't, and they were far better judges of horseflesh because their lives had always depended on it. Ours did not, but the success of the expedition certainly did.

I gazed across the stark landscape. It was deserted, a dust bowl. A blue sky curved and melted into the distant horizon. Tumbleweed blew across the parched red sand. Not a blade of grass could be seen anywhere; even the weeds couldn't get a grip. The mercury edged closer to a hundred degrees and the sun beat down mercilessly. It was as hot as hell, which I suspected it resembled.

We crossed the railroad tracks and illegally set foot in Mexico. This manoeuvre enabled us to claim that we rode over the border. Rusty clicked away madly with her camera to secure the event for posterity whilst Dube baulked furiously, shied away and strenuously avoided stepping over the rails. I dug my spurs in desperately trying to follow the others over the line. Nada. Moments earlier I had looked the essence of cool and highly authentic: Stetson, duster, leather vest, granddad shirt, a lucky white silk bandana and deerskin boots. My composure was badly dented because my bloody horse had become a mule, and we were going nowhere! Tiptoeing over, we promptly swung back into New Mexico, grateful the media were not witnessing the embarrassing debacle.

Leaving felt good. I felt ready for the pure freedom the ride had been promising. Five years of diligent research were to be tested to the limit, and I intended to make the most of my opportunity.

Joe led the party briskly. We weaved around sand dunes and mesquite. The first section of the ride took us through fifty miles of parched wasteland before reaching the Interstate. Our USGS maps (1:100,000 scale) showed desert paralleling the Southern Pacific Railroad tracks. The range was bare.

The first few miles were a blur. It was awkward towing packhorses, and we were immediately the victims of our own inexperience. When the horses were not continually jostling for supremacy, they hauled back and attempted to yank our arms out of their sockets. It was already proving more difficult than I had bargained for.

We shuffled through the rolling dunes, changing lead and swapping pack animals to ascertain who had the best pace and was most compatible. We rode down a steep, sandy slope, dropping under a ledge. It was a perfect ambush site. Astonishingly, even in 1999, the bandit threat was very real. Columbus and the surrounding country were teeming with drug-runners and bootleggers.

Were Butch and Sundance active in El Paso? No definitive reference says so. Pat Garrett (he who shot and killed the unarmed Billy the Kid) was sheriff of Las Cruces. By 1901, he was a customs officer in the border city. Butch and Sundance had escaped to South America by then, but other famed lawmen were also based in El Paso in the late eighties.

Jeff Milton, John Selman and George Scarborough are formidable men by any standard, and if underrated could easily become the nemesis of the Wild Bunch. Scarborough is a gunfighter, a former cattle detective, a sheriff until 1888, then by 1894 he is a Deputy US Marshal headquartered in El Paso. His friend Jeff Milton, a former Texas Ranger and railroad detective, is chief of police, and John Selman – who has worked on both sides of the law – has been a Constable for ten years. All have held different law enforcement jobs and have dealt with the likes of notorious killer John Wesley Hardin (whom Selman kills).

With such a tough bunch around it was maybe a little too hot in El Paso for Butch and Sundance. So where did they hide in Mexico? Closer inspection of history books and journals provided useful clues. The Cananea Cattle Company held vast tracts of land between the towns of Fronteras, in Sonora, and Ascensión in Chihuahua. A line anywhere between those remote Mexican townships would meet the needs of Butch and Sundance with some precision: safety south of the border from Texas Rangers, proximity to the Arizona and New Mexico state lines for tactical border-hopping, adjacent and secluded mountains in a crisis and (at the Chihuahua end) some Mormon settlements where Butch in particular would feel safe and very much at home.

And if any of the formidable El Paso lawmen sneaked across the Rio Grande border into the Mexican twin town of Juarez, the crafty outlaws could simply circle the metropolis and drop over the line without being noticed. Which was exactly what we managed to do.

RICHARD:

Back on the trail, the battle to get the horses moving along smoothly was becoming a war of attrition. We had grossly underestimated how awkward this form of travel might be. The horses were no more a team than we were. They were acquired from different *remudas* and constantly fought for the lead, swinging and jerking the lead ropes out of Barbara's and Simon's hands.

After a couple of hours trailing through sand dunes and scrub, two water canteen bottle straps snapped, adding to our frustration. Once we switched from the line of the railroad track to a compass heading, the navigation got much harder. Distant points of reference would disappear as we rode into dead ground. Altitude slowly decreased from 4,400 to 3,250 feet, and the heat rose commensurately. By four that afternoon, Joe decided to call it a day and we stopped at Strauss.

We pitched up near a homestead and coaxed the horses to a stagnant green pond, but they refused to drink. The homesteaders arrived, gave permission to use their corrals, pointed us in the right direction for tomorrow and wished us the best of luck, together with the cheerful information that they were currently in their seventh year of drought.

We picketed the horses in the corrals on "T" hitches to evaluate their suitability for later, laid our bedrolls, ate supper and by nine pm collapsed into our sleeping bags for the first night under the stars. All around, the hum and whirr of insects and other desert nightlife was punctuated by the snorting of our horses. Overhead, the clarity of the stars was reduced by the massive orange haze that marked El Paso. We had ridden a grand total of seven miles. I slept.

As I stirred early the next morning, I heard a commotion. Staggering to my feet, I hurriedly threw my clothes on and raced for the corrals, knowing something was wrong. Joe, Simon and Barbara were standing aghast. Barbara had gone to feed the horses at five and was met with another calamity.

During the night Rocket, Dube and Yazz had pulled down the metal "T" hitch to which they were tied. The result was grisly. Yazz had taken the full impact of a metal beam crashing onto his neck from fifteen feet above. Sustaining an ugly gash down to the cartilage, he had run onto a post and punched a trauma hole the size of my fist in his chest, which in turn revealed white muscle and blood. Somehow Rocket and Dube had held fast, which had averted further disaster. If they had panicked and bolted while tied to the beam, the entire string would have been destroyed.

I produced the vet kit. Joe gave Yazz the tranquilizers with local anesthetic. Scrubbing the wound with savlon solution, I began to suture the white muscle and torn skin tissue together and placed a vital drain wick in place. We began an antibiotics programme, dressed the neck and applied powder to Yazz's chest. It took half an hour. Barbara was unable to watch, and Simon was something of a Job's comforter. I understood his worry because of the possible consequences. We were under-funded to cope with any more horse losses, so the ride was already in jeopardy. And it was just day two.

We finally got going and rode parallel to the Southern Pacific Railroad. It was convenient and easier on the horses. Trains came and went, blasting their horns, crews waved as they thundered past. The horses were unperturbed by the racket. Eventually, we arrived at the Lanark water tank. Joe rode on for a pre-planned rendezvous with Rusty, who was hauling him back to La Mesa.

My thoughts turned to Yazz, and whether he would be out of the ride. We unloaded and tied off. I took a shower at a water tank and waited for the sun to dry me. Minutes later, a truck slowly appeared, bumping its way along a track parallel to the fence. The throbbing V8 engine cut, and out stepped a rancher who ambled over slowly and very politely introduced himself as Harold Clay.

"Hi! D'you guys know two other riders are heading north?"

Simon:

"No," I replied, doing my shirt buttons up. As we shook hands, I must have projected a strong whiff of fear. Was somebody else attempting to ride the Outlaw Trail?

"How long have they been gone?" I asked as casually as I could manage.

"A few days – a week. These yours?"

Harold pointed at the horses.

"Yep."

"He doesn't look too good," jerking a thumb at Yazz. "When'd he get injured?"

"This morning," I briefly explained.

"He mightn't make it. Let's look at the others."

"How old?" He indicated Rocket.

"Seventeen."

"Too old – what about the sorrel?" He pointed at Dube.

"Twelve."

"You want younger horses. Got a pair of Tennessee Walkers for sale. $7,500 the pair, they'll make it!"

Richard was busy preparing camp and Barbara had moved out of earshot. Harold was now inspecting our gear dumped on the floor. I waited for the criticism.

"You're carrying a load all right – boy!" Harold exclaimed.

I had to ask the question:

"Do you think we'll make it then?"

"Not a chance."

I wished I had shaken hands on the two Tennessee Walkers. Harold was the first of many experts we met along the trail. Some were well meaning; some merely scented a sales opportunity. But we were not changing anything just yet.

Joe returned with Rusty. Along for the ride was Anja Niebur, a German girl studying to be a vet. She looked closely at Yazz.

"He doesn't look good" was followed by "He might be out." We made no comment. I glanced towards the trailer. There were no replacement horses. Yazz was continuing regardless.

The day's heat quickly subsided, and a chill took its place. We made for the hearty fire and turned to watch sunset ebb into dusk. Richard poured steaming coffees to fortify us. Within minutes, another truck and horse trailer pulled over. The occupants, two cowboys, strode boldly over and introduced themselves.

"Hi, I'm Craig – this is John. We're riding the Outlaw Trail. Got stuck in Hillsboro," Craig pointed north, talking like a machine gun in short, rapid bursts.

"Really?" I replied, now totally pissed off. Harold Clay was right. Somebody was on our trail, riding our ride.

"Why are you back here then?" I was dying to know.

"A horse spooked, ran into a signpost and broke his cannon bone. We're trying to get a replacement."

We traded information to learn John and Craig were riding from their ranch in New Mexico to another in Big Water, Utah. Despite stating they were on the Outlaw Trail, they were not. Also, ahead, they had a driver running a rig with showers, feed and full support. Their budget was impressive. Barbara whispered indignantly that they were cheating. Richard shot her a quick glance. She had forgotten her own Russian trip, with four-wheel drive vehicle and everything including the kitchen sink!

We small-talked politely before the Armstrong party bade us goodbye, with firm instructions to call them from our next staging point.

We would head west of Hillsboro, the former mining town close to where on December 10, 1902, Henry Hawkins and Ed Kilpatrick, brother of the Tall Texan, held up the County Bank, rode out of town with several thousand dollars and vanished into the Black Mountain range never to be caught.

We elected to ride through the Mimbres Mountains, adjacent to the Black Mountain range. Henry and Ed would have lost any sheriffs and posses in the Gila National Forest.

I lay in my bedroll wondering what else the Outlaw Trail might throw at us. It had been a bad start. One horse destroyed, another injured. Nothing prepares you for things like that. Thoughts began to drift through my mind. Barbara, the horse expert, seemed mighty subdued and tended to distance herself from the realities. Richard maintained an air of underplayed confidence. I wondered about them.

We woke at the ungodly hour of four am, ate porridge, drank coffee, packed and loaded. It was after eight when we got going. The best part of the riding day was evaporating. We aimed for Aden Crater, a white, sandy depression. There was little to alleviate the boredom of this desolate stretch of nothingness.

However, we were not quite its only living occupants. Tiny, sandy-brown lizards darted from scrubby bushes, and above us, turkey vultures floated on the hot desert thermals contemplating us as we might size up the *table d'hôte* menu, and for roughly the same reasons. Not a happy thought.

RICHARD:

No routine was developing. It was essential to have foreknowledge of feed and water, and currently, we were riding blind. The horses did not always take water after morning feed, and often showed signs of tiredness after two hours' riding. They were unfit, and Barbara was very unhappy about the pace and the monotony. Hopefully the horses would harden up in time, but conditions were brutal.

Joe had made it known to me forcefully and in private that I must speed up the packing process, delegate more work to Barbara and Simon (before I dropped dead) and make camp by late afternoon, allowing a maximum of eight hours of riding. Leaving late meant using the horses during the relentless heat. Mileage projected at twenty per day was an overestimate. Locals reckoned fifteen if we were lucky. Barbara reminded us she rode thirty-five in Russia with no problem. But you would be hard-pressed to find anywhere less like Russia than our present location. By day three, it was evident twenty miles a day was a preposterous calculation. We were closer to ten.

The Chihuahuan Desert was already testing our mettle. I suppose we were lucky inasmuch as we did not have to cross some of the treacherous rivers over the border in Arizona. However, we missed our target, which was the McKenna Ranch, and could not find water around the White Flats area. At this point, Simon noticed his leather waistcoat was no longer tied to his saddle. It was anybody's guess where it had fallen. And it was stuffed with cash.

He walked back two miles to try to find it. He needed to be on foot to search properly, but Dube would not be led, so he had to walk both ways. He was sure he would find the missing garment near a railroad crossing at which our horses had baulked, but he underestimated both heat and distance. The exercise was futile.

Meanwhile, as we waited for him, a truck moved slowly by. I hailed the driver to ask where the nearest water tanks were. He stopped, but he was exceedingly cautious, and throughout our short conversation I could see he was keeping me covered with a pistol held almost out of sight below window level. He drove off in a great cloud of dust just as the weary and unhappy Simon drew near, complaining indignantly about our not recruiting the truck driver to help with his problem. I was very concerned indeed about the ominous start to our journey, and I had just been at the wrong end of a loaded gun (again!). I was very tough with Simon:

"If you can't handle it, get off the expedition."

I was being hard-nosed, but it seemed to me I had to get a grip on this mission. The waistcoat incident was childish, as was Simon's reaction to the truck's departure. He was tired and angry at the stupidity of losing his waistcoat and money. It didn't help that Barbara constantly drew attention to his lack of horsemanship, but what galled him most of all was that he knew she was right. We rode on in tight-lipped silence.

Simon:

The contrast between the three of us sulking grumpily and all the cheerful, joshing, buddy stuff in the Hill and Goldman movie would have been funny if it weren't so disappointing. By the third day, I was wondering why I had ever suggested the expedition. It had not been a great idea, and it was getting steadily worse. If I had seen this awful strip of land before, I would never have contemplated riding through it with horses.

Minus my lucky waistcoat, I was pissed off and silently cursing. To stave off hunger, I chomped into a strip of beef jerky, which burned my throat and tasted like dog shit. Precious pints of water were needed to get rid of the taste. I knew now exactly what was wrong with this trip: everything.

Then came the barbed wire fences that ripped our gloves and tore our hands. Miles of them, and for what? Nothing could survive here. Choking down dust under a burning sky, Barbara complaining constantly about the lack of feed and water for the horses; this was desert riding. At sundown, we rode carefully over a concrete bridge into New Mexico's finest hamburger stop: The Burris Bar.

Two young men invited us to corral and settle the horses, then showed us to a silver trailer. Spirits brightened. We smelled a good time looming. Proprietors Henry Elliott (Jake) and David Jones (Elwood) proved the "Code of the West" was alive and well. Inside the bar, they pulled the first beers, and we got in the mood for a piss-up. After heart-stopping quantities of steak, a huge bowl of spuds and pounds of sweetcorn, we could hardly move and had little desire to do so. I hoped this spirit would stay with us. It was highly evocative of what the ride was meant to be about. The more beer we consumed the less horrible the four-day ride seemed.

Loch David, the spitting image of Buffalo Bill, commanded centre stage and entertained with outstanding magic rope tricks. His sleight of hand was so remarkable I found myself unconsciously checking that my wallet was still in place. We downed more drinks until, suitably lubricated, we informed the locals we were Butch and Sundance re-incarnated. We escaped the bar long after midnight, and an early start next morning was clearly impossible.

Inside the caravan, I crashed out and hung onto the bed. My thoughts turned yet again to the outlaws. We were twenty-five miles west of Las Cruces.

On the afternoon of February 12, 1900, two horsemen ride into Main Street, Las Cruces. They dismount and enter Bowmans Bank. Cashier James G. Freeman and a woman bookkeeper are held at gunpoint. The bandits clear the safe of approximately $4,000, including the payroll for the Torpedo Mine. Bystanders watch them gallop out of town in the direction of the Organ Mountains. It is a clean getaway, the trademark of the Wild Bunch.

Nobody is 100 per cent sure who they are, but one of the culprits is almost certainly Tom Capehart, another alias of Harvey Logan/Kid Curry. Certainly Logan is strongly linked with a later and dramatic sequel to the robbery. The identity of Logan's accomplice remains uncertain. It might well be one of the Kilpatrick brothers, but it could also be Butch Cassidy or the Sundance Kid.

SIMON:

My head spun through the haze of too much alcohol. I began to recap the last four days. A shitty start, fifty measly miles ridden through the arse-end of New Mexico, wind, dust, low morale and serious worry about the further hardships the horses would have to withstand. The trek was underlining just how good in the saddle Butch and Sundance really were, but our own further outlook was, to say the least, unsettled.

STAND-OFF AT
OUTLAW CANYON

"I'm not sure we're accomplishing as much as we might."
ETTA PLACE

SIMON:

We woke with thick heads, which made for a late start. Barbara had fed the horses, so we ambled over the Interstate to the Lazy E Café. Affable proprietors Brent & Ida Houser supplied us enough hot coffee to melt down the after-effects of too much beer, then we despatched an enormous plate of eggs, hash browns and bacon. Two Border Patrolmen strode in and announced we were front-page news in the *Las Cruces Sun* newspaper.

"So how's it going?" one officer asked, removing his hat before sitting down.

In the comfort of the restaurant, we answered cockily:

"Well thanks."

We either had short memories or were good with the bullshit. Ours had been the slowest start in history. But life on the Outlaw Trail could only get better; it couldn't get any worse – could it?

Joe Armstrong visited that morning, bringing a fresh supply of antibiotic-injection tranquillizers, anaesthetic and dressings. We discussed Yazz's condition. I wanted a second opinion – should he be taken out of the ride because one of the outer stitches in his chest had pulled? After close examination and consultation, we decided that the horse could continue.

Waking late had cost half a day's riding. The plan was to stop at the Roberts place, water the horses, then overnight at the Lazy E Ranch just eight miles away. The heat was suffocating, and the horses reacted predictably. A pace of two miles an hour, and that was pushing it, meant the rendezvous was a guaranteed grind of over four hours in the saddle.

Tom Capehart (Harvey Logan) and his accomplice take this trail after the Bowmans Bank robbery in Las Cruces. It is a miserable ride through a wasteland. When Pat Garrett's posse light out after the hold-up, they never catch the bandits. They lose them northwest of the Organ Mountains where the outlaws almost certainly switch to fresh horses. The bandits are totally unaware that they are also hotly pursued by man-hunter George Scarborough, who never did, and does not now, give up.

Simon:

As we rode across that barren, sandy landscape, it was difficult to believe that Garrett's posse lost Harvey Logan. The terrain is flat and devoid of cover. Glassing the desert with my binoculars, I could see for miles. Maybe Garrett's instinct for self-preservation had been at work. Maybe he knew that his own biggest career coup, Billy the Kid, was a pussycat compared with Harvey Logan. Maybe he was just exhausted, very hot, and his volunteer posse thoroughly unmotivated.

The latter was certainly our situation, though we had to go on in these awful conditions because this was the way to Canada.

We rode fence silently for three miserable hours, dragging the packhorses behind. With your left hand holding the reins of your own horse, your right hand holds a lead rope of the pack animal. In theory, it is a simple task, but in practice, it is like riding two bikes at once. It was tiresome and a nuisance. Pace was agonisingly slow, and when a windmill that Sonny Diaz had reminded us to look for hove into view, we brightened. People were busy working in the corrals, so we politely hello'd and rode through the gate hoping for assistance.

Disaster struck. A pump started suddenly and without warning. The loud clanking noise spooked Yazz, and he shied violently away in panic.

Richard, leading the packhorses, was suddenly caught in the middle of a monstrous tug-of-war as Rocket and Miss-Ap instantaneously tried to escape Yazz's flailing hooves. Dallying Rocket's rapidly tightening lead rope round the saddle-horn had pinned Richard into his seat. Cowboys sometimes lose their thumbs that way. The result was inevitable. Saddle slip of alarming proportions gave Richard no opportunity to bale out to safety. He desperately attempted to re-align himself and stay on board whilst Yazz pitched feverishly.

Events played in slow motion: Richard freed the offending rope, Rocket and Miss-Ap peeled away to safety, Richard wobbled perilously and Yazz took a policy decision to empty his saddle forthwith. Richard was unceremoniously pile-driven into the dust. Fortunately, the horses didn't trample over him to add further injury to insult, but serious damage was done.

Barbara retrieved Yazz, who was shuddering violently. Richard's saddle was suspended beneath the horse's belly. The big black stood snorting in terror; even Rocket and Miss-Ap were shaking. Richard laid outstretched, face down and virtually unconscious. We were in shit street. Richard came round, staggered to his feet wincing and moved gingerly towards a water filler pipe. Mr and Mrs Roberts calmed our packhorses and suggested we ride for the Lazy E Ranch two miles distant and summon a doctor immediately.

Richard clutched his side and announced with the certainty of an old campaigner that two ribs were broken, possibly more. I re-saddled Yazz and fixed the outfit. Twenty minutes later, I heaved Richard onto his horse.

As we rode off grimly, a sense of impending doom choked the atmosphere. Heat had increased to the high nineties. The horses were virtually at a standstill. Within a quarter of a mile, Miss-Ap refused to budge, a clear indication that weight and fitness were, as we had feared, a major problem. Dube too required constant spurring.

RICHARD:

Simon led the packhorses with great difficulty, so Barbara elected to string them. I followed in suppressed agony, nursing damaged ribs. To get Miss-Ap moving through deep sand littered with prairie dog holes, we had to dump a sack of grain. Mr Roberts re-appeared, very concerned at my condition, and offered a ride to see a doctor. It was tempting, but there is precious little you can do for broken ribs. It helps to stop breathing, of course, but that can have serious side effects.

Self-examination revealed that I had fractured two bones on my right side. Concerned lest I had punctured a lung, or that excessive movement might cause such damage, I drew breath carefully and checked my vomit for signs. Apart from the pain, I felt okay. I saw concern in the eyes of Barbara and Simon and decided to continue, provided I had help mounting my horse. The alternative was to abort the ride or re-organize for the others to persist without me, hoping to catch them up along the trail later.

We arrived at the deserted Lazy E Ranch at seven. I was never so glad to dismount. Simon un-tacked Yazz and Barbara took over camp chores whilst pressing me to visit a doctor. Badly in need of rest, I declined. After the struggle to get into my sleeping bag was over, next came the awful test for the best position to lie. I took a course of strong painkillers. They had little effect, and around midnight I took more, a deliberate overdose.

SIMON:

As Richard lay in agony, I paced with worry, hoping the ranchers would arrive home soon. It was nearly ten when I heard the telltale sound of a truck. I politely introduced myself, explaining our predicament and why we were camped uninvited on private land. Leonard and Ethel Goad very generously offered Richard a bed for the night at ranch HQ, but Richard seemed unconscious rather than asleep. I didn't know he had overdosed.

I slept intermittently. Richard groaned and mumbled throughout the night. These were dark moments. I thought about Butch and Sundance. What happened when they had suffered the same sort of setback, or indeed gunshot wounds? It is seldom remembered just how much resilience the frontier demanded. People would ride seventy-five miles to see a doctor, but by the time they got there, they were either dead or well.

Would Barbara opt to stick with Richard? If he chose to quit, could

I consider riding to Canada alone? It was an impossible scenario to visualize. Was I being selfish? What really happened on a major expedition if you got hurt? Did you rule yourself out, or did the team decide? It was a tough call, and I needed Richard's leadership. To quit tomorrow would be a tragedy.

I drew the horse blankets over my bivvy bag. My thoughts drifted. Horses were docile creatures but Richard had come pretty close to violent death. When Yazz dumped him, he had narrowly missed splitting his head open on the edge of a stone water trough. Who was next to get the shit kicked out of them? I was clearly favourite.

Five days after leaving Mexico, the expedition was a shambles. This wasn't the deep understanding of the bandit life I had been hoping to acquire. Or was it? I was learning the hard way that this kind of travel was and probably always had been high risk stuff. It was certainly high risk for man-hunter George Scarborough back in 1900.

After the Bowmans Bank robbery, when Pat Garrett's posse throws in the towel pretty swiftly, lawman George Scarborough perseveres single-handed, pressing hard on the heels of the bandits. Tired of this relentless pursuit, Harvey Logan devises a plan to eliminate Scarborough from the chase – permanently. Near the Burro Mountains, the roles of hunter and hunted are to be reversed.

Scarborough is following a hot trail, and, seeking support, he telegraphs Deputy Sheriff Walter Burchfield, requesting they meet at San Simon. The pair ride across the valley and see a freshly slaughtered beef. As the trail continues higher into the mountains, Scarborough becomes very wary. The lawmen turn back near Triangle Springs, thirty miles out of San Simon, and then, perhaps unwisely, they follow a trail into a canyon.

Here they are ambushed, just before sundown on Tuesday April 3, 1900. At the sight of two saddled, rider-less horses, the lawmen pull up, but the outlaws immediately open fire with rifles. Both officers make quickly for cover, drawing their pistols, but Scarborough is knocked out of the saddle by a .30-40 cartridge and he goes down, to the evident delight of Logan, who gives a great whoop.

Burchfield immediately dismounts to help. The outlaw party very probably includes one of the Kilpatrick brothers who knew Burchfield,

*having worked with him previously on the Diamond A. Anyway, with or
without the compliance of the outlaws, Burchfield gets away. He tries to
save Scarborough and rides through snow to summon help at the San
Simon Ranch HQ. Scarborough has a nasty wound in his leg and is
further weakened by the severe cold. He is driven back thirty miles and
placed on the train for Deming, but dies two days later.*

SIMON:

The death of George Scarborough was a chilling reminder that these
were bandits, on the dodge, who prized their continued liberty above
the lives of other equally cold-blooded man-hunters. Most of the time,
life was a whole lot different from a witty, charming buddy movie.

The Outlaw Trail had many tributaries – one led to the Erie
Cattle Company located in Sulphur Springs Valley, near Tombstone,
Arizona. Their range stretched 20 miles northeast of Bisbee and at its
peak ran 20,000 head. On the payroll were Butch Cassidy and Elzy
Lay who worked there before moving up to the WS Ranch in Alma,
New Mexico. A safe house was a cow-camp at Mud Springs, suitably
close to the Diamond A. Here Butch and Elzy became acquainted
with Perry Tucker, ranch manager, who would take the same job
at the WS in 1899. The Diamond had a good rep despite hiring in
fugitives. Riding east, the outlaws could aim for Rincon, Seven Rivers
and Roswell, before dropping south along the Apache, Delaware and
Davis Mountain ranges into the safety of what today is the Big Bend
National Park, Texas. Heading north, they would pass through Las
Vegas, New Mexico hugging the foothills of the Sangre de Cristo
Mountains to Cimarron resting at another established den: Turkey
Canyon, hidden in heavily wooded country. Cleverly concealed it
could only be reached by two seemingly impassable, narrow, torturous
trails, round a massive boulder with a stream cascading into a canyon
or through a cut in the rock face.

I wondered if Butch and Sundance had also worked at the huge
Diamond A spread, whose horse camp in the Deer Creek tract became
a popular hangout for outlaws. The Diamond A was not averse to
hiring men from the wrong side of the law. Harvey Logan certainly
worked there in 1895. The record shows that "he was a good cowboy,

affable and rarely found fault with anything." Apparently, Logan had a unique whooping laugh, one "that could be heard for a mile." That distinctive hallmark is what linked him to the ambush and shooting of Scarborough at Triangle Springs.

We woke to a bitter, cold morning. Yesterday's offer of breakfast was too good to miss. We rallied and were called in. The smell of bacon, eggs and coffee was a joy. Inside, the decor was traditional ranch style; well-used, comfortable, chock full of western books, boots, range gear and ornaments to match furniture typical of the Western culture. Ethel Goad made my day by telling us she was a distant relative through marriage to Will Carver, a member of the Wild Bunch inner circle. You can't get that buzz by reading a book. It only occurs in the field, on the spot, and when it happens it is terrific.

After breakfast, Richard collapsed in a chair and virtually passed out. We discussed his condition with a view to returning to Las Cruces for medical assistance. It meant temporary cessation of the ride on day six, April 22. But a delay of just a few weeks would have us travelling through the desert sections of Arizona and Utah in high summer, when excessive heat would guarantee further misery and even slower progress.

Richard recovered and told us he intended to continue. I wondered which of us was dreaming.

We packed, dumping both axes and the heavy Dutch oven. Richard could hardly move without jarring his ribs. Despite the difficulties, we packed well and rode for Uvas Valley, squeezed between the Goodsight Mountains and the Sierra de las Uvas.

RICHARD:

Altitude around 3,800 feet, heat almost unbearable. Worryingly, our map showed more white patches, which denoted an extended wasteland. It was an endless raw expanse of sand punctuated by scrub, and it made for dismal riding. Another worry was that the condition of the horses was bound to deteriorate further.

We had an uneventful stopover and a very welcome night's rest at the Hyatt Ranch. With its enormous, heavily irrigated green pastures, it seemed like an oasis after the stark, unforgiving, brown desert.

Next day, I looked forward to reaching the mountain country. It became cooler in the rolling brown hills of Uvas Valley. Less happily, on taking a compass bearing towards Nutt, we hit enough barbed-wire fences to test the patience of a whole convocation of saints. They severely reduced progress, forcing us to criss-cross through pastures which doubled our mileage. It was very tempting just to cut the ranchers' fences and ride on, but we had been warned that such action would destroy any prospect we had of much-needed goodwill.

So Simon and I cut, heaved and spliced the wire together, suffering collateral damage in the process. Baling wire and our fencing pliers made good. It often took all our combined strength to afford the repairs, and did little for my sore ribs.

After riding across a dusty, trackless range for a day, we reached Nutt. It was virtually a ghost town, just a bar and broken down old wooden buildings. We left Barbara holding the horses (voluntarily) and went in to slake our thirst. The bartender viewed two very dirty cowboys very suspiciously before opening up a reluctant dialogue. Simon said afterwards that the telltale bulge of my pistol had been clearly visible under my waistcoat. After serving the beer, the barman suggested we ride for Sid Savage's ranch a few miles away, explaining that the other Outlaw Trail riders had put up there.

We left reluctantly, dragging the horses at a snail's pace. On arrival an hour later, a young Mexican boy rushed out to help put the horses up. Once they were tied to hitch racks, we began to unsaddle, but instead of waiting until the horses had settled, the niño eagerly emptied grain into the feed troughs. Instantly, the hungry horses went berserk, fighting to get to the precious feed.

Forgetting he was securely tied, Yazz lunged at Miss-Ap. Jerked back by the rope he lashed out with his hooves. The horses swung madly and the whole structure shook. Yazz was the biggest liability, so fearing for the safety of all concerned, we set him alone, and things calmed down.

Later, Simon and I took a much-needed shower in the cowboy outhouse. We stank dreadfully of horse and human sweat and other less delicate odours. Our fading clothes were filthy, we were sunburned and peeling, unshaven and scruffy, we looked as if we hadn't taken a bath for a month, and we certainly smelled like it.

Maybe the bartender at Nutt could be forgiven his unease at our approach. He probably got his first whiff of us when we were still a hundred yards away.

Next morning, the Mimbres Mountains came into view, another range that helps make up the backbone of the Rockies. We rode through the rolling green Greg Hills for Whiterock Canyon, a route over the lower reaches of the Gila Wilderness.

SIMON:

At Swartz, the road led north to Hanover. We hoped to camp on ranches, thus easing the problem of feeding the horses. I enquired at a house if there was somewhere to overnight. Mike Laney strongly advised deviating from our proposed bearing and suggested we rendezvous at a derelict bungalow set deep amongst the trees in Macho Canyon. We turned the horses out and secured fences. Feed was scant, and we feared an attempted breakout if they remained hungry.

Mike duly arrived and explained that our intended route would hamstring us in dense timberline, which was no place for horses. He proposed we rest, and then meet tomorrow at his brother's ranch further up the canyon. I thought the prospects for a hearty breakfast looked good.

However, our short-term situation left a lot to be desired. The abandoned homestead was a rat-infested dump. A brown shag-pile carpet proved to be a thick layer of vermin crap, and when I lit a fire in the old grate it roared up the chimney and threatened to set the house alight. To top off the evening, our shiny new Coleman lamp had gotten broken in the panniers, and we ate silently in total darkness before bedding down for the night.

Needless to say, we were up at sparrowfart and off to Pat Laney's, where, sadly, we got a cool reception. No water for the horses was offered, nor coffee for us. Promptly hustled out of the paddock and redirected towards Braddock Canyon, we were told to wait for Mike at a spring. The trail was an old Indian pathway.

The spring was perfect. The water looked pure enough to drink and lilies grew on the surface. A neat stone wall had been fashioned, and it resembled an ornamental pond but without the carp. All in all a beautiful spot.

Barbara watered Pistolera, Rocket and Miss-Ap then started to make temporary camp. Richard and I tied Dube and Yazz to a pair of thick posts sunk in the ground, which were clearly there for that purpose. We began to refill our canteens when without warning; Yazz spooked and made a series of terrifying rearward lunges to escape some invisible danger. Forgetting he was still firmly tied he promptly leapt into the spring and, when checked by the rope, kicked out with such force that he knocked the massive cedar post askew. Thoroughbred he may have been, but he had a kick like a giant mule.

Yazz lashed out again, and from where I stood Richard seemed to be right in the line of fire. I was sure the vicious kick had connected.

RICHARD:

It had. Fortunately, I had seen Yazz leap, and I took rapid action as he kicked. I was using a tin mug, another old friend of many sorts, and it took the full impact. The mug simply folded around my hand, nearly crushing my fist and jamming my arm into my broken ribs. More agony ensued, but there was the consoling thought that a foot closer to those flying hooves and I could not have survived the blow. Just as well I moved swiftly. There was nothing in the expedition's budget for funerals.

SIMON:

We grabbed Yazz and untied him. Being around such a neurotic horse meant living dangerously. The near-certainty of these violent incidents recurring guaranteed more close shaves – surely our luck would run out. And we hadn't reached the tricky Gila Wilderness yet.

We hobbled the horses for the first time, and watched their reactions closely. You cannot just turn horses loose, because they take off in a hurry. Hobbles are widely used but not foolproof. Some horses learn to move by a sort of two-footed hop forward with the forefeet, and then walk on with their hind feet to catch up. It was imperative to set a new routine for them where no corrals were available.

Yazz (of course) instantly hated the hobble. We tied him to a small tree whilst fixing a high-line picket. Moments later, he wound himself into a mess and yanked back. Thrashing in sheer panic, he desperately tried to cut loose. I had to sever the rope to free him. Yazz leapt away and stood wide-eyed, shaking and blowing hard through his nostrils.

"This damned horse is going to seriously injure himself, or one of us," I said, "We'll trade him."

"You're over-reacting," said Richard tersely.

"There's too much thoroughbred in him. He's a dangerous bastard!"

"He'll settle in time." Richard was dismissive.

"Sorry, I'm not convinced," I said.

"Richard knows what he's doing." Barbara's tone was patronising.

"So when the next person gets kicked to pulp, I'll remind you of that," I snapped.

RICHARD:

After settling the horses, I wanted to check Yazz's wounds. The lesion on his neck was beginning to smell, indicating an infection. I decided to unpack the wound, clear it without disturbing the sutures, and put in a drain hole with gauze to assist it to clear the build-up of pus. I injected Yazz with ten cc of tranquillizer penicillin prior to administering a local anaesthetic. It had no effect. I boosted the dose with another five cc. Seconds later, Yazz shook violently, stiffened just like Outlaw when we destroyed him, and promptly dropped to the ground. We were gob-smacked.

Yazz was comatose. His eyes glazed. As billowing dust cleared, I rapidly worked on the two unsightly wounds hoping he would come to life after the drugs had worn off. The cause of his problem with the neck was drainage. The wound had formed a hollow between cartilage and muscle, forming a reservoir that was holding discharge. Within fifteen minutes, the job was complete, and, to our relief, Yazz was back on his feet with no ill effect.

Our camp was dire. We were on a slope, it got very cold later and Mike Laney never showed. We ate our evening meal of pasta, tidied, picketed the horses and retired to our bedrolls bloody annoyed.

Our bivvy-bags slid gently for most of the night. There's nothing like sleeping on a stony hillside to guarantee a fast, early start next morning. It was the worst camp endured, and we rode off muttering good riddance oaths to Braddock Canyon and hoping for a better day.

SIMON:

It was crisp, cool and refreshing, but once in Taylor Canyon, we lost ourselves in a maze of small, apparently identical arroyos, which meandered through rolling hills. Inevitably, we picked the wrong one, and the track narrowed until small fir trees completely blocked our path.

We had to dismount, backtrack and claw our way through coarse undergrowth up a steep, sandy incline onto a ridge. The horses frequently baulked, and we hauled, cursed and cajoled them as they stumbled very reluctantly to the top with their "H" packs almost sliding off. It was a hair-pulling experience.

Once safely on the ridge, we had a clear view for miles. A herd of mule deer scattered before us. Richard checked the map and announced our location was smack on the Continental Divide at the appropriately named Outlaw Canyon.

Throughout a boiling hot day, we struggled through more draws and gullies, putting the horses under much duress. Then we rode down a stony wash into a lush Bermuda grass paddock. Five splendid horses, including a magnificent pinto, were enjoying a feast. Leaving Dube at the corrals, I walked round a tall hedge towards the pleasant adjoining bungalow. Maybe things were looking up.

Within seconds, the original Hound of the Baskervilles appeared, heading for me at warp speed, barking and baying in bloodcurdling fashion and clearly targeting my gonads. Luckily (I thought), his large owner was close behind, whose presence moderated the dog's behaviour to prowling, snarling and showing his ferocious, yellow canine teeth. But his glowing eyes never for one instant left my meat and two veg, which were clearly still on the menu.

"Good afternoon," I said, striving for confident and genial, but probably only achieving frightened and ingratiating.

"Which way did you come? You're on private property," the man stated accusingly. He stood as high as a barn door and half as wide, and he was nearly as threatening as the now slavering hound he made no attempt to restrain.

"Over the Continental Divide, through Gavilon Canyon," I replied. "We didn't see any signs."

"Nobody comes that way. What are you doing here?"

"Riding the Outlaw Trail to Canada. I wondered whether we could corral the horses and buy feed."

"I don't want to get involved. Ride back the way you came. Three miles down, use the old corrals there."

I thought quickly, then tried, "Come and meet my partners."

This he ignored.

"Ride back! Put up in the corrals yonder! Tomorrow get an early start to San Lorenzo. Fill your canteens at the irrigation ditch - there's a hose under a drain cover," he said, and marched off, followed by his no doubt disappointed dog. I realised I had been holding my hands half cupped over my crown jewels, like footballers facing up to a close-range free kick.

"Well, fuck you, mate!" I said with my usual flair for sophisticated repartee. But I said it under my breath.

"We're not back-trailing, we'll pitch up out of sight," Richard announced angrily.

We re-mounted and rode for half a mile, then we veered off down into a hollow, out of sight, trekked through a pasture and hid behind a huge clump of trees under a bluff. Thus ended, ignominiously for us, the standoff at Outlaw Canyon.

We were all furious. What really hurt was the denial of feed for the horses. Where was the much-proclaimed Code of the West?

"You know what? I'd like to run that bastard's horses off," I said furiously. "That's what Butch would have done."

In those parts, even to say that was not very smart. Maybe they don't actually lynch horse-thieves any longer, but taking a shotgun to trespassers would be the normal reaction if your person or your property were threatened.

In my sleeping bag, I checked the stats. They were frightening: we had ridden a grand total of one hundred and thirteen miles by day ten. Canada seemed light-years away. What a pain in the arse life was at that moment. To add to the gloom, Yazz promptly collapsed again next morning when Richard administered his daily dose of penicillin. Trouble was sticking closer to us than our skin.

Anxious to recover some lost time, we left Faywood and rode north. Route 61, a back road, was flanked by the Gila National Forest and Aldo Leopold Wilderness.

We hoped to find the Lazy S Ranch in San Juan, a charming hamlet of splendid houses set in orchards set back from the road. We couldn't and tried the Bie Belle Ranch. Again, their idea of the Code of the West was to set the ranch dogs on us. Two refusals in a row; a nasty consistency was becoming apparent.

Then, without warning, Rocket collapsed. Fearing an imminent horse wreck on the roadside, we quickly released Miss-Ap. We couldn't untie the rope to remove the packs, and cutting would leave us without a replacement. Unless we could get him up on his feet, the only hope was to shift the panniers and untie the securing knot beneath Rocket's belly. Fortunately for us, Rocket obligingly sprung onto his feet. What luck, but the day's riding was over.

We stopped at the Miller Ranch literally half a mile up the road on a junction. After hearing our plight, the family agreed to let us stay. Shown to a bunkhouse, actually a bungalow, we bought groceries and provisions off them, took a bath, shaved then cooked a slap-up dinner of thick juicy steaks, potatoes and a stack of fresh fruit, something lacking in our current diet. Miseries paled and discussion turned to Rocket and the grinding trail. We could hardly bear the thought of seeing another horse drop out of the ride.

After sleeping fitfully, we prepared for the climb to Hanover. Having saddled the horses, we started packing and received yet another nasty surprise. A small raw patch appeared on Rocket's withers, a sign of more serious trouble beckoning. Like a hole in a sock, a sore on a horse's back only gets larger and more uncomfortable. The problem was acute weight loss combined with prominent withers.

The added worry was that Rocket, Dube and Yazz were identical in conformation, and if they all lost weight, we would experience the same nightmare – and that meant more horses, with all the attendant (and impossible) financial and extra feeding problems. Or it meant the end of the ride.

Under the Tonto Rim

"No more of this jungle work for me."
Butch Cassidy

Richard:

David Miller smeared a number of potions liberally onto Rocket's red sore to ward off any infection that might build up beneath the horse blankets. Thankfully, Rocket was showing no signs of fatigue from yesterday's breakdown. We put the incident down to very mild exhaustion and pulled out from the Miller Ranch back onto the road.

We were grateful for the mountains, a welcome respite from the infernal desert. We felt for the horses, but we could not buy more animals to spread the total pack weight. Currently, the range was yielding barely enough feed for our five horses. Using more would only magnify the problem.

We trawled up the incline towards Santa Rita pit, tacking like sailing ships beating into wind, which whipped down. The temperature plummeted. Heavy grey clouds rolled in, spots of rain dampened our enthusiasm and we reached for our slickers.

When we reached the small settlement of Hanover we stopped at a garage to water the horses. There we were given directions to Fort Bayard, and advised to use the old military trail. The Wagon Road split between the Twin Sisters, close to 8,600 feet, which would lead us to Cross Mountain right on the edge of Piños Altos town. We were also warned not to deviate from the mule tracks. A mistake meant we would trail deeper into the forest towards Lake Roberts and get hamstrung in timberline for sure.

Hanover was six miles east of Silver City's metropolis. The idea was to ride into Silver, but we knew there were no corrals in the town centre. We rode instead for nearby Fort Bayard.

From 1875 to 1881, Fort Bayard houses a detachment of the 'buffalo soldiers' – Colonel Hatch's coloured Ninth Cavalry, who are stationed there as part of a chain of outposts designed (not always successfully) to contain the marauding Chiricahua and Mescalero Apaches under Victorio. In October 1879, two Troops from Fort Bayard under Major A.P. Morrow chase Victorio's band all the way to Mexico. The Apaches foul the water holes as they go. The soldiers struggle on doggedly, but they are so weakened by thirst and exhaustion that when they catch up with the Apaches, they are expertly ambushed and driven off, and Victorio's band escapes again. One of the Ninth Cavalry Troops is led by Lieutenant Charles B. Gatewood, the hero who in 1886 personally (and at great risk to himself) talks the great Geronimo into final surrender, for which he gets scant recognition.

RICHARD:

We cut a new fence and sneaked across the perimeter. Through scrub, rocks and sporadic vegetation, we topped a ridge and picked ourselves a hollow sheltered with trees for a dry camp with plenty of good grass for the horses. Once settled, we sat back and completed our mileage calculations: twelve days and a total of 140 miles. Progress was half as fast as predicted.

By morning, the horses had cropped all the good grass. We packed, took an old woodcutting trail looping the Fort boundary and easily picked up the mule tracks. The path became rockier as we climbed higher, and went deeper into the wilderness.

We entered the Gila. Soon engulfed by dense forest, it was spookily dark, silent and deeply oppressive. Simon in particular felt very claustrophobic as we threaded through this gloomy, eerily still woodland, keeping a watchful eye out for telltale mule droppings.

Three hours later, we trailed down a steep, rocky draw acting as a firebreak. Houses were hidden amongst the trees. The outer edge of Piños Altos loomed up. An hour later, we re-joined the tarmac road to town and stopped to scrounge water from a house. The horses had gone without water since yesterday morning and were desperately thirsty.

SIMON:

We arrived at the Buckhorn Saloon. Hitching the horses under the shade of a massive tree, we entered a dark and musty building, which dated back to the Butch and Sundance time. As I ordered cool beers from the old wooden bar, I wondered if the outlaws had patronised this place. The smell of barbecued meat wafted from the kitchens. A fat, juicy steak was too tempting to miss.

Cue Plan A: settle the horses safely at the Dunivans, our next port of call, and return later for a piss-up. So on eagerly to the Dunivan place, like camels scenting the waterhole. Unfortunately, after helloing, we realised it was deserted. Annoyed, we reluctantly left for Bear Creek Road. A man walking his dog informed us that Mrs Dunivan had just driven past.

Cut to Plan B: resigning ourselves to bedrolls for another night, we organised picket lines and camped.

It got very cold during the night, and we awoke to find frost on our sleeping bags. But a clear blue sky promised a fine day. We packed and moved out swiftly. Altitude reached 8,150 feet at Cherry Creek Canyon, which placed us twenty-three miles south of the Gila Cliff Dwellings. The tarmac road wended its way through the pines.

Reaching Scott Peak, 8,344 feet, we saw forest fires burning below, but no sign of fleeing game. Astride a horse, you are always thinking ahead. Which way now? Will it be safe for the horses? What will be the next problem?

We were nearing an amazing National Monument, where the ancient cliff dwellings perch around two hundred feet above the canyon floor, covering a time-span from around 100 AD to the early 1300s. Though tempted to sidetrack and visit, we continued northwest looking out for a small trailhead.

At Pine Flats, we located the Government Trail. This innocuous path took us through deciduous forest. An hour later, a horseman sneaked up on our tracks, unspotted. Butch and Sundance would have chastised us for our carelessness. Steve Harvill introduced himself as an ex-National Forest Serviceman, who now worked for the government as a freelance trailbreaker. Many trails were in serious decline, and his brief was to re-plot routes.

He raced ahead on a stocky cow pony, and we met up again at the Sheep Corral Camp. Steve showed us the box hitch, a useful alternative tie that allowed the pack panniers to be lifted off the horse's sides. He reworked the traces, tidied our rigging and directed us towards Sapillo Creek, warning us of a very steep, awkward descent into the canyon below.

Barbara led. We coursed down a tight, rocky path that twisted and turned amongst the trees. The trail roughened riding through a mini-gorge. Overhanging branches obstructed us, and we narrowly missed losing an eye every time one whipped back into our faces. The horses rapidly became uncomfortable with the weaving path. With no room for error, we stumbled along, getting jolted in our saddles. Despite the narrow passage, the packhorses came through unscathed, though the panniers took a bit of a bashing on tree trunks.

An hour later, the path dumped us on a windswept ridge, and we breathed a sigh of relief. The view was spectacular – a clearway stretching for miles across the grey, undulating hills. But some time ago, a violent storm had passed, snapping trees like matchsticks. The devastation was enormous – and worse, the track ahead was now obliterated.

How had Butch and Sundance coped with similar obstacles? Flattened landmarks gave no direction indication whatsoever. It was left or right. We wanted straight on. There was an uneasy silence. Richard consulted the maps, GPS and compass before deciding to proceed north along Snow Creek. At worst, it was a fifty-fifty chance, but my money was on Richard.

The trail into the canyon tested the surefootedness of the horses. My saddle slipped and Dube floundered on the rocks. We clattered over the stones and rode into a tight arroyo. A tree apparently blocked the path. Miss-Ap calmly picked her way round it, but Dube clumsily stumbled, and I pitched off. He turned tail and scrambled swiftly away, back the way we had come.

I was very scared, but Dube stopped a hundred yards away. I skirmished up to him extremely cautiously, lest I spook him into running. The horse allowed me to catch him, and I quickly re-saddled, re-checked my outfit and – suitably relieved – led the way back through the overhanging branches to join the others.

We passed a dead cow, its neck broken by a long, heavy fall. We traversed down the perilous slippery surface to avoid stretching the horses' tendons, and there was Sapillo Creek. Bingo! The canyon floor yielded a glorious riparian area abundant with luxuriant grass. Pitching camp by the river, we set up a huge roaring fire to stave off the cold.

RICHARD:

After eating a hearty meal of meat and pasta, I noted our mileage: twenty-three, the best yet. I stacked more wood on the fire, took coffee and crashed out in my sleeping bag, totally exhausted.

The Sapillo Creek took us west for two demanding days. Canyon walls two hundred feet tall towered either side of the river. It was hard riding, but a great improvement on the desert. We crossed the river countless times each day on desert horses that clearly preferred not to get their feet wet. It got a bit harder every time. The horses frequently lost their footing in the fast flowing river and scrabbled over rocks. Often, we had to work hard to get them to cross at all. Yazz and Dube baulked regularly, but we urged them on.

One additional worry was the possible shedding of horseshoes. Herb Greathouse had warned us that repeated dampening of the horse's feet over rocky terrain could loosen the clenches. If that happened, at best shoes would be thrown, or worse, a hoof might split. No foot means no horse. On no account could we afford to have trouble here.

On the equine management front, we began to ask ourselves if the horses were getting enough hard feed. Horses working extended hours in tough conditions require greater amounts of grain, oats or supplements to boost energy levels. Upping their grain intake not only increases their endurance levels, it also reduces the weight of their load – a clear double whammy. As it was, the horses were tiring too quickly, losing condition, and they were not hardening. Attempts to get Barbara to stop, even at lush areas by the riverside, completely failed. She was constantly worried about our frustratingly slow headway.

We meandered on, later getting a surprise when a pack of *cimarrones* – wild black cattle – emerged from a side canyon. These looked like Brahma bulls, with wicked looking sharp horns and a distinctive hump. They turned tail and fled crashing through the river and the undergrowth.

We stopped to check our position. I noticed an old corral tucked beneath a canopy of trees hard against the canyon wall. Why would anyone have a holding pen here? Nothing was marked on our map apart from the Diablo Mountain Range and Hidden Pasture Canyon. Was it was a remote pen used by a rancher in the vicinity? Simon, ever the romantic, wondered eagerly if it might have been an old outlaw stopover from Alma to Silver City. No way to tell.

In Alma in 1899, Butch and Sundance deftly outwit a Pinkerton agent who is hard on their heels. Operative Frank Murray tracks them down following the Union Pacific train robbery at Wilcox, Wyoming. He meticulously traces dollar bills stolen in the Wilcox robbery to Silver City, and to a bar the outlaws frequent. The artful dodgers quickly vanish into a hideout in or near Whitewater Canyon; nobody knows precisely where.

SIMON:

I pored over the maps and concluded there was a dim possibility. *If* Butch and Sundance had exited Alma via the Cardinal Gap to Angel Roost, it followed Whitewater Creek into the Mogollon Mountains where Butch hid out. Taking an indistinct trail to Lipsey Canyon, around Mogollon Baldy (at 10,770 feet), the track would drop them into Gobbler Canyon and finally Turkey Creek, close to Hidden Pasture and the mysterious old corral. Perhaps we had uncovered a secret path. Who knows?

History notes that Butch was always cautious. Using a busy

thoroughfare from Silver City to Alma was too risky for him. He and Sundance probably rode through what is now the Gila Wilderness to avoid detection. The outlaws used compasses, and Richard's course, plotted from El Paso, ran straight into the track from Piños Altos. We reckon that Butch and Sundance stayed hidden and rode the shortest distances available. We had probably ridden the same path they had taken a century earlier, and maybe – viewed from the outside world – we too had temporarily vanished into thin air.

Astride Dube, I could really feel the presence of the bandit duo. I imagined them swaying silently in the saddle, letting the horses have their heads. This was what the ride was about – not well-worn tracks but old, hidden trails.

At Turkey Canyon, we deliberated which direction to ride for Gila town. We heard an engine rumbling. Minutes later, an old, battered fifties truck appeared, bouncing along the rough track. It stopped. Danny Check was out on a fishing trip with two boys. We were surprised to see humans so far from civilization, and Danny was equally amazed to meet three English riders. He offered us a cool beer. It was the best offer since leaving the Burris Bar and it felt like a lottery win. Danny gave us directions and departed.

We followed a red sandy track along Brushy Canyon. It wove a trail up and over the rolling hills. Altitude had dropped to 5,800 feet. I stopped and took one last look at the imposing Gila Wilderness. The sun's rays cascaded down over Watson Mountain. We were virtually through and unscathed; it was a very good feeling. The horses were tired with the uphill slog, and dusk began to close in quickly.

We stopped for the night at another deserted old corral. It was a dry camp with no feed or water for the horses. The wind returned with a vengeance, and dust came whipping over the ridge top. We draped tarpaulins over the barbed wire fence as a windbreak and huddled in their inadequate shelter. Supper was wolfed down, and we turned straight into our sleeping bags, ready for another cold night under the stars. We had cracked the Gila. I gazed at the heavens, but could not imagine Butch and Sundance camping here. It was too exposed.

Our next major obstacle was the Mogollon Rim. East of Phoenix where the cooler highlands rise into picture perfect forests, the landscape mirrors that of southern Sweden or the Northern Plains.

The Mogollon Rim is a long, timbered, rocky escarpment that stretches for 300 miles from New Mexico into the heart of Arizona. It boasts the world's largest Ponderosa pines.

A road climbs up through mountain resorts into Zane Grey country, where the popular author wrote – and located – many of the yarns that fuelled over a hundred early Western movies, like *Riders of the Purple Sage*, *Wild Horse Mesa* and *Under the Tonto Rim*. He thus played a key role in the birth of a film genre, which eventually reached its pinnacle with *Butch Cassidy and the Sundance Kid*, for which a great many owe his memory a very special debt; myself in particular. I tipped my hat to him.

Ascending out of the Tonto Basin's elevations of 5,000 feet, on the Rim itself you climb to 7,000 feet. It is spectacular country normally seen from the comfort of an air-conditioned car. Tonto means foolish, but I felt we were very smart to be drinking in this wonderful vista on horseback. It really is the only way to identify with outlaw country.

RICHARD:

In the morning, the horses were alert and restless. Something had spooked them and since they would smell danger long before we could, we looked around carefully. Then I spotted it. I pointed wordlessly to where, less than three hundred yards from our camp, a big black bear was ambling up a slope. We were grateful he was not going in our direction. Our packs contained fresh meat amongst other goodies, and a bear clawing its way through our outfit was no way to start the day. Also, while our .30 calibre Winchester with its 30 grain cartridge would doubtless have the stopping power to drop a charging angry bear the size of Godzilla, I was in no particular hurry to test the theory.

It was May 3. We planned to reach Gila Town for vital re-supply. Packing quite briskly compared with our earlier efforts, we proceeded along a dusty track for around three miles until the first few houses came into view. Simon had elected to introduce himself to the first residents we saw for guidance, so he rode up a drive to glad hand in his own inimitable way the unsuspecting victims as they tended their garden.

"Hi! How far to the general store in Gila?" he boomed.

"Bout five miles. You Australian?"

"English. Simon Casson."

He offered his hand.

"Oscar and Sue Davis," said Oscar. "Where've you ridden from?"

"Mexico – we're on our way to Canada," Simon replied proudly.

Oscar stopped to digest the remark, then very kindly suggested we unpack and rest the horses in their paddock. It was far too good an offer to refuse.

Later, inside Gila's general store, we were introduced to the locals as the "Outlaw Trail riders". This was meat and drink to Simon.

He shook hands cordially with just about everyone, but I noticed that they all backed off pretty swiftly. It took a minute or two for the penny to drop, then I posed the obvious question:

"Do we smell?"

Oscar laughed, "You'd better take a shower when we get back!"

The Davises dwelt in an interesting home made up of four buildings scattered over a wide desert plot. Each comprised a kitchen, bathroom and master bedroom. The main house incorporated a splendid chapel, office and tack room constructed out of dense straw bales, rendered with plaster and topped with white paint. From the outside, the building looked like typical southwest adobe.

We relaxed in the warm kitchen and drank coffee, savouring our first day off since leaving Mexico sixteen days and two hundred desolate miles ago. Oscar and Sue invited us to stay overnight, saying that their two friends would like to meet us. We accepted gratefully.

It was pleasant to be civilised for a spell. Scott and Shelley Victor joined in cheerfully, and we settled down to good conversation and wine. Scott talked with us of bears, mules and horses. He shared Simon's interest in the Wild Bunch in Bolivia, and also Barbara's fascination with Mongolian culture. I was "volunteered" to cook steaks for supper, and they all gathered round with beer, advice and friendly abuse.

Later, Sue pressed special herbal treatments into our hands for our impending travels, warning us about the perils of sunburn. I also took the opportunity to clean our weapons and to re-divide and lighten the loads for the trail ahead.

SIMON:

Butch and Sundance had left us few known trails in New Mexico, but anyone who has done any research knows about their times at the WS Ranch in Alma. Which way had the duo ridden out of the Gila Wilderness, to Silver City and beyond?

We rode out over the Shelley Ditch irrigation channel along a dusty track towards Sacaton Mesa. Despite a fine, blue-sky day, the wind relentlessly spat dust into our faces, at times seeming to blow us backwards. The horses loathed it, and we continued grimly to Mud Spring Mesa. Mogollon Baldy towered over us in splendour at 10,770 feet, and the vast open space shrank us to insignificance. We stopped opposite Rain Creek Mesa. The range was devoid of grazing, so we were forced to corral the horses, unwilling to risk turning them out on hobbles.

Barbara announced that she was unhappy about the lack of progress, and about the horses' workload. She also suggested we were on a wild goose chase. The reality was simple: we were all going through a process of toughening. We were on a rapid learning curve, and the first thing we had learned was that our earlier calculations were too ambitious.

Our maps suggested there were no easy trails in any direction, only high desert. In all likelihood, Butch and Sundance rode at night, avoiding the more heavily travelled route from Mesilla to El Paso. Unlike us greenhorns, they almost certainly had the sense never to trail through the southwest desert by day at this time of year.

Tomorrow promised a long ride to Alma, and it was twenty-four hours since the horses had had a drink. Also, we had only a limited amount of sweet-feed to offer them as sustenance. Supper was consumed in deathly silence. A line of trees sufficed as shelter, and we tucked ourselves beneath the overhanging branches. The horses paced madly and chased one another round the corral all night. That meant they would be unrested and tired tomorrow. In short, conditions were shit.

We packed lightning-quick and left, stopping for water at a cattle sinkhole. Predictably, the horses flatly refused the brown, stinking liquid, so we rode to the Siggins Ranch. Two miles later, the track turned into Little Dry and Big Dry Creeks.

Near Big Dry Creek on December 18, 1885, an Eighth Cavalry detachment commanded by Lieutenant Fountain is ambushed while pursuing the elusive Geronimo. The troop starts out from Fort Bayard, and two-thirds of the way up Soldier Hill, the advance party is met by a volley of gunfire from front and sides. Concealed behind cedars and brush, the Apaches kill six soldiers in the gun battle that follows. Fifteen minutes later, the main body under Fountain (who has a bad case of dysentery) comes up to find the Indians have removed guns and ammunition from the dead men and vanished without trace.

SIMON:

We rode round the "S" bends, noting it was a great place for an ambush. On reaching Glenwood, I foolishly believed the day was virtually over and it would be a formality to ride to the WS Ranch, but on seeking directions, we were told we were still seven miles from our destination.

The news was like a death knell. It equated to two extra hours of riding on fit horses, or three and a half hours on ours. Shit! We gritted our teeth and mounted, riding through Glenwood's sleepy suburbs. Our morale drooped with the slowly sinking sun. Where could we camp if we didn't reach the WS by nightfall?

Eventually we made it, virtually in the dark and exhausted, to be greeted by current owner Margie McKeen. I was very relieved. Just two hundred and fifty miles from the border, we had reached our first milestone: an important way station on the Outlaw Trail.

Little did we know that Joe Armstrong had requested Margie to keep us there at all costs to rest the horses. After thirty miles, much of it near vertical, they were definitely in no condition to be used tomorrow.

THE BLUE WILDERNESS

"Horses ain't good for much more."
THE SUNDANCE KID

SIMON:

We anchored ourselves at the WS spread for a well-earned and much-needed four day rest. The ranch and indeed the nearby town of Alma are major landmarks on the elusive trail of Butch and Sundance. There is no trace of them in the town – only a few old corrals and a trading post remain of Alma's original site, though both ranch and local community are rich with oral memories handed down from generation to generation.

Still in its early years, the Alma story is broadly the story in miniature of much of the American southwest during and after the Civil War. Settlers arrive from the East and set up communities in a land so desert it can barely support its indigenous, mainly Apache population. There are minor frictions and skirmishes, but the serious problems only arise when gold, silver or both are discovered. Then follows a swift population influx, a boom in the micro-economy and lots of jockeying for the most likely land. This results in displaced Indians and leads in turn to a sharp increase in Apache depredations, but also in the government's willingness to send more and better soldiers to protect its citizens – and especially their gold mines!

Typically, then, the discovery of gold and silver at the Cooney Mine boosts Alma's economy and the tiny township suddenly boasts a steam and stamp mill, saloons, general stores, a hotel, blacksmith, shoemaker, physician, Justice of the Peace and a population of 150. The original location of the town is the east bank of the San Francisco River, north of Mineral Creek.

Close to Alma is the eastern boundary of the WS. This big spread is the last ranch at which the outlaws work stints in 1898-1899. Butch Cassidy, Elzy Lay, Ben Kilpatrick, Harry Longabaugh and Harvey Logan all, under their various aliases, spend time in this neighbourhood.

The WS is one of seven or eight ranches along the Outlaw Trail where a cowboy can rein in and sign on for work with few questions asked. Beneficially from the outlaws' viewpoint, the WS is located about a hundred miles north of the equally outlaw-friendly Erie Ranch, across the state line in Arizona.

The WS lies in a flat valley that runs along the San Francisco River. Harold C. Wilson, a British businessman and investor, founds the spread in 1882 and manages until it until 1887 when it is taken over by Captain William S. French, an Englishman and former soldier who resigns his commission to raise cattle in America. The WS doesn't own much more than 1,500 acres, but the range is extensive, extending from Alma on the east to the Blue River in Arizona, a distance of nearly twenty miles.

RICHARD:

I logged our mileage. It didn't look good, just two hundred and fifty-one completed in nineteen days. Mathematically a week overdue, daily averages stood at 13.15, or 1.6 miles per hour, over an eight-hour day in the saddle.

The following morning, we met for breakfast with Tom Klumker in the Red Hen Café. Tom was a wiry frontiersman with much to offer, having spent twenty-five years outfitting horse trips and hunters in the Gila and Blue Wilderness regions. We reflected on the trip to date, and Tom pointed out to us that if riding had been tough so far, it was to get much worse.

He absolutely guaranteed that the next section – which ran through the Blue Wilderness, cutting through the Mogollon Rim into the hot, flat east of Arizona – would prove even harder going. Barbara expressed her frustration, repeating her deepening alarm over the expedition's timeframe.

"How can we speed up?" she pleaded.

"Well, you jest cain't do that," Tom replied impassively, sipping hot coffee.

"What about trotting the horses?" Barbara queried earnestly.

"Nope. Not with them packs, and they're not fit enough anyways."

That did it! Our prediction of a three month ride had stretched to four, then five – maybe more. Speed depended on the condition of the horses, plus a measure of luck when battling against the relentless Sonora Desert. At the two hundred and fifty-one mile mark, more cracks in our plan were appearing. We needed to know much more about horse management, compared with which actual riding skill was turning out to be irrelevant, a point not lost on Simon, our most-criticised equestrian.

Back at the WS, Tom quickly assessed the condition of the horses. Rocket, Miss-Ap and Dube, though muscling up, had lost considerable weight. No amount of dressing and padding would render Rocket fit for another day's packing. His withers were totally beef-streaked and Miss-Ap's were deteriorating. It was too late for solutions. The conversation turned to buying two extra horses. Simon suggested hauling Rocket up the trail later. Tom dismissed that notion.

"He's not gonna be fit before you guys make Canada."

We urgently needed a replacement horse before leaving the WS. The first string of five was down to three. Yazz, although slowly mending from the trauma at Strauss, had two new circular swellings on his flanks. Tom inspected those too, then my heavy roping saddle. Apparently, the O-rings beneath the tooled leather skirts were compressing the horse's sides. This promised more sores if he continued to lose condition. The major problem was to keep the horses fat in such a hostile environment.

Tom could see our dream fading rapidly. He provided a very generous quick fix, offering to lend us Bones, a hardened mountain horse – Rocket to be swapped as a temporary exchange until the end of the ride (which at that particular moment looked like this year, next year, sometime, never). Bones, an eleven-year-old dark bay mare of fifteen hands, had been a reliable mount on numerous trips into the Gila and the Blue, and was easily up to the task either as a pack or saddle animal. We needed time to consider Tom's handsome offer – like about one and a half seconds – then Simon accompanied him gratefully to help re-shoe her.

Our string now comprised three mares and two geldings. We could look forward to a new equine contest to establish the pecking order amongst the mares.

SIMON:

Later, I talked to Hugh B. McKeen II, the current WS ranch owner. I wanted to understand more about the West today and about his family who had pioneered the ranch, so I cross-examined him on a number of interesting topics, to which he responded willingly.

McKeen's great-grandfather is from New York of American Revolution ancestry. He migrates across the West to Texas. His father is born in 1863, but around 1880, the family moves to Arizona and finally locates in Silver City around 1882. Buying mule teams, McKeen organizes contracts with the railroad and moves to Mexico. Eventually, he arrives in Alma, going to work on the WS. By spring 1889, a move to Cooney, shrewd trading and hard work combine to extend his ranch and cattle holdings to the point where he becomes a major force in the New Mexico cattle world.

Today, the ranch remains in private hands, jointly owned by Hugh B. and his Uncle, John McKeen. It is still a rawhide outfit – horses do the work they did over a century ago. The only building remaining from the outlaw times is a white adobe wall covered by a barn.

We learned that in some states, much of the land along the Outlaw Trail now belongs to big corporations, with the result that traditional ranching values and the pioneering way of life are eroding steadily. Government agencies have begun to take a heavy hand in altering agendas. I asked about the National Forest Service:

"They want ranchers in their present form out, and they want control of the land, killing off homesteading and water rights and only issuing permits for the short-term," said Hugh.

On the land itself:

"It's changing, it's not grassland – there's more trees that have continued to be a real problem, whereby cutting and burning operations have been restricted."

On ranching today:

"It's being controlled by bureaucrats and their endless processes, with penalties for exceeding cattle numerage per acre, and rotation rulings, along with constant modifications to the utilisation guidelines."

On threats for the future:

"The rivers are drying up and have been for years. Over thirty-six years, there's been erosion and more trees. In my grandfather's time, the watershed was in better shape."

On horses:

"Horses are smarter today with different breeding. In the old days horses did pretty much everything you wanted. They weren't so intelligent."

On the outlaws:

"I don't remember many stories. When they worked for the WS, there were no problems, they were just good old boys. But there were far more Indian problems then, and a lot of people lost relatives."

Butch first works at the WS in 1896. He arrives not with Sundance, but with his other good friend, Elzy Lay. Captain French urgently needs capable, trustworthy hands, and when the pair shows up in the company of a ranch ramrod named Perry Tucker, French agrees to terms. Tucker takes over the day-to-day running of the outfit, with Butch (using the alias Jim Lowe) and Elzy Lay (calling himself William McGinnis) in support.

French is impressed. He notes of Lowe that he is solidly built and can probably handle himself if things get tough. He records that McGinnis seems several years younger, much taller and darker – in fact, quite a good-looking young man, debonair, with a bit of a swagger. He seems clearly a cut above the ordinary cowboy and undoubtedly has more education.

French adds that now Jim and Mac are in place the flow of new hands seems to increase more or less when required, which brings a change to the previous range problems: the way they handle stock is a marvel, and the rustlers are suppressed.

Hands come and go, and, despite French's worry when good hands leave, he comments that Jim replaces them with others equally capable. Even the infamous Harvey Logan (known here as Tom Capehart) makes a lasting impression on French as Jim Lowe's right-hand man. French regrets seeing the man leave.

Over the three or four years that follow, Butch and his friends return several times to work at the WS for brief spells. And these competent, hardworking and always welcome cowboys are the very same desperadoes the law enforcement agencies are so intent on exterminating.

SIMON:

In everything he said, Hugh B. McKeen II was frank and open. He hurt over the erosion and potential closure of a way of life, which was happening in other parts of the West too. Governing bodies were now dictating the terms to pioneering families which had been around for seven generations. I understood the mistrust and anger clearly because I too have always hated bureaucracy, rules and red tape.

Running cattle alone is almost unworkable today. Dude ranching has become important to many families in the West because it is the only way to generate more income. There are close parallels with the development of popular tourist attractions at Britain's stately homes – undignified, but profitable.

RICHARD:

Barbara seemed to be distancing herself from us and clinging to Margie for support, leaving Simon and me to get to grips with the expedition proper. Margie looked the horses over and told me that Dube had a large swelling on his near hind leg, and also that a few horseshoes were loose. Having stood idle, Dube's leg had filled up – a phenomenon peculiar to horses when they rest after heavy exercise.

It caused him slight lameness, but a cold compress helped. Despite the horses being leaner and muscled up, the awful prospect arose once more of further unaffordable changes in our *remuda*.

We were begged, again, most generously, to extend our stay. It made every kind of sense, especially considering the horse situation. We hosted a dinner to show our appreciation for the warm hospitality extended to us, and later we all piled into the Blue Front Saloon to enjoy a very cheerful get-together with Tom and his family. The jovial host, Bucky Alred, delighted Simon by introducing himself as the grandson of the owner of the original bar used by Butch, Sundance and other known outlaws, a bar which has its own small place in history.

The reason Pinkerton agent Murray is able to trace banknotes from the Wilcox, Wyoming train robbery to New Mexico, and specifically to a bank in Silver City via a local store in Alma, is that in dynamiting the express safe, the robbers blow one corner, the same corner, off every single bill!

Murray identifies himself to William French as an operative of the Pinkerton National Detective Agency, currently investigating a train robbery. He explains that the storekeeper in Alma confirms these bills were cashed by a WS employee named Johnny Ward, who in turn says he got the money from another WS hand, now departed, on a horse trade. Murray is hot on the trail of the culprits, and French is shown a picture of wanted man Butch Cassidy, whom he now realises is his trail boss Jim Lowe.

Murray actually enters the saloon where Butch is tending bar and asks questions about the gang's whereabouts. He is treated to a drink by the very man he is looking for.

When Jim Lowe returns to the WS, French tells him of Murray's visit. Lowe grins and replies that he knows the detective is in the area and that he and Capehart bought Murray a drink. Much later, Murray claims that he was in fact well aware of the true identity of "Jim Lowe" and "Tom Capehart" but was forced to turn a blind eye to save his own life; an episode he omits to mention in his report when he gets back to headquarters.

SIMON:

We finally departed from the splendid, irrigated WS pastures. Lining up for final photographs was a proud moment. I was looking forward eagerly to the next section, conquering the tricky Blue. It promised to be difficult and challenging riding. Tom Klumker reckoned that nobody had ridden deep into the Blue Wilderness on horseback for years.

The dusty trail meandered along Keller Canyon for thirteen miles, rising over rolling hills into Spring Canyon. Four hours later, we arrived safely at the Arizona state line – a barbed wire fence. It was a minor landmark, the departure from New Mexico into the next state. Richard pointed out Horse Mountain at 7,907 feet.

RICHARD:

Over Alma Mesa, the trail got steeper and rougher, trees hampering our progress. Deadfall and jagged rocks were extremely hard on the horses' hooves. Barbara took a shortcut into Yam Canyon where wolves had been re-introduced. Simon and I followed, creeping slowly up the rocky slope. Barbara, towing the packhorses, soon disappeared over a ridge.

Concerned for Yazz's flanks, I had decided to ride with a very slightly looser girth. It was my downfall, literally. As we scrambled up the rocky slope, ducking and weaving to avoid low branches and tree roots, my saddle slipped. Yazz panicked and resorted to a frenzy of bucking and kicking like a rodeo bronco, which dumped me unceremoniously. He tried to run away from the saddle, now hanging beneath his belly, and my kit – including pommel bags, slicker and water canteens – was strewn over a large area. My pride was damaged along with my hurt ribs, which had not yet healed.

Next, Yazz bolted towards a dense thicket, thundering through vicious thorny brush with saddle and reins catching and snagging on substantial deadfall. It was unnerving as well as painful, but fortunately, he stopped two hundred yards away, snorting, blowing hard and sweating profusely. Simon retrieved him for me, we collected my scattered kit and when Yazz calmed down we re-saddled, re-packed and continued on our now rather careful way. We had just missed the calamity of losing another horse.

As we proceeded still cautiously over Alma Mesa, the narrow trail took us deep into a juniper and pine forest. At the fork of Yam Creek we edged down a tricky mud slope. The sun quickly disappeared over Horse Mountain and dusk loomed. We struck camp close to Little Blue Creek in the midst of trees. There was no grass or water, but it was an uneventful night.

In May 1885, Captain French is with five men on a routine trawl of wild cattle to increase the WS herd. Not very far from Little Blue Creek, they spot turkey buzzards wheeling, then dead horses with their throats cut. They also find bodies which they can identify as the Luther brothers, who have been shot and clubbed to death.

Their worst fears are confirmed. The Apaches, tiring of their new agrarian lifestyle, have once again broken out of the San Carlos reservation, skillfully dodging the cavalry posts. As usual, Geronimo gets all the national headlines, but it is actually the much less famous Chihuahua and his band who raid, slaughter and create mayhem for three weeks in southern Arizona and New Mexico, evading over twenty Troops of searching cavalry before slipping invisibly over the Mexican border.

RICHARD:

Next day, we moved ahead on foot for three hours, clearing deadfall. Progress was agonisingly slow, our pace less than one mile an hour. Hemmed in a deep *arroyo*, the horses thrashed, staggered and stumbled amongst the rocks as we picked our way down the uncompromising trail. It took four gruelling hours to reach Bear Valley. We had made a total of two miles. I sat pensively checking the map and looked ahead. There had been what looked like a serious forest fire. The trail ahead was once again obliterated.

The Blue Wilderness is an area of around 222,000 acres of pristine terrain, the last remaining primitive area of National Forest land. It is a special place, far from the metropolis and with limited access.

The incredibly harsh environment has anyway kept visitors to a minimum.

At higher altitudes, we were surrounded by ponderosa pines. Sharp-eyed travellers are often rewarded with sightings of lizards, javelina (a pig-like mammal endemic to the American southwest), coyotes, turkeys, mule deer, black bears, wolves and the occasional mountain lion. The racket we made while travelling ensured we saw nothing! We rode blindly through the forest trying to pick out a kind trail for the tired horses. Looping too far southwest, we squandered valuable time.

Ahead lay the infamous Mogollon Rim, a hundred-mile mountain stretch, which culminates in a natural escarpment over half a mile high, beyond which there is a fifty-five mile expanse of very hostile desert. It would be tough going. Here we would be following Coronado's Trail – the Spanish had called this part of Arizona the *desploblado*, "a howling wilderness that took fifteen days to cross" – this part of the journey alone had nearly killed Coronado and his men. I wondered if we would suffer an identical fate, and sat tight on Dube hoping my sphincter muscle would hold out…

We followed Little Blue Creek and left Bear Valley at 7,200 feet. Bear Mountain towered at 8,550 feet. Riding down the narrow path despite the map showing a trail at Largo Creek, I found myself hoping we would not end up facing a blank wall with no way through. Suddenly, we were out of the woodland and onto a bluff, where we stopped to take in the panoramic view. I checked the map very carefully. We were adjacent to Lamphier Canyon, and had somehow cut through the Rim itself, which was very good news.

SIMON:

A white, sandy, switchback path descended to the Blue River. We stopped at the corrals. I announced to Barbara that I would try to make a call ahead to warn the Marks family of our late arrival. A ranch house was conveniently opposite. I crossed the river, and after endlessly helloing, I was cautiously invited inside. The owner remained on guard, very suspicious of me. I noticed a rifle strategically propped up against the sofa, right in front of the window, where moments earlier I had been standing.

On my return, Barbara warned me with glee that Richard was furious with me.

"You've done it now," she exclaimed, crowing with satisfaction.

Richard strode over and literally threw the maps at me:

"If you don't trust my map reading, tell me where we are then!"

I was stunned.

"Hold on. I went to make a call ahead, to say we're on our way, that's all."

Richard had taken my action as a location check and a personal insult. I saw Barbara was hugely enjoying the moment. She had not informed Richard of my virtuous intentions. He and I were nose-to-nose, adrenaline pumping, only a few seconds away from fisticuffs. We cooled down, but it was an ugly scene, and I severely reprimanded Barbara for her dishonesty. She blatantly ignored me, and immediately became very pally with Richard. I felt rejected and humiliated.

This episode fuelled a growing suspicion. Was Barbara attempting to divide the team? She had agreed we would both write the book of this trip as a joint effort, but she was now dismissing this notion. We were crumbling fast. I found myself seriously wondering, was this part of a bigger plan? Was she out to hi-jill my expedition? Just because you are paranoid, I reminded myself, doesn't mean the bastards aren't out to get you.

Later, Richard asked me how I had met Barbara, and how much information I had been given about her Russian ride. He told me bluntly that he had rescued her on a commercial basis for her then-husband, Giles. She was an excellent horsewoman but not an expedition rider, and she rode like an old colonial. It was a bombshell. I was alarmed, angry and felt I had been duped. The horse expert was no expert, and to cap it all, Richard and I were scrapping like schoolboys.

The distinct possibility of a split-up was in the air. I mistrusted Barbara, fearing she harboured ulterior motives. I seethed with rage, and decided nobody would usurp me. My feelings were running pretty deep. I had spent years working on this challenge, with all sorts of other possibilities hanging on its success.

Another valuable lesson I learned about expeditions is that the rules must be agreed in writing before the start. Not having done this, I needed to keep a close guard on my contacts and forward arrangements. They were my only bargaining tools, and my sole insurance against a *Red River* scenario. (Howard Hawks's *Red River* movie was a Western cattle-drive version of *Mutiny on the Bounty*!)

I dug deep and prepared to do whatever had to be done to maintain a truce with Richard, despite our differing views. As for Barbara, whenever I looked at her, my head was filled with the haunting refrain of the *deguelo* – "cutthroat," the Alamo promise of "no quarter." From this point on, I adopted the outlaw mentality of self-survival at any cost. We had ridden a mere 280 miles, and the team was splitting apart at the seams.

We rode into the beautiful Marks ranch at the base of a small canyon close to Clifton some twenty-nine miles from the WS. It was a great, little-known hideaway. The 1891 ranch house hewn out of thick cedar logs, and with a stone chimney, had been splendidly restored. A brand new corrugated roof protected it from the elements. The property was set amongst the firs, and it was idyllic. The fifth generation family still operated the ranch in the old style.

Clifton is the outlaws' favourite recreation base when they plan a celebration. In Alma, Butch keeps the gang on their best behaviour – Clifton is the party place. From Alma, Butch and Sundance usually take the Buzzard Canyon trail from the ranch, riding over Sunflower Mesa round Charlie Moore Mountain and Maple Peak before following a winding trail past Horse Canyon through Morris Day Gap. This connects to Wild Bunch Canyon where Butch and Sundance ride south through Salt Ground Canyon before crossing the San Francisco River.

Party place or not, Clifton's bank is not sacrosanct – it is robbed by Harvey Logan and Ben Kilpatrick on February 20, 1898. The outlaws plan a good escape route making use of a long, deep arroyo a short distance out of town. There are no crossings, but Logan carefully trains his mount to jump across the arroyo at a feasible but still alarming looking point. Kilpatrick, too heavy for his horse to follow suit, elects to wait with fresh mounts ten miles out of town.

Logan holds up the bank single-handed and gets away with

$12,000, an excellent haul. Cunning as ever, he runs to a nearby hill and waits until the posse has set off in the most obvious direction before riding towards the arroyo. He is spotted, but it is no problem. He easily clears the tricky cleft, leaving the posse literally standing, and rides off to join Kilpatrick.

The noose tightens after the Southern Pacific train robbery at Steins Pass, New Mexico, on December 9, 1897. George Scarborough, Jeff Milton and a hardened posse pursue the bandits into Arizona, stopping at the Cienega Ranch of the San Simon Cattle Company. Finding the culprits, including Tom Capehart (Harvey Logan) gone, they pick up the trail heading south, eventually converging near the Chiricahua Mountains, 120 miles away and track up Tex Canyon, another outlaw rendezvous. As described by rancher Jesse James Benton, "I run onto a ranch in wild beautiful locality, at the south end of the range, a wooded region with a pretty spring and a chinked log house in a clearing. When I saw that place my heart skipped a beat I wanted for myself... smoke was coming out of the house, so I rode up and were surprised to find eight outlaws there, all wanted men and tough hombres. Some of them took part in the Steins pass train robbery... I asked if it was for sale. It was not. I knew why. It was an ideal hideaway." Tom Capehart was arrested with several others after the crime. Cipriano Baca, Marshal of Clifton, Arizona was in the posse. Clifton was a Wild Bunch party place. Did Baca know Butch and turn a blind eye to certain visitors?

SIMON:

That night we slept in a barn on hay bales. The following morning, it was freezing, the mercury recording minus one. After breakfast and the formalities, we set about packing pretty briskly.

The main concerns were Miss-Ap's and Dube's withers. Richard had cut away the blankets to relieve the pressure, but enough damage had been done travelling through the higher reaches of the Blue. Once a horse gets a sore back, that is it, so I reluctantly accepted the inevitable – and unaffordable – need to replace the mare. We stopped en route at Jim Joy's on the Blue Crossing to re-shoe Dube, Miss-Ap and Pistolera, re-packed and were on our way. It was to be a short riding day.

The heat returned with a vengeance. Near Jackson Canyon, we made camp at Upper Blue. It made a welcome change to quit early and have an easy time. We turned the horses loose to graze contentedly. We had clear running water nearby and plenty of wood for a fire.

I had time to consider my stomach. It felt like lead because our diet had lacked fresh fruit and vegetables. Crapping in the wilderness was a great leveller. Crouched behind a convenient tree, I was torn between tears of joy at finally doing the business after a four day interval and the undiluted agony of passing what felt like a rectangular house brick.

RICHARD:

The San Francisco Mountains rose to over 8,600 feet. The deserted road wound back into New Mexico for a mile. At Whispering Pines, we started a long, hard slog up Turkey Canyon. The trail climbed sharply (altitude was close to 7,200 feet) and we had to tackle it in stages to rest the horses.

Arizona was green and water plentiful – by contrast with New Mexico, which offered neither. Riding the high country was excellent. Soon, we passed our first country club. All this way, and then a bloody golf course! It was like climbing Everest and finding a McDonald's at the summit.

We rode into Alpine. Settled in 1876, it owes its name to the mountain scenery that surrounds it. At the local store, we bought ice cream, cookies and Coke, and then rode for the Robart's place in the hope of camping overnight.

Dink Robart spotted us riding across the meadow a mile away. We were cordially invited into their house, which was full of character. A Cambodian pot-bellied pig had to be negotiated in the hall, and a goat was asleep on the sofa. The goat's name was Piddle; we did not care to ask why.

We slept under the stars, and then the following morning, we made for Bear Wallow Café and met Judge Bernardo Velasco. Simon asked the judge about the penalties for horse theft.

"You can still get seven years and a few thousand dollar fine, depending on the value of the horse," said Velasco. He pondered for a moment, then added:

"Take my card, in case you get trouble."

Clearly, Simon was still fantasising about stealing that handsome pinto, property of the hostile giant near Outlaw Canyon, the guy with a dog as big and menacing as a Mexican fighting bull.

Dink was short and bearded and wore overalls and a baseball cap. After carefully checking the horses over, he applied cherry juice, a secret red concoction for sores which he produced from a huge outside fridge that doubled as a medical cabinet. It contained a vast array of potions, needles, syringes and lotions – including teat balm, an item that seemed to Simon to be full of intriguing possibilities.

North of Alpine, we passed the Continental Divide. The mountain scenery melted away as the terrain flattened. The Outlaw Trail runs its course along the Little Colorado River starting at Nutrioso Creek. We were four miles west of the Escudilla Wilderness, one of the few reserved for foot and horseback travel only.

We made eighteen miles and camped near Nelson reservoir, altitude 6,500 feet. After unpacking, I noticed Dube's and Miss-Ap's sores were getting worse. Cherry juice and teat balm were no use for injuries as advanced as these, although I continued applying them in the hope of preventing infection.

Barbara suggested we trade the worn horses for mules, and Simon agreed grudgingly that it was a good idea in principle. Miss-Ap would have to retire and another horse needed to be bought. The budget was spiralling upwards. Later we returned to our sleeping bags under the stars feeling a bit down. It was very cold that night, and there were coyotes close by, yelping and barking across the meadow. Our horses were restless, moving uneasily on the picket line.

At 0400 hours, I climbed out of my sleeping bag and put the coffee on. The sun's first rays scattered shadows over a cool earth. Watching dawn break has always been one of my favourite moments, and it was quietly satisfying to have the wilderness to myself before the others rose. At first light each morning, I would prepare the nosebags for the horses, start a fire and serve hot coffee to Barbara and Simon as to the manor-born.

BEHOLD: A PALE HORSE

"You can come with us, but the moment you start to moan and whine,
I don't care where we are, I'm dumping you flat."
THE SUNDANCE KID

"Don't sugarcoat it like that, Sundance – tell her straight."
BUTCH CASSIDY

SIMON:

Once back on the tarmac, the heat was cruel. Near the rodeo corrals on the outskirts of Springerville, a small truck pulled over. Alert driver Terry Wagner was interested to learn why three lunatic riders were out in the midday sun. A good question! I briefed him on the ride in a few sentences. He seemed a friendly and knowledgeable guy, and we agreed to meet at a feed store a mile yonder.

Richard wanted to grain the horses before riding on, and while we were removing the packs, Terry saw the damage to Miss-Ap's withers. He whistled, and immediately made a strong recommendation that we go and ring our outfitters immediately. I was feeling very nervous, and Terry was convincing, so I hopped aboard, and we left Barbara and Richard to their own devices.

"You want mules," advised Terry as I slammed the truck door.

"We've got horses," I replied, missing the context.

"What I mean is you ought to use mules for your pack animals."

On the way, we drew into the 26 Bar Ranch near Eager. It had belonged to the greatest screen cowboy of all time, John Wayne.

Busy cutting bulls and choking down dust in the corrals was Joel Quisenberry. I had to do a double take – he was the spitting image of film actor Sam Elliott (Virgil Earp in *Tombstone*). Terry described our plight whilst Joel got on with his tasks. I smiled weakly, shook hands and accepted a typically spontaneous and kind offer to stop at his place at Salado. I did like these Westerners.

We returned to Springerville, telephoned the Armstrongs and left instructions where they could find us, then went to rejoin the others. Richard had vanished, and Barbara was anxiously walking Dube round in circles.

"Dube's got colic and looks sick, and Richard's gone off to the vet's," Barbara announced.

Dube was sweating profusely. Richard soon re-appeared with syringes, needles, medicine and Dean Berkey, a friend of Tom Klumker's who was expecting our arrival. He had been on the lookout for us.

"Your horse is in trouble – give him those shots and see what happens," Dean advised.

Richard jammed the needle in. Dube suddenly coughed and shook violently, then hawked up a lump of mashed green pellets. The improvement was rapid. So the problem was not colic; small, dry alfalfa pellets had gotten stuck in his throat. No water was available to wash down the hard feed, so it was like asking humans to eat a packet of dry Jacobs Cream Crackers with nothing to drink. Relieved, we reloaded and hit the trail.

The Little Colorado River cut through a flat landscape of scrub, sand, cactus and shale. After a few miles, the fertile high country melted into desert. The lower altitude signalled greater heat, less water and scant feed – it was back to the grind. Meanwhile, the wind chucked squalls of dust into our faces.

To Richard's disappointment, Springerville had proved to be an inconsequential town offering zero excitement or entertainment.

"Isn't there a decent place in Arizona to find some excitement?" he asked.

"Winslow – maybe Tuba City," I answered.

"Christ! I want to relax and enjoy myself, we haven't done any of that yet!" Richard was fed up.

"A hundred years ago, these towns were happening places, but not today," I said, rubbing salt into the wound.

"God, I hope it's not like this all the way. I'm bored and pissed off!" snapped Richard.

I had a quiet smile. At best, the towns on our route were one-horse outfits – until our five horses made them six!

We rode on in the baking heat, with Richard muttering and cursing. Not that I had much to smile about. My idea was to enjoy the experience, the country, people, places and the fun of being outdoors. So far, it was falling short of my expectations too. We weren't gelling as a team, which was deeply depressing. And the roadwork was wicked.

Motorists waved, thoughtless truckers blew their horns and some drove so close to the horses their slipstream almost knocked us over, spooking the horses. I hated the road. It was a time of stress mainly for the unpredictable reactions of the horses, in particular the pack animals.

The Little Colorado River was to be our guide for the next few hundred miles, so the navigation was a doddle. We moved steadily along, enduring endless, monotonous, flat, barren terrain. I completely understood Richard's desire for some "excitement." No wonder cowboys used to ride in and hooraw the town after a cattle-drive, letting off their guns, riding their horses along sidewalks and sometimes even into saloons, as portrayed in Michael Winner's excellent *Lawman* movie.

We trudged on. Not a blade of grass to be seen, and the heat was melting the tarmac. Soon we would be approaching the Painted Desert. A state penitentiary loomed up. What a perfect location; no way would anyone risk escaping from here to die of heat exhaustion or thirst. Talk about mad dogs and Englishmen. If any of the inmates had scanned the road with binoculars that afternoon, they might have seen five horses and three clowns.

Late in the afternoon, Joel Quisenberry overtook us and stopped his vehicle to introduce himself quickly to Richard and Barbara.

"Not too far now, my place is on the left, you can't miss us. See you later," he said cheerfully and disappeared over the horizon in a cloud of dust.

We rode for hours. Our pace was pathetic. Dusk was gathering and night riding might be on the agenda. Then Joel re-appeared with a huge horse trailer hitched behind his pick-up.

"The traffic's way too risky for riding along here. I'll haul you guys the last two miles," he announced. It was a generous offer. I asked myself, was this cheating? The reality was that at any moment, we could be wiped off the map by a speeding juggernaut. This was not a hazard Butch and Sundance ever had to face.

RICHARD:

We opened the rear door. Miss-Ap and Bones, the packhorses, jumped in and were secured. Yazz suddenly barged past Dube, who promptly slipped and fell on the smooth aluminium floor. He lay thrashing about, panic-stricken, desperately attempting to get to his feet. Yazz, never one to disappoint, immediately baulked. I feared a serious horse wreck with me squeezed inside. Simon yanked on Dube's lead rope, deftly steering clear of Yazz's flailing hooves, and Dube regained his feet. The mares ignored the commotion created by Yazz. It was another close call; lucky no harm was done.

I climbed quickly up through the roof of the trailer, and then hopped into the flatbed. Joel gunned the engine and increased speed to fifty-five, wholly unperturbed by the incident. Barbara was looking mortified. I watched her periodically holding her hands over her face, tense, clearly awaiting disaster. The horses? They stood rock solid and unruffled. Simon and I smiled knowingly, because that's how horses are transported in America. They are habituated, no fuss. Barbara saw our smiles and made another entry on her already lengthy mental black list.

SIMON:

It was dark when we led the horses to the corrals. Halfway down a rocky slope, the procession abruptly halted, and Dube planted his right fore hoof firmly on my left foot. Oops! The weight of a thousand pound horse crushing my toes had an impact equivalent to Mike Tyson punching my jaw. I collapsed for a count of as many as you like.

It felt as if an anvil had just been dropped on my foot. In response to my scream, Dube kindly lifted his hoof, thus freeing me to roll about clutching my foot in agony and terror, which seemed an excellent idea at the time. Barbara was dismissive:

'It's *only* bruising and par for the course!'

On a horse, Barbara prided herself on having a good seat. Which is precisely where I would have booted her, if only I could have stood properly. My toes throbbed, and my boot felt far too tight for comfort. Turning Dube loose, I limped to the house. I decided to postpone removing my footwear. I don't want to sound overly squeamish, but I dislike the sight of crushed flesh and bone. Especially when it is my own. My policy was to grin and bear it, painkillers at the ready.

Joel's very relaxed wife Donna welcomed us into her home and set down a splendid chicken dinner. We ate heartily and chatted. I learned the town of St John's was only seven miles away. The Quisenberry property had once been a line-camp, and part of the famous Colter Ranch.

Could Butch and Sundance have stopped here? Little is known of the Wild Bunch's movements in Arizona, where they were mostly lying low. Possibly, Butch's careful discipline ensured their safety. More likely, the outlaws were all using aliases that remain unknown today. Often in the company of good Mormons, Butch and Sundance were usually pretty safe.

Yesterday had been a record twenty-nine mile day and the horses were very tired. Our stats read twenty-four days on the trail and 351 miles, still averaging only 14.4 miles per day.

Joel suggested a rest before resuming our journey. There was no argument. Apparently, Joe and Rusty Armstrong were already on the way from Las Cruces. We visited town, purchased a few things and caught up with our laundry.

In our absence, Joel and Terry had scrutinised the horses, back at the corrals. All was not well. Terry was polite but emphatic:

"You ain't gonna make Canada with those horses, except for the bay mare maybe," pointing at Bones. "They're tired and their sores are getting bad. You won't get a trade either – they're out."

We knew the horse situation was not good, but Joel and Terry's certainty was a bit of a bombshell. We entered into a protracted debate – mules versus horses. Barbara liked the idea of mules, despite not being competent to handle them.

RICHARD:

Horses or mules – it didn't matter. No more funds meant no nothing. Maybe the ride was ending right here on mile-marker 351. Our horses weren't increasing weight or building stamina on the move. Miss-Ap and Dube were out. With three horses down, two were left out of a string of five, not counting the death of Outlaw. The horse usage was alarming, and Barbara was incapable of handling the situation. She was way out of her depth – her Russian ride had taught her nothing about conditions as tough as these.

Terry broke the silence.

"Which way are you heading out of Arizona?"

Simon replied that we intended to ride through the Navajo Reservation, over the Vermillion Cliffs and then onto the Kaiparowits Plateau up to Hite.

"You'll need permits to cross the Res, if you can get them, and the horses will need vet papers. You can't trail horses through Glen Canyon either," Terry remarked.

"We've got papers organised in Las Cruces, Terry," Simon answered tartly.

"You'll have trouble. You can't get through. Your firearms will cause problems, too. They don't allow them – I used to be a police officer, I know. It's a separate nation, and you've got hellish country in Utah to negotiate. You won't make it," Terry replied, bullet-pointing his remarks.

Joel suggested a coffee.

SIMON:

What I really needed was half a bottle of Jack Daniels. My life was changing shape very swiftly. Was I losing it? I glanced at Richard, his face black as thunder. I felt deeply weary and disillusioned. The expedition was teetering on the brink of failure unless we bought another string of horses. The cost? $10,000. That could not be the solution. Quite apart from the money crisis, we couldn't go on spoiling horses in batches. We needed to re-think our horse management methods.

"Well, what now?" I asked Richard.

"What do you mean, what now?"

"You guys better come up with a plan, 'cause our horses are being used up systematically. As the historian, I'm not responsible for animal welfare."

I jerked my thumb towards Barbara who was sullenly chain-smoking across the yard.

"She is…and she can't cut it!"

There was a pause, then Richard said slowly, "Then I'll have to take over the horse management."

Something clicked. Richard was absolutely right. I realised – perhaps belatedly – that Barbara's credibility, and with it our already damaged working relationship, had been totally destroyed. With hindsight, the writing had been on the adobe wall from the corrals at Blue River, when Barbara maliciously stirred it up to make unnecessary trouble between Richard and me.

But right now, hard decisions had to be made. Quitting good jobs, torching savings, adding new debts and departing my sick mother's side were all tougher decisions than removing the bad apple from the barrel before the other two were irreversibly tainted.

Failure to me was unthinkable. Out of the window would go all those years of reconnaissance, research and planning, plus my credibility, any future projects and a potential publishing deal. Whatever commitment Barbara may have had to the expedition was already long gone. She had to go, and I must think about when and how.

I was still thinking two days later, when the arrival of the Armstrong party had a seesaw kind of effect on our morale. First we cheered to see them, and then, after warm greetings and introductions, we got down to business.

Joe and Rusty inspected the existing horses and were visibly shocked, although they brightened briefly at Yazz's improvement. Rocket, the old packhorse, was almost ruined. Joe, speaking softly, announced that Miss-Ap and Dube were definitely out, and Pistolera must return home to New Mexico.

Praising Richard for his excellent doctoring on Yazz, he nevertheless reminded us that the ride ahead promised further hardships. We had only come one eighth of the way. The big question was, how much further could we go against seemingly insurmountable odds?

There was a gloomy silence. Joe was confirming what Joel and Terry, and earlier Tom, had all said, but with even more authority. Then Rusty spoke:

"But we've brought you some replacements…"

The thought of fresh horses instantly lifted our spirits. The first out of the trailer was a pretty strawberry roan quarter horse mare named Imasizzlin'lady, aged twelve, standing at 14.2 hands. Next was Sunday, a grey mare quarter horse and thoroughbred cross, aged nine, at 15 hands, both of these being ex-ranch horses. Pancho completed the trio: a fourteen-year-old grey Arab gelding and a proven endurance horse. He was a personal favourite of Rusty's. According to Joe, all three both saddled and packed, thus enabling us to rotate duties.

The offer of new horses was mind-blowing. Not only did it mean we could go on, but it also meant that expert and responsible professionals like Joe were taking our project seriously, and considered it worth the risks involved. It was a tacit thumbs-up of approval without which we would have been foolish to continue.

So after all the alarms and pessimism, we were going on. Richard would continue with Yazz, and the grey mare would become my saddle horse.

"And I looked and behold, a pale horse…" I hoped fervently that the gloomy passage from the Book of Revelation would not prove to be an ill omen.

RICHARD:

Barbara confided in me that she wished to pull out of the expedition and continue alone. Simon told me she had made secret phone calls at Alma to the Armstrongs to the same effect. I was not best pleased. Joe was still concerned about Simon's riding ability and horse management skills, although Simon regarded the latter as Barbara's department, not his. Simon had stuck to his side of the bargain, having conceived, planned and organised the ride, but I noticed he was now playing his cards very close to his chest, and keeping to himself all details of his contacts along the route.

Barbara later notified me formally that she would continue as far as Hite, Utah before making her final decision. She could no longer tolerate Simon, saying he was incompetent, lazy, cruel to the horses, and no gentleman. As far as I could see, these charges were mostly based on fairly minor matters, like Simon's farting and peeing openly and sometimes pulling the bit too hard against Dube's mouth.

SIMON:

So what was wrong with a touch of *Blazing Saddles*? And taking a leak in the desert was no big deal. Anyway, our diet plus the *al fresco* lifestyle inevitably made the bodily functions a bit conspicuous. Most of the time, there's only a ten per cent chance of a tree to go behind. Besides, there's no way you can be refined about four days of constipation followed by the kind of mammoth bowel movement that would have flattened the Ruhr dams in World War Two. And I defy even Houdini to get his trousers off with one hand while holding on to an interested but anxious horse with the other.

In summary, of all the possible reactions from an involuntary spectator, straight-laced prissiness was the least appropriate.

RICHARD:

As for the horses, even mothers get cross with their children from time to time. It was that or put up with constantly being given the run-around. Whilst leading Bones, she continually snacked at clumps of grass on the move. Each time, it felt like having your arm wrenched out of its socket. For most of a day, every time Bones put her head down I tugged on the lead rope, bringing the knotted end down on the side of her neck. She eventually got the message and stopped snacking.

Barbara glared at me throughout the process but made no comment. She thought I was being harsh, but I knew the horse only needed to learn which of us was boss to accept the rules.

I agreed with Simon's view of Barbara's attitude to the horses. She was simply unable to come to terms with their demanding workload on a major endurance ride. Her attitude to handling and management was undoubtedly coloured by her experience of owning horses for pleasure, and virtually as household pets. By contrast, the much more experienced Armstrongs had gone to great lengths to support us.

Bringing in new horses was legitimate because, as Simon pointed out, Butch and Sundance had switched to fresh horses whenever required. However, horses today are mostly recreational animals, seldom used for serious work. This meant that if we incurred more fitness problems along the trail, we would find it tough to find suitable replacements.

SIMON:

Researching other equine expeditions had provided some useful insights. While no world-class rider, I observed, listened to, and sometimes quoted the experiences of others. Barbara's mindset on these occasions was always to drive another wedge into the growing split in the team; any advice or observation offered up by me was dismissed out of hand, and rudely.

Nevertheless, we set off with the new horses in fairly good heart. It was great to have a fit, fast team. Yazz was improving, Bones was fresh since swapping her for Rocket, and since Sunday and Imasizzlin'lady were infinitely better horses than Dube and Miss-Ap, we hoped for faster progress. We sped along the road and soon arrived at the small town of St John's without incident. It was another Mormon community, formed in 1874.

Around 1883, Matt Warner, one of Butch's earliest sidekicks, carries out his first successful armed robbery in St John's, holding up a combined store and bank. He rides in at midday and cleans out a large safe which stands open all day behind the counter while (to use his own words) "prosperous Mexican rancheros and Mormon freighters is bringing in scads of mazuma."

Using the classic Wild Bunch tactic of spare horses stashed in an arroyo, Matt and his accomplices get clear away, though they are pursued by a posse through cactus and chaparral for most of the 250 miles to the safety of Robbers Roost. Unlike Butch and Sundance, Matt does not make the national headlines in a big way, and so doesn't become a household name. However, again unlike his friends, he does leave an ill-written, undated but vivid record.

SIMON:

We rode through suburbia. At the sound of our horses' hooves on the road, dogs chained to link fences raced over, barking their heads off. Once through the town, we melted back into the great wide open, and for miles, yellow-gold burnt grass stretched to the horizon. We notched up another highly creditable mileage and arrived at a miniscule settlement known as Hunt.

We reined in at Rick and Robin Cumming's place. Conversation moved onto guns over dinner. Rick proudly showed us his firearms, and was keen on the Winchester I was packing. He carefully queried whether we had "beans in the wheel."

"It's loaded, so is the pistol," Richard remarked.

"Keep 'em that way," advised Rick. He stressed that carrying unloaded guns could be dangerous. If they were visible, they were assumed to be loaded, and people would react to that assumption in different and sometimes unexpected ways, according to their mood or nature.

After a fine meal, we crashed out contentedly and departed early the next morning.

Back on the trail, the heat was fierce and the melting tarmac shimmered. There was no shade from bluffs or rolling hills; it was billiard-table flat. We rode on grimly, hot saddle leather creaking gently and the horses snatching at passing clumps of grass.

We rode for Woodruff, a tiny Mormon settlement at Silver Creek on the Little Colorado River. Gazing across the barren vastness, we wondered where camp could be struck. Late in the afternoon, we stopped inside the entrance of the Petrified National Forest and picketed the horses between two telegraph poles.

In Arizona, day temperatures were high and nights were cold. Prime feed was only available on the roadside, and the horses begged for it.

Frequent stops became necessary, which meant unpacking for just an hour. Richard and I preferred to keep riding and get mileage under our belts early, before the sun was high. But we had begun to master the fine art of packing and could now whip the bucks, panniers, "H" packs and ropes around the horses in impressively quick time.

The following morning, it was Sunday's turn to be packed. Sawbuck firmly on and cinching up, I hooked the first pannier over. I was just going to sling over the other when Sunday exploded into a ferocious bucking sequence. She pitched feverishly, unseating the offending boxes and jerking the lead rope out of Richard's hand. Next she bolted, swerved towards a haystack, narrowly missed a JCB digger and just avoided shredding herself on a lethal barbed wire fence. The panniers were duly dumped on the deck, and she made off on a dead run. It looked like we were in the shit yet again.

For ten minutes we watched Sunday race round the massive feedlot, evading every attempt to stop her. When Richard and Barbara finally cornered her, she was miraculously unscathed. Another close call, and (contrary to what it had said on the label) another mare not suitable for packing.

A plan to depart swiftly for Winslow was foiled when Yazz threw a shoe; we had to fit an easyboot over the bare hoof, which proved tediously difficult and wasted hours. We rode in to the LX Ranch for the night, camping in a hayshed. Owner JR de Spain, who welcomed us, said the ranch used to be part of the infamous Hashknife, a ranch which harboured some very dubious characters, some of whom were involved in Arizona's Pleasant Valley range war. Fictionalised by Zane Grey (and later filmed by Henry Hathaway) with the dramatic title *To The Last Man*, it was interesting history, but not on our agenda this trip.

We pressed on and crossed with some trepidation, but without incident, the narrow metal bridge which spans Chevelon Canyon a hundred feet below. We camped in Winslow. Mileage totalled 559 in thirty-six riding days from Mexico, an average of 15.5 miles per day, precisely as the experts had predicted.

Just as I relaxed in a chair after a hot shower, Richard warned me that Barbara was again expressing great dissatisfaction with the ride, my presence, the horse usage and the lack of grazing. Further upsets were imminent.

"What does she expect?" I asked, exasperated.

Richard explained:

"She wants to quit because the expedition isn't going her way and the outlaw aspect is of no interest to her. She says she simply can't bring herself to ask the horses to continue."

"Too bad – but we change nothing," I replied succinctly. Was this the chance I'd been waiting for?

I strode into Barbara's room and tackled her head on. Not mincing words, I told her that her years of riding and the experience gained on her Russian trip were useless on this expedition. She gave me a look that would have drawn blood at twenty paces. I told her she was just not up to the Outlaw Trail.

In fact, the next section of that trail, between Page, Arizona and Hite, Utah, now lay submerged many fathoms beneath the surface of Lake Powell, which was the end product of a major dam project completed in 1963. Environmentalists were still up in arms over the scheme.

The consequence for our expedition was that we had to circumnavigate part of the eighteen hundred miles of shoreline, encased in orange and red sandstone walls and now a popular National Recreation Area. Whichever route we took around the huge lake, it was a massive detour over alien terrain, with severe hazards for the horses. Not a problem for Butch and Sundance – no dams and no lake in their day – but a big problem for us, and in her present mood, an impossible one for Barbara.

The logistics involved seemed unfathomable, so I phoned my first guide to Robbers Roost, expert outfitter AC Ekker, to seek advice. He strongly recommended us not to ride over the Kaiparowits Plateau, since we'd never get through on horseback. Our only option was to ride from Cameron to Mexican Hat, then into Fry Canyon, before taking the Orange Cliffs trail. Even that route was debatable. We knew feed and water were non-existent – it was naked wilderness, and, for horses, decidedly dodgy. AC reckoned a month's riding on the trail before we reined in at Robbers Roost.

There are no guarantees on any expedition. Barbara declared she wanted to leave the ride and then, to my sheer amazement, said she would return to Alma on my horses, to have her own adventure instead. I burned red:

"We're riding north, not south. You won't be taking any horses; I won't allow it, and I stop for nobody!" I bellowed.

Richard joined in:

"You're not fit and strong enough to pack, and you can't manage the gates either."

Barbara sat and glowered at us. If looks were Gatling guns, we had just been mown down.

"I didn't do all that research for you to hi-jack me. We'll be taking the full string to Canada," I added.

Unexpectedly, Richard then remembered his initial promise to Barbara's family – he would have to stay with her. Thanks a bunch, I thought.

"Well, you'd better take Yazz, Pancho and Bones. Joe will pick you up from Alma, if you make it," I said calmly. Then, pointing at Barbara:

"You've relinquished the book deal, you don't have the moral right to it," I concluded, and left the room.

Ten minutes later, Richard rejoined me, grinning, and plonked himself down in a chair:

"She's changed her mind. She'll stay with us to Tuba, then decide her future there."

I didn't know whether to laugh or cry.

RICHARD:

Simon could be hard going. After a month on the trail, he still hadn't mastered some of the most elementary horse management and packing skills. Barbara's unwillingness to adapt and become a team member was equally wearing, as were her attempts to isolate herself from us, and her constant disapproval, to which Simon's invariable reaction was to provoke further rather than to conciliate. Both with Barbara and generally, he operated on a pretty short fuse.

A visit to a country and western bar offered a brief respite from the punishment and boredom of the trail, so Simon and I went to check out the scene. The bar was a typical prefab with no soul. A few guys were playing pool, and in another dimly lit room, a deejay was bashing out Willie Nelson songs. We propped up the bar and drank a few beers. Winslow was just not happening. Simon quoted Brad Dexter's line in *The Magnificent Seven*:

"We had a pretty wild evening. We got to talking about the weather, and didn't break up till nearly sundown."

After a while, we left and went to feed and check the horses, who were fine.

So they ought to be. Earlier we had been held to ransom by big Charlie, one of life's loveable rogues, full of blarney and out to make a fast buck. His shoeing rates and his hay prices would get through to the playoffs for the highest in the USA, but he had us over a barrel, so we paid up and looked cheerful. While I did the deal with big Charlie, Simon was obtaining clearance from the Tribal Police to cross the Navajo Nation, en route for Mexican Hat, so we were in good shape.

Butch's buddy Matt Warner gives us a very fleeting glimpse of his flight across the nation:

"We made a record run through the Reservation, covering more than a hundred miles of very rough country in twenty hours of runs and rests."

Man-hunter Charlie Siringo rides through that same country after leaving the Mormon town of Kanab, chasing Butch hard all the way to Alma, New Mexico. According to Siringo:

"Kanab was the last settlement for hundreds of miles. A three day ride over the Buckskin Mountain and down the Colorado River brought me to Lee's Ferry and I found water scarce and far between. Not a habitation or a settler was seen between Kanab and here. Another three days over uninhabited desert country brought me to the Indian trading store at Willow Creek. From here I turned due east across the Navajo Indian Reservation and through the Moqui Indian country."

Butch and Sundance ride northwest of Cameron, following the Little Colorado River till it joins the Colorado itself. Continuing upstream for sixty miles, they stop at Lee's Ferry to re-supply, then ride along Glen Canyon to the White Canyon, a total of two hundred and twenty-odd miles. Then they cross Andy Miller Flats to the foot of the Flint Trail and ride into Robbers Roost.

SIMON:

We could never get through the reservation as quickly as the bandit riders. This was a hell of a trail for horse work. Riding through at our slower pace still allowed us to share part of the experience with the outlaws. But we thanked our lucky stars not to be riding in their footsteps all the way.

The creation of Lake Powell had spared us, and more importantly the horses, from riding an unusually troublesome stretch. Instead, we would head for Mexican Hat, Utah and evaluate our options from there.

A deserted tarmac road led north into Indian country and more adventure....

Showdown at Mexican Hat

"That settles it – this place gets no more of my business."
BUTCH CASSIDY

RICHARD:

Seven miles north of Winslow, we entered the Navajo Indian Reservation. The road evaporated. We chose to track the course of the Little Colorado River, bang on the edge of the Painted Desert. Lack of topographical maps meant dismissing the idea of camping at Bird Springs oasis. We didn't fancy our chances of locating the spot by wandering randomly across a desert region larger than Belgium and Holland combined.

We did not see a living creature until late afternoon when a tree line hove into view. Opposite, ramshackle houses and old battered cars were dotted haphazardly. Rubbish was strewn, dogs milled, children played noisily on swings nearby and Navajo men sat unsmiling in rickety chairs, eyeing us with suspicion and following our every move as we rode in. It was clear no hospitality would be offered, only grudging directions to water. The reservation was depressing and poverty-stricken, with none of the glamour that greets tourists at, say, Monument Valley.

We had been warned to exercise extreme vigilance, particularly with regard to the horses. Since over-cautious is always safer than under-cautious, I selected a campsite in a large thicket, which formed a rudimentary natural zariba: *easier* to see out than to see in, and if worse came to the highly unlikely worst, easier to defend than to attack. On the same over-cautious principle, I posted sentries overnight in three watches.

Once settled in, I cooked, and we ate well on our core diet of meat and pasta. Simon frequently had two helpings, partly to avoid waste, but mainly because he had heard and approved the military adage that you are never sure of the next meal but one. I may say he was the only one who held his body weight.

Whenever Simon and I sat round a fire stuffing ourselves, he would goad Barbara with (accurate) taunts that she ate like a sparrow, and ought to eat and drink more to keep her strength up. To which her reaction would invariably be spirited but irrelevant, like calling Simon a greedy pig. Whereupon Simon would wolf down a third helping, emit a huge belch, break wind loudly and tender his compliments to the chef.

Simon loved winding Barbara up like this, but health was a serious issue, and Barbara really did look emaciated. Eating minimally and drinking frugally, she was continually tired and short of energy. We consumed at least a gallon of water a day, but I had lost about thirty pounds following my accident. The horses required fifty gallons per day – ten each. When taken out of their comfort zone, they react much as humans do.

A common mistake amongst inexperienced desert travellers is to try to conserve water. The body reacts very negatively to water shortage. In desert conditions, you can easily lose a gallon of water in less than two hours by doing all the wrong things. Your mental capacity, specifically your judgement, upon which all actions depend, is drastically impaired, so if you have ample water, it is important to drink as much as you want when you want.

There were no unwelcome visitors in the night. We broke camp and departed beneath heavy grey clouds. Temperature dropped, rain spattered and the dusty road turned gradually to mud. We rode across a landscape that was flat, colourless and uninspiring. The wind increased and the rain turned to hail. As conditions worsened, the horses put their backs to the wind and refused to budge, which forced us to give up the struggle. Imasizzlin'lady began to fly-buck and kick, so we re-packed her twice, checking her blankets for burrs. So passed most of the day.

After a miserable ride we arrived in Leupp. The Navajo call Leupp "Tsiizizi", which translates as "scalps." Sodden from the earlier downpour, we camped in the rundown rodeo corrals to contemplate the route ahead. The vast American desert system between Mexico and Canada occupies one million square miles, or thirty percent of the continental United States, and we were getting mighty weary of it. These desert crossings were very hard work, but (so far) not impossible.

At times, the sheer monotony of endlessly unchanging scenery got me down. To defeat this, I made up songs, composed magazine articles, thought about the horses, and learned what I could about the stark but striking terrain.

The vividly coloured Painted Desert runs southeast from the Grand Canyon. The land is scored by jagged canyons and dominated by sandstone skylines of cliff, buttress and spire. The oppressive heat sucked the body fluids out of us like a dehumidifier, silently drying us out. We did not sweat a drop.

SIMON:

Grand Falls was grand all right, but minus its falls, following the dissipation of the spring run-offs. While we pondered where to camp, a Navajo landowner suddenly appeared in his truck, blocked our path and stated curtly:

"You're on private land."

"The road's for public access," I said politely.

"But my land's either side," he shot back.

We stared. Did we need this asshole's permission to camp?

"We're on a historic ride, and we've come up from Mexico," I said, hoping to avoid a deadlock.

"Get a lot of white people making noise and interfering with my cattle here."

Hmm. We looked at one another, each wondering what the next move might be. Dusk was drawing in and the horses were tired. It would be hopeless riding on.

He suddenly relented. It might have been Barbara's winsome smile – who knows? We shook hands and the ice was broken. I left Richard preparing camp and accompanied Jerry Tso, our Navajo landowner, to procure hay. Jerry was located near Mormon's Crossing, a historic landmark about four miles south of Leupp, which was a trading post originally established by Andrew Wolf, a German immigrant who settled there in 1876.

Butch and Sundance very likely stop in Leupp to stock up on provisions. There is a network of such trading posts. One is due north at Willow Creek where man-hunters Charles Siringo and WO Sayles re-supply after chasing Butch to Alma in 1899. Beyond Willow Creek another is in Hanksville, Utah. A general store-slash-hotel there is operated by Charlie Gibbons. Earlier Butch was a cowhand working for Charlie and his partner in the Henry Mountains.

It is common knowledge that the Wild Bunch regularly buys supplies whilst hiding out at Robbers Roost. Without established safe trading posts and stores, Butch and Sundance find it impossible to subsist in such remote country.

That night it was very warm and I slept atop of my sleeping bag. Waking at four, when Richard put a steaming mug of coffee by my side, I noticed something move out the corner of my eye. It was a small sandy-coloured scorpion, perched on the edge of my sleeping bag. At an inch long it looked harmless, but not wanting to be stung on the left cheek I cautiously unzipped the bag, edged out, turned my boots upside down, shaking them vigorously before kicking the stinger out of harms way. A ridiculous sight, yes, but it beat accidentally squashing the arachnid and getting a foot full of poison!

RICHARD:

For the next two days, it was slow going to Cameron. The only landmark was Humphrey's Peak towering at 12,643 feet, the highest point of the San Francisco Mountains, and our instructions were far from clear. Any cattle we saw were scattered, and the water troughs were dry.

Eventually, we came to a completely derelict homestead. Luckily, searching the ground above it we found a tank brimming with good water. The horses crowded round and filled to bursting, having learned – as range horses always do – to drink every chance they get.

When we struck camp, we bedded down where we stood. Against every rule of desert work, we were travelling during the heat of the day. To compound our worries about feed, I thought I saw Jerry Tso's pickup disappear behind a ridge, never to be seen again. It had our bales of hay on board.

Next morning, we passed an empty reservoir and an abandoned farm; a trough, but no water. We could only ride on and hope the horses could handle it. In the Painted Desert, not a blade of grass was to be seen. Miles later, opposite a series of greying rocky outcrops, we spotted a pair of massive water containers, a bit like smaller versions of the artificial *ballehs* they used to build between the scattered oases in the Horn of Africa. Our luck was holding.

Once the land was fenced, many natural sources of water were cut off, so ranchers had to tap into the water table, sink a well and install a pump. A little wind and a good water table then ensured a plentiful supply. These windmills often baled us out of trouble. Once again, the horses jostled round and filled their empty tanks.

Two hours later, Cameron appeared. A bridge spanned the Little Colorado River gorge, and volumes of traffic thundered past on their way to Lake Powell and Monument Valley. It was a dangerous crossing, so we diverted into a trailer park opposite a venerable tourist trap called Cameron Trading Post. We hitched the horses, then bought ice creams, and two charming ladies made a great fuss of Yazz and insisted we call them when we got to Tuba City.

Simon:

We corralled and ministered to the horses, checked into the hotel, got showered and changed, then dined like greedy lords in the restaurant – even Barbara. For purely therapeutic purposes of course; we needed to restore our lost body weight. Well, that was my story.

Next day, we were en route for Mexican Hat – where we were to liaise with AC Ekker – and then down to historic Lee's Ferry, where Butch and Sundance had crossed the mighty Colorado River.

Lee's Ferry is named for John Doyle Lee, the first settler and ferryman. It is probably 1884 when Matt Warner arrives here with Tom McCarty, and another character, Josh Sweat, after a monumental chase of over three hundred miles across Arizona. Matt writes of the chase afterwards:

"We rode like hell in short runs. We felt sure no officers would go through hell, or would know horses as well as us. As we rode down the canyon leading to the ferry, imagine our surprise when we saw a bunch of deputies close behind us."

Warner yells a fifty dollar wager to ferryman Johnson that he cannot make the shore in two minutes. Thus motivated, the Swede pulls the boat in just as the posse closes the gap. Warner and friends quickly lead their horses on board, pay up and urge haste, but Johnson says he had better wait for the approaching lawmen, now very close. The outlaws at once draw their guns and announce that, "they wait for nobody." Finding their arguments persuasive, Johnson casts off and heads for the distant far bank in the nick of time.

When the officers ride up they yell to Swede Johnson to turn back, but no way can he comply. The river is too wide to shoot across, and once over, the outlaws are safe. Being very cool customers, they rest their horses, have a meal, and take a bath, all in full view of the frustrated officers. Then, up early after a night's sleep, they ride off, turning Johnson loose to begin the long, slow, double river crossing in his own good time.

Warner writes, "what saved us was the fact that we start out with a fresh relay of horses, as a chase continued, our horses and the horses of the deputies naturally slowed down. We started on a dead run, slowed to a gallop, then a trot and finally a canter was the best we could do. Fresh horses widened the distance between us – we felt good and followed the regular trick of outlaws in a hot chase. It was the beginning of a long experience and training in outlaw flight that made up such a big part of outlaw operations".

SIMON:

We crossed the bridge spanning the gorge. Traffic slowed, with the exception of one selfish idiot: a huge pickup towing a speedboat raced past at fifty-five miles per hour, little more than two feet away from the horses. In reaction, Sunday swerved towards the bridge parapet and I very nearly went over the edge. The fall of around two hundred feet would definitely have made my eyes water.

I cursed and shook my fist, in the hope that the driver would stop. He didn't, which was a pity; I was all set to play out a favourite scene from Serge Leone's *For A Few Dollars More*, where Clint Eastwood invites the miscreant at gunpoint to say "sorry" to his horse.

We rode out on the edge of the Moenkopi Plateau. A series of broken buttes loomed, and beyond them, the horizon fell away behind a yellowish carpet. After three hours crossing a hard-baked desert floor in appalling heat, we reached the base of a towering grey wall. I led through clumps of brush up a steep, rough trail.

At the summit, we turned to gaze back towards Cameron. It had disappeared into the haze, some twelve miles distant. Here was an awesome overlook – the stuff Western movies were made of. Then the horses perked up and quickly broke into a trot. Over a faint ridge, a windmill was pumping water into a brimming trough. Spared again.

RICHARD:

Tuba City was ahead. A deep river valley presented an obstacle and a new fence hemmed us with no gates to exit. We line rode, right then left, for over a mile until Simon lost patience and cut a hole through. Less than fifty yards later, in a hollow, we came to a gate. I swore at our laziness and impatience.

Once at the main road, a pickup suddenly pulled out and approached us. A Navajo announced:

"We've been waiting for you."

It sounded very ominous, and I was sure we were in bad trouble for criminal damage. But Simon gently reminded us that the friendly ladies at the Cameron Trading Post had instructed us to look out for George Begaye. And George it was, thankfully.

We tracked through town and penned the horses at the Animal BIA Sanctuary. George took charge, and set about rebuilding the horses with extra feed and supplements.

We checked in at a rather drab motel. Given some time to reflect,

I decided our pack weight needed to be reduced before tackling the San Rafael Desert. Temperatures were soaring, and for the horses' sake, we should shed all unwanted gear, so I planned to continue just with the canvas "H" packs. All unused equipment, Barbara's spare rucksack (eighteen pounds) Simon's boots, other extra clothing, books, maps and a fax modem would be returned to the Armstrongs along with the four panniers. We were gratified to find we had saved a hundred and twenty pounds – the equivalent of one pack load.

We realised we would have to spend an extra month on the trail. In thirty-six days riding days, we had covered 559 miles, just 15.5 miles per day. As we sat and digested the gloomy stats, Barbara revealed for the third time that she was leaving. She said that up to Springerville Simon had been her problem. Then by Winslow, the punishing schedule had seriously aggravated her, and now I was to blame. Nothing was right, and she loathed the trip. I was slightly taken aback, but Simon, I knew, was delighted.

"I'll be doing my own expedition next time," Barbara announced confidently.

As will already have become clear, our mutual hostility and behaviour to one another had deteriorated by now well below the level of nursery spats. We greeted Barbara's announcement literally with hoots of derision. After the problems she had caused, it seemed the funniest thing we had heard. Simon in particular laughed till he cried.

"You didn't know what you were doing in Russia, and you still don't!" he jeered.

I tried to advance a few more practical arguments, to which Barbara turned a deaf ear and fumed.

SIMON:

The following morning, Barbara knocked brightly on our door with important news. After protracted telephone calls with her daughter Katy in England, she had decided to stay with the expedition after all. Bugger!

We set off to the laundry in disgust. There, a charming, incredibly sexy Navajo lady invited us to participate in a "sweat." As tourist attractions go, it sounded enticing. We imagined ourselves lolling in a baking, steam-filled stone room, drinking whisky half-naked, and being fêted by beautiful women in like state. I thought of the "other" cult outlaw film of the sixties, Sam Peckinpah's *The Wild Bunch*, where a similar scene occurs before the final, mould-breaking shootout. Then it was back to reality. In our dreams would a couple of dirty, scruffy Anglo cowboys be offered an afternoon leg over in Tuba City!

This was the major town on the Navajo Reservation, and nothing to do with brass wind instruments. The standard rig for men was jeans and Stetsons, while the women dressed in their traditional long velvet skirts. Everyone seemed to have braided hair. The Navajo people were incredibly polite, hospitable, keenly interested in our quest and willing to pull out all the stops to help us. Barbara fell in love with them.

Two days later, with provisions and human batteries re-charged, we roped the "H" packs firmly on the horses' backs and set off, well pleased with our drastically scaled down equipment. Within minutes, we were turning back in disarray. The horses were upset; the top-heavy "H" packs were starting to slip beneath their bellies. There was nothing else for it. We had to retrieve the panniers and revert to the original packing assembly. Our clever plan to save a hundred and twenty pounds of weight had been foiled. *Damn!*

RICHARD:

We rode twenty-four miles for the tiny outpost of Tonalea. The temperature cooled dramatically, the biting wind increased and rain forced the mercury down to zero. We endured ten hours of misery riding through uninspiring Middle Mesa country, rolling sand dunes and scrub to the Hopi Indian Reservation.

It was dusk when we closed on Charlie Dandy's homestead. Charlie showed us to our sleeping quarters: a Hogan. The traditional eight-sided building, which used to be made of wood and mud, is still favoured by the Navajo. We passed a comfortable night, but we seriously disturbed the sole previous resident, an insomniac mouse.

We were riding on autopilot. Even Simon was beginning to tire of the everlasting, undulating, reddish-brown landscapes. At Begashibito Wash, a young rider waited patiently on his cowpony. Royce Maloney greeted us, and offered corrals, oats and a place to camp. We promptly quit for the day. Royce was busy breaking and training hardy-looking horses that could easily take the physical punishment of the Outlaw Trail. Aged twenty, a roper, horse-breaker, trainer and farrier in the making, with plans to go to college too, Royce impressed us.

I served dinner, and we mellowed out around the fire with coffee before setting our bedrolls. It was cool, and I drew the hood tight on my four seasons bag and soon fell asleep. After a disturbed night – Simon had some very bad dreams, and yelled his head off – I awoke to a promising day with a snap of frost in the air. When I presented Simon with his mug of coffee, he had absolutely no recollection of what took place during the night.

We packed quickly. Royce brought tasty, piping hot Navajo fry bread and rode out with us towards Black Mesa. There we became the focal point. Simon always attracted most attention when we met tourists. Tall, slim, in traditional Western garb, his Stetson at a rakish angle, he resembled one of his own dashing Western heroes – Bat Masterson, or whoever.

A little later on Simon was lucky not to have his legs broken.

The Sharndi place was empty and we turned back to secure corrals opposite the garage. The hosts kindly agreed to put the horses up, and began moving foals out of three pens to make room. One bolted and Yazz panicked, taking flight with Bones still tied firmly onto my pommel. Simon was blocking Yazz's escape route and couldn't step out of harm's way. Wham!

SIMON:

A hoof smashed into the base of my shin then crunched my left foot. Remember, I still had two broken toes. The pain was immense. I screamed. It felt far more serious than the previous bone-crushing incident with Dube. My foot began to swell alarmingly and I could hardly put it to the floor. Hindsight plugged in and switched on. Why hadn't I let the horses stand where they were? It was stupid. The Navajos were extremely embarrassed, but I waved off the incident.

Two hours later, I gingerly re-inspected the damage in my sleeping bag: one toe broken, and two re-broken. I considered myself lucky, after all I might have been felled and ridden over.

We rode for Kayenta in freezing conditions. Drizzle added to the misery. A lady drew alongside in an old car, said the Navajo Police were looking for us, then promptly drove off with no explanation. It sounded like a warning. But we had the right permissions, guns and ammunition were properly stowed, and we had given the Tribal Police our itinerary through their Nation. What had we done? Then my thoughts turned uneasily to my mother, who on the last report in Tuba City was heavily sedated, and resting long hours.

Within an hour, a police patrol vehicle stopped and the trooper called out my name. I stepped off Sunday, introduced myself, shook hands and asked if we were in trouble.

"Not at all," replied the officer, "I have an urgent message. Call your outfitters – there's an emergency. The nearest phone available is at Tsegi Canyon eight miles on."

The patrolman wished us good luck. Instantly fearful about my mother, I re-mounted and relayed the message to Richard and Barbara. We pressed on hard, and found the café busy with tourists. The other two held the horses while I went to make the call in absolute dread.

Rusty told me my mother had died early on the morning of June 4th. My legs almost buckled. I was in shock, and images of our last moments together in the nursing home coursed through my mind. I walked blindly outside. Richard sussed the situation at a glance and gripped my shoulder sympathetically, but I needed to get away – it was no place to surrender to my emotions. I mounted in silence and we got to riding.

What should have been the very special approach to Monument Valley passed in a blur. I vaguely remember a long stretch of road before we reached the monoliths. At the Blue Coffee Pot Café we sought out Roy Watson, our next contact. Roy was away but neighbour Don Polich kindly offered us the use of Kayenta's rodeo corrals for the night. We duly camped outside the corrals and contemplated the next move. Barbara stayed with the horses whilst Richard and I returned to the Circle K shop for provisions. I could hardly concentrate.

That night I dreamed that my mother's death had itself been a bad dream. Waking early, I realised my subconscious had played a mean trick on me.

We resumed our usual duties and, thanking Don, rode for hay at the crossroads as the horses were forced to subsist on oats last evening.

A stocky, affable Navajo parked in his battered car eased the window down and greeted us cheerfully with an offer of assistance. He, James Cly, could guarantee our success in traversing the last section of the Reservation by organising stops in Gouldings and Mexican Hat. He then told us proudly that his grandparents had worked with John Wayne, who of course starred in most of John Ford's Monument Valley Westerns.

The heat returned. We rode seventeen miles through dust and scrub to a vast flat where the dramatic climax of *Stagecoach* was filmed. We finally stopped at Gouldings, where James's friend Leroy Teeasayatoh was already busy fixing corrals for our arrival.

Over a fairly silent dinner, my thoughts were constantly of my mother. I had missed her birthday on May 1st – she was sixty-seven when she died. Then I remembered the last gift she had given me that Christmas was a John Wayne anthology video. Here of all places, it was a deeply poignant thought.

RICHARD:

Next morning, we woke to see the sun's rays glowing on the etched sandstone spires, pinnacles and buttresses. The sheer majesty of scale of this uniquely sculptured red rock landscape defies description. James guided us on horseback through an almost empty Monument Valley, from Eagle Mesa about half the way to Mexican Hat. Then he gave directions to a watering hole en route, and left us.

We were crossing broken ground – bluffs and *arroyos* alternating with barren, red, sandy flats – and navigation was difficult. Finally, we made it to Mexican Hat, named after a sombrero-shaped rock formation.

We unpacked at Burch's Trading Post, stacked our gear in a shed and turned the horses into a corral overlooking the river. We bought some hay from Suzy, the proprietor, whose terms were so generous that we all ended up sitting on her back porch, sipping the ice cold beer we had provided, while we watched the sun dip below the horizon.

After quite a few very refreshing beers, we booked in at the hotel, showered, changed, and emerged in the state specified by the Manual of Small Arms for every soldier's rifle: clean, bright and lightly oiled. We chose a Western theme restaurant to have dinner, to which we had invited James and Leroy. What followed was unique in my experience of eating out in America, especially in a tourist zone where normally food, service and value are so impressive I worry for the UK tourist industry.

SIMON:

First we were ushered to our table by two breathtakingly rude young waiters dressed as cowboys. We ordered some coffee, then ten minutes later repeated the unfulfilled request. What was plonked on the table in a blatantly hostile manner was tepid and so disgusting we would not have risked tipping it into a healthy potted plant.

Next we ordered from the limited menu, expensive to say the least.

"What salad dressings are available?" I asked.

"One the chef makes," came the unhelpful reply, delivered with a lot of attitude.

I smelled trouble. In fact, the whole place stank of it.

An age later, lukewarm, expensive, unappetising tourist dinners were unceremoniously slid under our noses. The food was garbage. The restaurant was almost empty, and now we knew why. Within minutes of our starting to eat, a bill was placed on the table, apparently inviting us to leave ASAP, whether or not we had finished. I scrutinised the bill and found that a mandatory ten dollar tip had been added.

Richard reached over, took the offending paperwork and made for the bar. Leroy suddenly seemed nervous and said maybe we should have dined at the bridge restaurant instead. Too late.

Richard was taking an age. I glanced towards the bar. An earnest conversation was taking place, and the body language denoted growing hostility. So me being me, I ambled over slowly, to be greeted with:

"Well, here's another asshole gonna contest the check."

It was the proprietor, a fat greaseball slopped on a barstool with an enormous beer gut sagging over his belt.

"*Me?*" I queried, recognising the unmistakeable preliminaries to fighting talk.

"Ain't nobody else behind you!"

I thought: one good shove, mate, and you're on the deck with my boot firmly on the bridge of your nose.

"We're not paying a tip. The meal was poor, the service non-existent, and that's the last word," I said curtly.

Fatty looked very angry, but stayed on his stool. The cocky cowboy waiters were tense behind the bar. A red-faced chef holding a large metal poker shuffled crabwise to the left of Richard. It was four against two, which was a little unfair. Since our team comprised a former marine commando and a seasoned street fighter, I felt we outnumbered them.

I waited for the poker-toting chef to raise his hand. That signal would be the "on" button, and he would not get back the use of his poker without rectal surgery.

At this point, Fatty threatened to call his friend the sheriff.

"You do that, but you still won't get your tip."

Mrs Fatty, an angry hippo wallowing at the fringes, suddenly interjected:

"We always add tips but Europeans never pay them."

Our policy in a nutshell.

"Service is rewarded; you didn't provide and you know it," said Richard brusquely, and offered to pay the bill minus the ten dollars.

The response was abusive threats and raised fists. It was unbelievable: the proprietors clearly wanted trouble over the equivalent of six bloody quid!

"Pay the total," they yelled.

Silence. Menace. What would their reaction be? Did they have firearms concealed behind the bar? Possibly. One thing was for sure: we didn't.

"You're not getting it, so don't threaten us for ten bucks!" I snarled.

"Get the sheriff," said the chef.

I was hopping mad by now. I *wanted* a breach of the peace. This was the Wild West, we were in a bar with a big mirror, tables, chairs, bottles and a poker, all the props in place – it was shaping up just like the saloon brawl in *Dodge City* (give or take sixty extras). We remained tense. I noticed that the rest of our party had beaten a strategic retreat. Meanwhile, the poker-toting chef looked committed to grievous bodily harm. No more verbals, then.

At this point, Richard, who had kept his cool throughout, tossed the money onto the bar, minus the tip.

"Get off our fucking property!" screamed Mrs Fatty, "And don't ever come back!"

We moved outside onto the sidewalk where the others waited anxiously.

"Are you going for the rifle?" asked Barbara, but whether fearfully or hopefully I never found out.

I shook my head.

"Sons of bitches!" I said.

Then Leroy gunned the truck engine and we all jumped in for the short drive to the hotel. So ended the showdown at Mexican Hat.

Soon we all said goodnight and walked to our rooms. The ugly episode stayed with me. Was it all over or would they seek revenge, this very night perhaps? Always a firm believer in the soft word that turneth away wrath, I sneaked out to the shed and collected the Winchester and some shells. Just in case.

RICHARD:

Simon contacted AC Ekker. The visit to Monument Valley had been a digression, so we arranged a haul back onto the main stem of the Outlaw Trail at Hite. The alternative was three days over desolate country without feed and water. The climb out of Mexican Hat alone would equate to a day's work in extremely dangerous conditions.

By this time, Barbara was pushing hard for Simon to return to England for his mother's funeral. She hoped she and I would continue alone. Maybe Simon could catch us up later. Maybe…

I expressed my own view, which was that Simon should tough it out and stick with the expedition, despite the personality clashes. He had told me how at their parting his mother had urged him, perhaps presciently, to finish the trip come what may. Besides, it would take three days to be in a position to quit America from our present location, and longer if transport connections were dodgy. A double disaster like blowing the expedition *and* missing the funeral would leave wounds almost impossible to heal.

Simon made the right decision, no doubt aware that my advice was disinterested – which unfortunately could not be said of Barbara's.

SIMON:

That morning we were badly jolted by a phone call from the Hans Flat Ranger Station. I had misunderstood the rules about permits for horse riding in the Canyonlands National Park.

"Horse travel is suspended in this section," I was told politely but firmly. The ride was once more in jeopardy.

"What do you advise then?" I gasped, my heart sinking like a millstone.

"AC Ekker has informed us of your historic ride. We'll support it as a one-off and map a route that's easy on the horses. We'll specify where you camp and where you'll find water, and we'll track your progress. If you don't stay on schedule, we'll assume you are in trouble and we'll come and find you, so don't wander off course just for the hell of it."

I tried not to whoop for joy! Without approval from government agencies, we were riding nowhere. AC had come up trumps again. We would after all be able to tackle the next arduous stretch; to ride through the Canyonlands – hostile, desolate terrain, one of the least populated regions of the United States, with one of the most monstrous climates. Lucky old us.

ROBBERS ROOST

"Which way?"
THE SUNDANCE KID

"Hell, it doesn't matter – I don't know where we've been and
I've just been there."
BUTCH CASSIDY

SIMON:

For Outlaw Trail buffs, the jewel in the Canyonlands crown is the legendary Robbers Roost, a term loosely applied to 300 square miles of desolate land in the high desert of southeast Utah.

The weather here has a 144 degrees annual temperature range, one of the widest in the world. Daily variations of 50 degrees are not uncommon. It does not make travel difficult: mostly, it makes it damn near impossible.

In Butch and Sundance's day, there were two principal crossings of the Colorado – Lee's Ferry and the Dandy Crossing – and they are 170 miles apart. Pasture is sparse, water is in short supply and ranching is marginal. In short, most of the Canyonlands region is pure wilderness.

Our concern was for the horses. We planned to reach Hite then the Roost Flats before negotiating the awkward San Rafael Desert. Careful attention to our detailed instructions was vital to make it safely to the town of Green River. Yet again, we had been unable to obtain ordnance survey maps. All we had was an old two-dollar BLM map showing four-wheel drive tracks.

Waiting for Dennis Ekker to arrive with a trailer and haul us out, I assessed our achievements to date in terms of my original objective, which was a unique understanding of Butch and Sundance – what they experienced physically and how they handled themselves.

Despite our catalogue of errors as tenderfoot travellers, we had learned a great deal you could never get out of books. We had now proved that the Wild Bunch were finely honed experts at much more than just robbing banks and trains.

Without straddling a horse for weeks on end, experiencing the conditions at first hand, no one could truly understand just how hard it was to ride unsupported along some parts of the Outlaw Trail. Butch and his fellow outlaws displayed a remarkable feeling for geography; their ability to remember vast tracts of land in close detail was extraordinary with only rudimentary maps or none at all. They also excelled at horsemanship and horse management of course, and in their ability to cope with adverse terrain, climate and supply situations. These, along with their highly intelligent advance planning, were the component parts of their unique escape and evasion record.

Before we started this ride, like so many others, I knew they were exceptional outlaws. Now I knew in a deeply personal and private way that they were also exceptional travellers.

RICHARD:

Dennis Ekker duly arrived with a trailer. We loaded and hauled out. The truck roared to the top of Moki Dugway overlook. The steep, narrow track made us nervous of passing cars on the tricky switchback ascent, especially with horses on board. It didn't help when Dennis pointed out the wreckage of a trailer that didn't make it. But as we climbed higher, the view became breathtaking. The splendid Valley of the Gods unfolded in the haze. Red and orange sandstone monoliths were dotted across the plain for miles beyond.

Altitude rose progressively to 6,997 feet along White Canyon. The country was dramatic. Bleached beneath the burning sun, mile upon mile of white, slick rock craters were flecked with stunted junipers. It was a moonscape. No grass; the only water lay trapped in rock pools. We were grateful not to have to ride this section, or make the trek to Dandy Crossing.

In 1899, legendary man-hunters Charles Siringo and WO Sayles are chasing the notorious Harvey Logan and Butch Cassidy after the Union Pacific train robbery in Wilcox, Wyoming. Information leads the two man-hunters to ship their horses to Marysville and make a fast ride to the Dandy Crossing ferry in the hope of heading off the robbers.

Siringo writes that two men have just passed there going south. They are driving thirteen head of good horses, have been seen in Hanksville en route to the Dandy, and are undoubtedly the train robbers they are after.

In Hanksville, Siringo and Sayles question Charlie Gibbons, who runs the mercantile store and hotel, only to learn that two characters with thirteen horses have crossed the Colorado River at the Dandy Crossing about ten days ago. A week later, a third man with five head of horses crosses. From the description given he is evidently Harvey Logan.

SIMON:

Staring out of the window as we barrelled along, my admiration for Siringo and Sayles increased. I knew the bandits had no fear of riding vast distances through extremely unwelcoming land. It was also significant that when on the run, Logan and Butch travelled with half a dozen horses a head. No wonder they got away from the posses so often. Of course, if our funding had stemmed from successful armed hold-ups we too could have ridden with ample spare mounts, and more than doubled our average daily mileage.

At Hite Marina, we crossed a bridge, turned off the highway onto a dirt track and unloaded. Dennis briefed us that when we got to the heart of Robbers Roost, we should get a message to the Ekkers via the Ranger station, and AC would fly out to the landing strip to meet us. Bidding Dennis thanks and farewell, we struck camp and took stock of our surroundings.

There are three dirt-road trails into the Roost. All can be traversed in a car, but to ride like the outlaws, the trail from Green River runs from the Roost flats through the sand dunes, then passes Jack's Knob (you'll never guess what shape that was!), along the North Spring Wash, where it meets the San Rafael River, crossing the Horse Bench through fifty miles of sand, stunted sagebrush and little else.

From the Horseshoe Canyon hideout, Butch and Sundance ride to the head of Robbers Roost Canyon, past Dead Man Hill, turning west on the Angel Trail to Angel Point. After watering their horses at Poison Springs, they'd make for White Canyon, eventually reaching another ranch hideout located east of the Colorado River near Monticello. Conveniently placed for fast riding into Arizona or New Mexico, Monticello lies in the Abajo (Lower) Blue Mountains.

Butch and Sundance probably pass Maverick Point before taking a track to Shay Mountain and peeling east to the Carlisle Ranch five miles north of Monticello. The Carlisle is similar to the Erie and WS Ranches. Started in the 1880s, many outlaws ride through, stopping a mile north of the ranch HQ where a hay thicket is kept. This is to avoid suspicion that the Carlisle is actively harbouring criminals. Butch is never credited with being a hand there, though his younger brother Dan Parker is prior to arrest for his part in a stagecoach robbery.

Siringo, living in the saddle, pursues the outlaws like a dervish. He sets out from Grand Junction, Colorado after Sundance and Kid Curry, and trails them south to the Blue Mountains. Three weeks searching this region teaches him a few secret trails and also the names of some fringe members of the Wild Bunch. Siringo tests the mettle of a few local sheriffs and comments:

"No wonder the Blue Mountains have been an outlaws' paradise for so many years."

SIMON:

We sat back and enjoyed sundown. As the sun's rays ebbed slowly over the walls of Rock Canyon, the hue of the towering Orange Cliffs was stunning. Around the campfire, I enjoyed the tranquillity of the moment. The only sound to disturb us here was the desert nightlife slowly increasing in volume as dusk gathered. Soon the last of the sun's rays flickered and shrank into darkness. I was left to think alone, but this was my favourite time of day. It grew chillier, and I turned into my sleeping bag. My last waking thought was that mother's funeral would be the following Monday, June 14. I hoped I had done the right thing, staying on the ride.

In the morning, we rode the ten miles across Andy Miller flats to Cove Canyon. Sporadic clumps of grass and brush scattered over the warm sand, and lizards and jackrabbits darted from beneath coarse scrub. The morning sun lit up the white-crested shades of orangey-red sandstone bluffs, creating a painter's paradise. Hot rays radiated welcome heat after last evening's cold. I was thoroughly enjoying the ride and had the sensation of coming home. Within two days, we would be at the Roost, and I relished the prospect.

We arrived at Cove Canyon, striking camp at midday and hobbling the horses on a generous patch of purple grass. I relaxed and roved the landscape with my binoculars. The haze shimmered. White rocks burned. Buzzards wheeled in the distance, floating on the desert thermals. It was quiet here.

Next morning, we continued along a reddish dusty track between the Cove and Red Point. We got mildly lost looking for Waterhole Flats, which completely eluded us. That was why Butch and Sundance liked the Roost country: it all looked the same.

Waterhole Flats is a useful stopover. Butch and Sundance can use it before reaching the Dandy Crossing. A convenient jump-off for Spanish Bottoms, the route eventually leads towards Colorado. Acknowledged to be a rugged trip, it necessitates crossing the treacherous Colorado River. The outlaws traverse innumerable hidden valleys into the Needles district before vanishing deep into the myriad of canyons connecting into Elephant Canyon and the Abajo Mountain country.

SIMON:

Camp here was pleasant (apart from the pesky mosquitoes) and we sat back to enjoy the afternoon. It felt a little odd not to be in the saddle all through the grinding midday heat – but nobody was complaining.

The following morning, after enjoying a lazy afternoon and evening at Waterhole Flats, we were up early, eager to roll towards the Robbers Roost. Blanket on, I heaved Barbara's saddle onto Bones – Barbara suddenly shrieked in surprise, dropping the cinch and stepping back, as she prepared to tighten the girth. The problem? A small sandy-coloured scorpion, it fell to the floor, only to be scrunched by my boot. It was the second close call with the arachnid. Bones would not have been bothered, but a sting for humans was certainly unpleasant and possibly threatening.

We returned to the crossroads. Sunset Pass (another Zane Grey and Henry Hathaway movie) led due west and Telluride east towards Spanish Bottom. Zigzags scored a vertical orange canyon wall. This was the daunting Flint Trail. The surface was a hard-packed dirt track winding upward, tricky for horses. We dismounted, led the horses up through the junipers and found ourselves perched on a rock ledge with a dramatic drop of around 1,500 feet just to our right. The combination of climb plus vertigo literally took our breath away.

Twenty miles distant across the lower plateau was the Canyonlands "Maze" district, a wild, remote cat's cradle of interlocking, vertical-walled canyons. We broke for lunch in searing heat, camping behind a clump of bushes. Mosquitoes were minimal, but our water supply was dangerously low. Luckily, the horses had a patch of decent grass, and they tucked in with gusto.

We relaxed during the hottest hours, then set off once more. Richard led up the incline. The orange wall towered. Soon we were out of the saddle again, with a stop every two hundred yards to let the horses rest. We twisted and turned upward. Puffing and panting to the summit, we took an hour to climb. Altitude nudged 6,275 feet.

Beyond Hart's Point, the valley opened, and a green swathe of junipers carpeted the mesa. Another gorge in the landscape led to the foothills of the La Sal Mountains, with white fluffy clouds resting on their shoulders.

We hobbled our tired horses on some excellent pasture, but the joy of negotiating the Flint quickly evaporated as our situation hit home. Based on advice that water was bound to be available at the denoted campsites, we had miscalculated. Two gallons had sustained us through breakfast, lunch and the toilsome climb. We were now out. Richard said he would find the spring and disappeared with our empty cantinas.

Barbara calmly announced:

"I've got water, but I'm saving it."

I couldn't believe my ears.

"What the hell for?" I asked incredulously.

"For the horses – to mix with their grain tomorrow," she said, adding, "It's a good job some of us don't drink all our water isn't it?"

Speechless and smoking with anger, I awaited Richard's return. For two hours, I also searched unsuccessfully for water.

RICHARD:

Respect for Barbara took another plunge when Simon quietly relayed their brief conversation. Her refusing to share water for the evening meal was beyond belief, and, from that moment, she ceased to exist as part of the team. While my water had been used earlier for the benefit of all, she knew we regarded hers as our reserve. Barbara's reasoning about the horses was ill thought out, too. Grazing was close by and would be heavy with dew in the morning. It was just a typically selfish decision, made worse because she had endlessly refused to pack a second canteen. Our current overall capacity was just two and a half gallons, which a very thirsty man could consume alone. I remonstrated with her, and she retired to bed in a huff without food.

Later, Simon and I picketed the horses on a high-line. Despite the rarity, I informed mountain lion tracks abounded in our vicintiy. We knew the cats were expert night hunters, employing stealth and power for a stalk then ambush - they could even take down a horse.

SIMON:

Charles Kelly it was who said: "The view from the summit of the Roost country is either sublime or depressing, depending upon the amount of water in one's canteen and one's knowledge of waterholes." He knew his stuff.

We made an early start and arrived at Frenches Seep by nine. Water was plentiful, and the horses fought madly for it, having gone without for over twenty-four hours – as had the humans. The bad news was that there was no grazing at the site, so thirst quenched and cantinas refilled we rode immediately for Crow Seep. The heat nudged the hundreds, and by the time we got there, the horses were almost at a standstill.

Butch and Sundance's most desolate rendezvous was virtually unchanged. The Henry Mountains formed a splendid backdrop sixty miles distant. The stucco ranch house sported a new back door, and the adjoining cedar log cabin (where writer Pearl Baker grew up) was still keeping the elements at bay. We almost breathed in the history. With increased restrictions on horseback travel in Utah's wilderness, we might very well be the last to have the privilege of riding through here.

I felt this was very important, and so (to my surprise) did Richard. I am not saying he underwent a dramatic conversion like St Paul on the road to Damascus, but here at the heart of Robbers Roost he was for the first time soaking up outlaw history and atmosphere like a sponge. We cooked a special celebratory breakfast.

At nine that morning, I looked across the desert. The Henrys were a dark, distant shadow against the pale blue sky. I reflected that back in England my mother's funeral was just beginning. Mixed feelings of loss, guilt and the finality of death.

Life might be more bearable if we were a more harmonious unit. Though, strangely enough, I felt Richard and I were slowly moving towards becoming a cohesive two-man team. Could it be the ghostly influence of Butch and Sundance, which was almost tangible in these parts? It would be good to think so.

RICHARD:

Compared with camping on the trail, the ranch house offered us welcome mod cons. There was a cooking range inside, a well-stocked freezer and storage dugout for the benefit of passing ranch hands. Simon and I pumped up fresh water from the well and refilled the container on the roof of the outdoor shower, which was a cubicle made of rough-hewn planks. With the sun's help to heat the water, we enjoyed a half-decent shower whilst taking in the panoramic view across the desert. I delighted in cooking fresh steaks garnished with a huge can of chilli beans. We ate our fill at a table, and relaxed afterwards on a sofa. Luxury.

After supper, we had a visit from a Ranger, just checking up on us and surprised at how fast we had moved in the latter stages. We explained how we were driven by our pressing needs, first for water and then for grazing. He went off promising to cue our flying (literally) visit from AC.

I have to report I thoroughly enjoyed the Roost, and increasingly found myself reflecting on Butch and Sundance's travels too. They might have made the identical journey from the Dandy Crossing in one day. It took us four! Simon pointed out that, driving their spare horses ahead of them, their fastest route would have been along the Dirty Devil River past Red Benches, round Poison Springs Canyon and into Larry Canyon. The trails used by the Wild Bunch still remain the routes into the maze of canyons.

The first to use the Robbers Roost are horse thieves, followed by cattle rustlers who know the country thoroughly and have no difficulty eluding pursuit from lawmen. Some suggest the Roost has been used as early as 1883, citing Blue John Griffith, Silver Tip, Jack Moore, Gunplay Maxwell, the McCartys and Tom Dilley, to name a few who drift in around that time.

Butch and Sundance use a number of places here to hide out. The best is Horseshoe Canyon located northwest of the Maze, some twenty-five miles east of Hanksville. Access is by one trail over the eastern rim of the Horseshoe Canyon. Tents are set and supplies are brought in by wagon, a slow journey across the desert. An alternative route is via Dennis Canyon, later renamed the Spur Fork; the entry point is protected by a ten-foot gap, which discourages all but the ablest and most confident horsemen.

Here Butch and Elzy Lay plan the remarkable Castle Gate robbery, training and preparing their horses for the sortie.

SIMON:

AC had guided me into Horseshoe Canyon in 1995. We didn't need to make the big jump – rock-falls and the passage of time had smoothed the trail. Also, AC's horses were brilliantly trained – he rode and guided like the very best of the old-time outlaws. Later, I learned that his great-grandfather was *the* Charlie Gibbons, friend and employer of Butch Cassidy – another big buzz.

AC flew over us next morning, blipped his engine to signal his presence, and then touched down on the nearby landing strip. We had a friendly, typically laconic reunion, and then he handed over a few provisions – not enough to constitute cheating – and strict instructions for our next leg. He made no adverse comments whatsoever about the condition of our horses or the way we were operating which, given his vast experience, expertise and habitual candour, gave us great comfort. Maybe we were learning.

Richard settled the bill for the aircraft charter and contents, we said our farewells and he took off into what little wind there was in a cloud of dust and noise. We watched him make a banking turn over the Horseshoe Canyon, then head off back towards Hanksville.

We departed across Roost Flats, passing a long mound called Dead Man Hill, where once perished a young horse-thief, shot by an irate posse and buried on the spot.

RICHARD:

Roost Springs was six miles away and awkward to locate. Every feature looked identical. After riding over a series of sand dunes, Simon recognised an old chimneystack, the remains of an ancient cabin. The water troughs had survived, brimming under a rock ledge hemmed by a small semi-circular wall. The horses drank copiously.

It was uneventful riding. We made camp at North Spring Wash. The heavens opened. We used an empty grain bin for shelter and piled our saddles and gear in the dry.

Next morning, we rode into a small canyon across the flats towards Moonshine Wash. North of the Roost promised nothing but sandy terrain. The dunes slowed progress. Traversing the San Rafael Desert was no fun.

Charles Kelly records that the desert and canyon country between Hite and Vernal, through which the Outlaw Trail passes, is the least known and most isolated of any section of the West. Riders who pass along that trail are men of iron, accustomed to the roughest sort of life, able to ride day and night without rest over dry deserts and through dangerous canyons. When required, endurance and courage are paramount – those who lack either are quickly eliminated.

SIMON:

Seven miles west the Flat Tops, a series of reddish buttes marked the southern approaches of the San Rafael Desert. Near Antelope Valley, Barbara spied a four-wheel drive track. We used it to ease the going for the horses. The heat was alarming, in the hundreds. Compounding the problem, there was no water. All our canteens were empty. At Lookout Point, Richard placed our position west of Keg Spring Canyon. I glassed the range, hoping to see the greenery that indicates a spring.

We deliberated. Ride towards the ominous Labyrinth Canyon to locate water there? Beyond laid Hell Roaring Canyon and Deadman Point. Somebody named those unfriendly-sounding places for good reasons. We were out of water and in trouble.

The mistake was leaving the sand dunes. North Spring Wash ran into Saddle Horse Spring to Moonshine Wash. Without decent maps we were riding blind. Instead of reaching Saucer Basin we had unwittingly aimed towards Keg Spring Bottom and the Green River. Cut off by Labyrinth Canyon, another four-wheel drive track turning north looked promising. We followed it. It dumped us on white, slick rocks west of Bull Hollow.

I knew we were floundering but I tried not to get edgy. Meanwhile Richard was working on re-connecting with his usually reliable sixth sense. Over a sandy wash, we found a tiny rock-pool of water. Only Sunday would step into the depression to drink. The other horses required the canvas bucket even though they fought to quench their thirst.

Hindsight: we should have ridden north then west of Three Canyon on the dirt track. Instead, we had ridden up a gradual incline and over a rocky wall onto a bluff. At the edge of the precipice, we were rewarded with great views over the San Rafael Valley, but zero views of a trail or of water.

Marooned the wrong side of Three Canyon, we stopped to contemplate. To add to our problems, Richard's GPS was playing up, and we could not even get an altitude fix.

Our only option was to ride south to find a way to exit the bluff. I was seriously dehydrated and beginning to struggle. I stopped sweating and began to heat from the inside, a warning sign. Feeling light-headed and sick, we traced our way down a rocky *arroyo* onto more slick rocks. A gorge blocked our path, with a sheer drop of two hundred feet. Shit! We were in a dangerous situation. No water and no determinable way out.

"I'm off for five minutes," Richard announced calmly.

I stood there holding the horses and wondered what next.

"Hey, here's water!" Richard called:

"I've found a spring, there's even a frog in it!"

Consuming six pints and rapidly re-hydrating, nobody cared about boiling the fluid or chucking in purification pills. We had won another close-fought round, and that was good enough.

Once replete, I asked Richard how he had found the water:

"Was it the famous sixth sense of the veteran traveller?"

"Not this time," he said, "I just went behind a rock to have a pee, and there it was!"

"I hope you peed somewhere else!"

He gave me a ghost of a smile:

"Wouldn't you like to know."

RICHARD:

Dusk was creeping in. Barbara wanted to press on to find grazing. Wiser counsel was to stay close to water. I made the decision to turn back to the spring. Barbara was mortified. At the spring there was no feed for the horses, but a greater concern was nowhere to picket them. I chose a flat spot with small fir trees growing out of the rocks that we could just get a line onto. The rains came as we secured the horses. If they made a break we were finished. Simon had a sleepless night, relieved to count five horses the next morning.

We broke camp early to make up mileage. It was overcast and cool. Fresh batteries restored my GPS, and I took a check and a compass bearing as Simon led the party south onto a game trail, through a small canyon. We topped a ridge and hit a dirt track, the one we should have been on yesterday. We were back in business. I reflected how easily we had lost ourselves. Presumably, old-time lawmen had the same problem.

The Roost is a no man's land. Sheriffs and other lawmen do not search here for Butch and Sundance. As a safe haven, it grows steadily in popularity with outlaws over the years. The law rides into the Roost just once, in February 1899 in pursuit of Blue John Griffith, Bill Wall (aka Silver Tip) and Indian Ed Newcomb, who have stolen horses in the area. Sheriff Jesse M. Tyler takes up the chase, rides to Green River, and with the assistance of a guide, manages to find the stolen horses grazing on a mesa above Robbers Roost Canyon.

The posse plans to ambush the outlaws early next morning. On March 5, 1899, Tyler orders an assault, but, unluckily, he is seen on the bluff opposite by one of the outlaws fetching water from a spring. There follows a prolonged fusillade. The outlaws scramble up a narrow trail, reach their horses and escape without loss. The posse, stuck on the wrong side of the canyon, waste two hundred rounds of ammunition.

Matt Warner confirms that for a quarter of a century – from 1870 to 1895 – Robbers Roost is the greatest outlaw hideout in the US.

RICHARD:

The horses were performing well. We passed around Three Canyons to Moonshine Wash and stopped at the San Rafael River to rest and feed the *remuda*. Later, formidable black clouds enveloped the horizon. A desert thunderstorm descended. Lightning bolts danced across the sky as the storm raged overhead. The heavens opened, and in minutes, the drenched horses turned their backs on the driven rain, which swiftly turned to hail. Periodically the sky lit up as if switched on and off. It was a fantastic spectacle, but sitting on horses made us potential lightning conductors.

When the storm passed, the horses' hooves started to ball up in the muddy track, and we knew this would slow us even more.

SIMON:

At Horse Bench, a dry *arroyo* had turned into a raging brown river. The flash flood carted off vast quantities of wood, cactus, tumbleweed and other debris. Massive black clouds passed overhead. The temperature dropped considerably, and I longed for heat. Our problem was where to camp. My thoughts turned to the outlaws, as they frequently did at difficult times on the trail.

After Butch, Matt Warner and Tom McCarty rob the San Miguel Valley Bank in Telluride, they race into Utah through the Blue Mountains. Stopping at the Carlisle Ranch to change horses, they run for the Colorado River at Moab. Once across, they ride through the Arches with a posse already hard on their heels. In Whipsaw Flats, south of Thompson Springs, the outlaws leave the trail to slip through an opening in the cliffs. Matt Warner describes the chase as "hell proper."

Posses are out scouring the whole country. The outlaws run into fresh parties of the widely spread lawmen at regular intervals, and have to change direction suddenly, dodge into a rock or timber hideout, backtrack, or follow long strips of bare sandstone where they won't leave tracks.

The trio ride into a box canyon where they are effectively trapped. Luckily for them, the posse continues north into the open country. The outlaws bypass Thompson, guessing there will be a posse waiting there, as the town is on the Denver & Rio Grande Railroad line.

SIMON:

We headed for our next scheduled rendezvous, which was with Jay Ekker. We topped a sandy rise and saw corrals but no feed or water. We had resigned ourselves to another night under the stars when a truck appeared. Chris Ramsey leaned out of the window, surprised to see riders appear out of the desert:

"Where the *hell* have you guys come from?"

"Robbers Roost," I replied, adding: "We're due to meet Jay

Ekker."

"I know Jay – hop in. You won't make it before nightfall, not across town on horseback anyway.'

I hopped in. Five minutes later at the Ekker residence (a two-hour ride on a fit horse), Jay opened the door and smiled at the dirty cowboy on his neat front lawn.

"Get the grain I sent?"

"Yeah, thanks. We got hung up on Three Canyons," I replied cheerfully. "Didn't think we'd make it tonight."

"We'd have come and gotcha anyway."

Chris drove off to collect Stephen Ekker and the trailer. No sense in riding horses through a town in the dark. Jay arranged our hotel; we found Barbara and Richard waiting at the edge of town. We were euphoric.

The brutally tough fifty-five mile San Rafael Desert section had been completed. Our welcome had been fantastic, unprompted and unexpected. Perhaps our arrival was a kind of endorsement of our acquired resilience. Let's face it, who rides a horse across a desert these days?

We unloaded into a restaurant and gorged ourselves on a fine steak dinner. Beer flowed and spirits were high. Above the din, Jay affirmed the loan of a truck for the duration of our stay. Knocked out by such generosity, we knew we were meeting real Westerners and set about enjoying our brief sojourn in Green River.

DEATH OF A LADY

*"Someplace out there must sell some horses. I'll get the best
I can with what we've got left."*
ETTA PLACE

RICHARD:

After our bad situation at Three Canyons – which could have gotten a great deal worse – I wanted to make quite sure there would be no repeat problems on the next leg. AC Ekker had informed us enough feed *could* be procured along the Green River to Vernal, but it wasn't guaranteed. This was another no man's land to trek through. Feed or logistical problems meant putting extra pressure on the horses. We also discussed the Castle Gate option, in essence using Route 191 to Sunnyside and Wellington, before heading up the Nine Mile Canyon to Myton.

Butch Cassidy is planning a big hit at Castle Gate, Utah, and spends the winter of 1896 in the desolate Horseshoe Canyon at Robbers Roost. He forms the nucleus of an outlaw gang to carry out the robbery. In addition to Elzy Lay and the Sundance Kid, likely candidates are Joe Walker, a Texas cowpuncher whose specialty is stealing horses, and Bub Meeks, a veteran of the Montpelier bank raid. Butch and Elzy plan to relieve the Pleasant Valley Coal Company of its payroll. It is probably the most difficult robbery Butch has ever tackled.

The Company effectively owns the town of Castle Gate. It employs most of its citizens and is one of the largest mining enterprises in

Utah. Every two weeks, the payroll is brought in on the Denver & Rio Grande Railroad from Salt Lake City. The operators know that running regular shipments is tempting to bandits, so to reduce the risk, they pay out fortnightly on different days of the week. The workers don't know which day is payday or on which train the money is coming in until they hear a specific blast of the mine whistle, indicating their pay is waiting at the paymaster's office.

Butch needs a brilliantly simple plan to overcome such an ingenious defence system. There are some special problems. First, Castle Gate is not a cow town, which means that mounted cowpunchers are not a usual sight. Added to this, the paymaster's office can only be reached by a fairly narrow outside stairway at the side of the building. Finally, every payday, a bunch of hard-bitten miners mill around at the foot of those steps, undoubtedly ready to tear limb from limb anyone who tries to come between them and their well-earned pay.

The key question Butch and Elzy face is this: if cowpunchers are unusual in the town of Castle Gate, then what other kind of rider isn't? Discreet research reveals that the locals are used to seeing racehorses in town. Horse racing in Utah is as popular as it is in Colorado. Ergo, no one will be suspicious of seeing jockeys exercising their mounts regularly.

Butch and Elzy visit the town, suitably attired, on a daily basis and engage in casual conversations with the miners. They watch and wait patiently, listening for the telltale whistle.

On April 21, the payroll arrives at Castle Gate station at noon. Butch is already loafing in front of the company store. Around the corner from the stairs, Elzy is astride his own horse and holding onto Butch's. The whistle blows and the paymaster collects the payroll from the express car messenger. The payroll, in a leather satchel and three sacks, totals $9,860 in currency, cheques, gold and silver.

Elzy unties the horses ready for the escape. Butch watches paymaster Carpenter and clerk Lewis enter the station, then return minutes later with the money. As they reach the stairs, Butch steps out, points his gun and relieves a stunned Carpenter of his load. Lewis tries to make a break for the front door of the store. Frank Caffey, a miner, rushes to see what the commotion is about and Elzy, still mounted, points his six-shooter and says:

"Get back in there, you son-of-a-bitch, or I'll fill your belly full of hot lead!"

Butch tosses the sacks to Elzy, who promptly drops the reins of Butch's horse.

Excited, the animal spooks and promptly starts to bolt.

Butch warns the crowd:

"Don't anybody make a mistake. Everything's going to be all right!"

Somehow Elzy blocks the runaway's path with his own horse. Butch catches the bridle safely, mounts and the pair gallop swiftly out of town. It is a close call.

Minutes later, Carpenter tries to telegraph the sheriff. The line is dead. Carpenter climbs into the locomotive cab of the noon train still standing at the station, and orders the engineer to head for the county seat of Price. Butch and Elzy race for Helper, ditching the bag of heavy silver and the satchel full of cheques. The escape is planned meticulously. Following the main road until Spring Canyon, they take a trail circling west to bypass Helper, Spring Glen and Price. Ten miles further, near Gordon Creek, they change clothes and horses.

Carpenter, in the locomotive, reaches Price and alerts sheriff Gus Donant to put out a call for a posse. Butch and Elzy return to the main Cleveland road, cutting more telegraph wires. Sheriff Gus Donant has already spread the alarm, and posses form in Huntingdon, six miles west of Cleveland, and Castle Dale, ten miles further south. Incredibly, the Huntingdon posse is led by Joe Meeks, a cousin of Bub who is a confederate of Butch's. One of the horses Butch uses in the getaway belongs to Joe, who has lent it to Bub.

Butch and Elzy slide through the net. They ride east to Desert Lake then south to Buckhorn Draw, where they meet Bub waiting with fresh horses.

Most of the posses are tired and dejected and soon turn for home. But the one led by Deputy US Marshal Joe Bush continues south towards the Roost and gets almost within shooting distance near Wildcat Butte. The outlaws are comfortable entering the forbidding canyon country, but Bush decides it has become a potential ambush situation, in which Butch, with local knowledge and extra support, will have the upper hand. So Bush heads back for Price. Once again, Butch achieves a major coup, escapes the authorities and disappears into the void.

147

RICHARD:

I had already been alerted that the route Butch and Elzy had ridden on the Castle Gate robbery could not now be used due to road closures. We re-thought our direction north and decided we had no better option than to endure the forbidding Book Cliffs.

It was June 19 and day sixty-four. A truck appeared while we were preparing to depart. Driver Jim Wilcox introduced himself, asked about our route, then informed us it was not viable: high water levels meant swimming the horses across the deep river, which was not possible with a pack train. Instead, Jim suggested we use Tusher Canyon as our entry to the Book Cliffs. This proved to be the most fateful decision of the entire trip.

We stopped to let the horses graze before pushing on to our designated campsite. I was feeding each horse a minimum of ten pounds grain a day, equating to one sack. We packed two sacks in the panniers, tying another on top. A hundred and fifty pounds was three days' feed.

As evening descended, I decided to camp by a tiny water source. The horses were tethered to a low picket line and grained while I cooked the evening meal. Later, I retrieved the feed and re-filled our canteens. We noted that the horses immediately locate the best grazing even when hobbled. We learned that it was madness not to tether them in this situation, particularly at the beginning of the day.

Barbara in particular would waste hours trying to coax the horses back into camp, catching and leading in one, then going for the next in the vain hope the first one would remain still. It became a futile exercise, a joke. I felt neither Barbara nor Simon ever really grasped the way horses behave.

SIMON:

We pressed on. Between towering sandstone rock walls, junipers and dense undergrowth hemmed the dusty red path. At Cow Springs, the horses drank their fill. A combination of heat and the steady incline reduced our mileage. Mildly dejected, we stopped for lunch.

Richard and Barbara slept under the junipers to escape the burning sun, whilst I elected to watch the horses. Our three-hour break was ruined when all five horses began to move purposefully back down the hill in search of decent grazing.

The Western practice is always to tie securely a saddle horse, so that should the string bolt you have a mount to help recover them. Foolishly, we had failed to observe this rule, and we were in danger of finding ourselves afoot.

I managed to grab Sunday and Imasizzlin'lady, but as I did so Yazz, Bones and Pancho scattered rapidly into the dense undergrowth. Richard heard my woeful cries, came to the rescue and caught Yazz. We eventually retrieved the horses without incident, but I felt very chastened and vulnerable.

RICHARD:

After a long, tiring haul up Tusher Canyon, we arrived at the Seismic Camp, a bluff overlook with limited grazing. I went off to reconnoiter the trail for the following day. We couldn't complete the steep climb up over the canyon wall before nightfall. The route was a trail that climbed steadily along the east side of the canyon. The gradient was manageable, but the path itself was only about two feet wide and very close to the edge of a drop which in places was vertical.

We settled down around the campfire. The horses were hobbled to graze on the lush grass, and later, we picketed them in the cottonwoods. It began to drizzle, and we turned in early, only to be woken after midnight by an invasion of wild cattle. The horses were restless for the remainder of the night, and nobody slept well. I was happy to rise at four.

The trail out promised to be hard graft, so we prepared to set off early. The saddle horses were never fully cinched up until the pack horses were ready to travel, and while I was packing Imasizzlin'lady, Yazz suddenly and inexplicably bolted, taking off on a dead run. My saddle and equipment were emptied in all directions as he raced across the old camp. Stopping abruptly where it fell away to the river, he turned and thundered down the slope towards Green River. I tried in vain to head him off. The remaining horses, despite being hobbled, were in full flight and discarding their loads. Simon's reaction was to explode: *"Fucking hell!"*

SIMON:

Boy, was I angry! My first reaction was to give the other two, the so-called horse experts, a bad-tempered dressing down, but I don't believe my very explicit criticisms made the slightest dent. Remembering my own performance watching the horses the previous night, there may have been a "hark who's talking" element in their wooden response.

Meanwhile, Barbara and I were holding on to Imasizzlin'lady with all our might while the other horses were a quarter of a mile away going hard.

"Bastards!" I yelled as they took the first curve and disappeared in a cloud of dust.

Richard quietly retrieved his scattered pommel bag, saddlebags and water canteen. Stunned and dejected, I set off on foot to follow the horses.

It was a long walk. Passing blankets, canteens, pommel bags and other items strewn along the trail, my worries increased. I spied the horses still going flat out. I had hoped they would pull up after the first curve; instead, they thundered on. Shit!

I was also keeping a wary eye open for my pommel bag, which contained money, credit cards, used film and camera – all the important stuff. I hadn't seen it amongst the debris at camp.

I marched furiously. Twenty minutes later, Barbara caught up riding Imasizzlin'lady bareback. Mentally, I was already prepared to walk towards Green River town in the hope that the horses would tire and come to a standstill. I reprimanded Barbara again in my usual calm and measured fashion:

"For fuck's sake!" I yelled. "You just can't do anything constructive. It didn't need three of us to hold one horse."

What concerned me more than the scattered kit and the hike was the possible collateral damage. If the horses ran into thick undergrowth, we would have cut chests, shredded flanks, torn legs, even broken bones to cope with. Helpless and both close to tears, we continued to backtrack, hoping for the best and fearing the worst.

I tried to forget that Bones and Pancho were not our horses and damned Barbara again.

Five miles on, as we turned a corner, we spied the horses – bar Pancho, Rusty's valuable endurance horse, who was missing. The others, blowing mildly, had stopped where we lunched yesterday, bang opposite a bluff. I caught Yazz, Bones and Sunday, being careful not to spook them. Thankfully unmarked and still with their saddles intact, they were sweaty but seemed remarkably calm.

Thanking God, I mounted Yazz and began to tow the two mares back towards the Seismic. We had been lucky, but what if Pancho lay badly injured? I would have to ride back with Richard and shoot him, and then inform the Armstrongs that our stupidity had done the damage.

"Find the Arab!" I shouted to Barbara, and made off.

In little over an hour, I arrived back into camp with all our belongings.

"Where's Barbara?" asked Richard, looking relieved.

"Hunting for Pancho. Bastard's done a runner. What's missing?" I asked.

"Nothing. Here's your pommel bag."

Phew. Anxiety about the horses had driven the precious bag out of my mind.

Barbara arrived twenty minutes later with Pancho. He had galloped another mile and halted. It was lucky, but we wasted five valuable hours catching and re-packing the horses. Which paled into insignificance compared to the next incident.

"Right. Let's get going before the heat hits," said Richard as we finished loading the packhorses. He mounted and led us through the cottonwoods. We followed a faint cow trail. It promised to drop us on top of Tusher Canyon. From here, we would slowly trace our way to The Basin, forking away from a forbidding sequence of interlocking canyons.

The next canyon was Flat Nose George, named for one of Butch and Sundance's fellow outlaws. Unlucky George Currie was ambushed here in 1900. All around, the names identified with outlaw history: the McPherson Range, Wilcox Point, Horse Canyon, Walker Draw and Moonwater Springs. We were penetrating deep into Wild

Bunch territory.

Danger was close at hand. The narrow path required very careful negotiation. Five hundred yards up the track, Imasizzlin'lady (currently packing, and towed by Barbara) made a wild charge past her leader. Plunging uphill and swerving left, she slipped off the path and crashed through the undergrowth. The noise was incredible as branches snapped like matchsticks. Her action was a total shock. You don't expect to see a horse pitch off a track. Stunned, we dreaded what we would find.

Leaving Barbara holding the horses, we scrambled down a muddy bank. The Sizzler was on her side. Pinned by the weight of panniers, a puddle of water was slowly trickling into her nostrils. Unravelling the rope, we set aside the panniers and "H" pack. Richard tugged on the lead rope, and the mare scrambled to her feet, heavily caked in mud but showing no sign of injury or fear.

"That was close," I said.

A grain sack was split in the fall. We filled a nosebag and gave the mare a feed to calm her whilst quickly re-packing.

"All done," said Richard, as the rope was tied off, "Barbara can take her, but just stay back."

I settled in the saddle, relieved that the danger had passed. Mobile again, we moved ahead a hundred yards. The track narrowed. Richard started to urge Yazz up the slope when Imasizzlin'lady panicked again and charged past Pancho. Plunging forward, she stumbled, slipping on the loose dirt. She righted herself momentarily, only to lose her footing on the edge of the track, and seconds later, the mare toppled backwards from the ledge. It was like a bad dream – in slow motion, yet no time to react. Richard, busy leading, hadn't witnessed the disaster. A few seconds of shocked silence – then the crash. The Lady had run herself to death over a precipice.

"Jesus Christ, the horse has gone over!" I yelled in disbelief.

The horses floundered and surged together, barely under control.

Barbara wailed: "Oh, Lady – she's done it again."

Richard was speechless. We immediately rode for a small clearing ahead. I handed my reins to Barbara. Tempted to take the rifle, I left it in the scabbard. I hoped that Lady was dead on impact.

"Hold the horses, I'll go down," I breathed.

Where the mare had toppled over was a sheer drop, so I backtracked a hundred yards and scrambled down the steep slope. I trudged up the gorge to find the mare dead on her side, pack gear smashed to smithereens. It was horrendous. The fall had broken Lady's neck and back. Richard joined me moments later.

"What now?" I asked faintly.

"Take the horses back to Seismic," said Richard. "We'll haul the gear up and take it from there."

That was the lowest point on the expedition. We switched to autopilot – Barbara capitulated. Visibly pale and very shaken, she stayed with the horses whilst we took Bones and returned to the grisly scene to manhandle the remnants up the slope. Inspection of the equipment within yielded a destroyed stove, folded plates, flattened pots, pans and mugs, liquid containers burst and various foodstuffs melded into a gooey mess. After careful salvage, we cached the smashed gear in thick undergrowth.

Miraculously, we had avoided losing any more horses. Bones was promptly packed, and we rapidly set off for the grim thirty-one mile return to Green River. It had been wickedly hot earlier; ominous black clouds swiftly enveloped the sky, and a heavy cloudburst deluged. Literally and metaphorically, we rode in deep, deep gloom.

Emotionally, the journey was becoming demanding and for Barbara, unbearable. Had our romantic quest for some sort of equine grail placed our horses in jeopardy? The honest answer had to be a rueful "yes."

Barbara was in deep shock. When it came to the crunch, her continuous anxiety about the horses hadn't helped or been relevant. I felt sorry for her. As for Richard and me, we were only there to overcome difficulties and risks. If those elements weren't present, neither would we be. But a mare falling to her death was a stark reminder that risks can have tragic consequences. We gritted our teeth.

One thing was clear: as the yawning gulf between our horse management skills and those of the outlaws became more apparent, the more crucial it was that we at least matched them for determination, endurance and grit. There was no turning back. Despite the awful loss of a valuable horse, we would find a way to continue.

Two days later at the Nelson Ranch, Bruce Nelson phoned Jay

Ekker who quickly dispatched Jim Wilcox to the rescue. Jim appeared within twenty minutes. He was a third generation rancher whose family homestead was close by a well-known outlaw way station, and his grandparents were on friendly terms with Flat Nose George Currie amongst others.

To us, in our distress, he was like an uncle, sympathetic about our bad luck and reassuring us that others had lost horses in the same fashion. It was not our fault, and horses could do those things; we should not blame ourselves. Jim's kind words were little comfort; I was ashamed that a horse had been killed.

We unloaded into Robbers Roost Motel. I phoned ahead to Ray Hunting in Vernal to advise delay and the urgent need to buy a replacement horse. AC Ekker rang in later, having learned of our disaster. Bad news travels fast in Utah, but a horse was for sale in Montrose, Colorado, 170 miles away. It was ours if we wanted it. Locally, horses were unavailable. We considered the options. Buy a replacement horse, or ride to Vernal with four mounts and a reduced pack train. It was a difficult call. Richard had run out of cash and Barbara was still waiting for the insurance payout from Lloyds.

Barbara made herself scarce, and once more, I sensed strong disapproval. I focused on hitting the trail again. Yazz and Pancho needed a new set of shoes before leaving, and I mentioned this to Jim Wilcox, who brightened, stating:

"Boys, I'm the best around. Let's get some beer and go shoe a horse."

At the corrals, I caught Yazz and Pancho. Then Jim discovered the remnants of the pressure sores on Yazz's flanks. They had virtually healed, but the sight ignited the blue touch paper, producing a totally unexpected and extremely hostile response.

"Real cowboys in this country wouldn't ride a horse in that condition," said Jim aggressively. I felt very uncomfortable.

"You cain't ride a horse like this, it isn't done," Jim went on, "You should swap him out."

I explained that we were already looking to buy another horse, maybe two if the price was affordable.

"Promise me you won't ride the black," Jim demanded, pointing at Yazz.

"Jim, he's okay," Richard replied calmly, hoping to defuse the situation.

Jim literally threw away his hammer.

"People can get the shit kicked out of them for less. I *won't* shoe this horse – that's it! You don't know what you're doing and you know nothing about the outlaws," Jim cursed, his face brick red with anger.

I was mad as hell but I bit my tongue. We returned in silence to the Robbers Roost Motel. I apologised. It was no part of our plan to make enemies. Richard busied himself. Jim wanted us to promise not to ride Yazz and to buy an extra horse. We agreed. No horses were available within our budget of $1,500 per mount. Those offered were over double the price. Financially, the expedition was in deep trouble. We couldn't expect anyone to lend us a horse, nor did we have $3,000 in spare cash. It was stalemate and four horses.

I was deeply distressed by Jim's sudden and dramatic switch of mood. One minute we were all buddies, revelling in our shared interest and his family's historical link with the Wild Bunch. Just one glimpse of a (nicely recovering) set of pressure sores and we were suddenly unacceptable frauds, not fit to be allowed out on horseback, and he wanted nothing more to do with us, all said in the most aggressive and offensive terms.

Richard in particular came in for undeserved abuse. No one could have displayed greater concern or taken more trouble with Yazz than Richard had done, not only patiently forgiving the black his many alarming and dangerous displays of temperament, but also nursing him carefully and skillfully back to health after his injuries, in a manner that consistently won the approval of the highly experienced Joe Armstrong.

Sure, we were learning the hard way, and sure, it was tough on the horses, even tougher than it might have been because of our inexperience. But long distance horse-packing in this terrain and these conditions is a testing business – it was then and it is now. Good as they were, don't tell me the Wild Bunch never injured or lost a horse.

We were sad to have upset Jim and sadder still to have apparently lost his friendship, but this huge gulf between the theorist and the practitioner was precisely why we were doing this trip. Enthusiastic locals, proud relatives of outlaws, historians, film buffs, even equestrians, all know the history, but if they haven't ridden the ride, they just cannot know what the risks are about. As a hobby, the Old West is great fun and make-believe. Trying to experience it for real is demanding, and on occasion dangerous for riders and horses alike.

Meanwhile, we were in deep shit.

RICHARD:

The Bush Telegraph was in good working order, and Ted Ekker had heard of our plight. He contacted local horse and mule trainer Kurt Olsen. Another trail could be taken from Thompson Springs through Thompson Canyon.

We phoned the Armstrongs to report the loss of Lady, and announced our departure with four horses. It caused great consternation. One packhorse was deemed not enough to carry for three riders. Rusty organised a replacement pack outfit and sent it to Ray Hunting's. We hoped to purchase another horse in Vernal.

I arranged with Ted the retrieval of our cached equipment. I also mentioned the run-in with Jim Wilcox, fearful that we may have dented our reputation locally, but apparently this was not the case. We drove to the Seismic camp and walked to the site of the accident. Lady still lay untouched by predators, but Ted assured me the cadaver would be picked clean within days. The place where the incident occurred showed no threat and the trail was firm, albeit close to the edge. It was easy to see how unlucky the mare had been to lose her footing.

Ted was totally behind our expedition. In his sixties, rugged looking, forthright and happily retired, he had successfully outfitted on the Roost for a number of years with AC and knew of the inherent dangers when working with horses.

Kurt Olsen, a young, blond-haired, mustachioed cowboy arrived, and we did a deal to box our horses to Thompson Springs for the re-start. Having covered thirty miles of reverse mileage back to town, Simon accepted that it was okay to haul directly east – but not north!

With one or at most two notable exceptions, everyone was heart-warmingly generous and helpful. The Code of the West was alive and well at Green River.

RIDING THE HIGH COUNTRY

"What are we doing here?"
THE SUNDANCE KID

SIMON:

June 24. Kurt Olsen hauled us from Green River. We passed through Thompson Springs, a remote outpost comprising a few wooden buildings and a deserted railway station. The southern gateway into the Uintah and Ouray Indian Reservation, this country is usually reserved for intrepid hikers, extreme cyclists and hunters – not three lunatics on horses. The most prominent landmark is a massive bluff overlooking the town.

Kurt's truck crashed and banged up the dusty, rutted track towards Sego, a mining ghost town that was nothing more than the ruins of stone buildings crumbling into dust. Brush and vegetation slowly strangled and reclaimed the canyon floor. As we trundled past, I wondered what this rowdy coal mining camp was like in its heyday.

1897. Accompanied by a driver and buggy, Butch and Elzy Lay drive a fine string of horses through Sego on their way to Arizona. Butch pulls up to ask the storekeeper, Bud Milton, for permission to water the horses. Bud keeps a fine string of racehorses. He notices Butch's outstanding mounts but doesn't venture outside to parley. The Wild Bunch uses Ballard Brothers Store, maybe quite often. Joe Walker, who is a fringe member of the gang, runs cattle and horses on Florence Creek with Jim McPherson and needs to re-supply locally.

SIMON:

I tried hard to imagine Butch and Sundance being here, but somehow it didn't feel like their kind of place. Remote mining towns were too rough and ready for the real sports, and we know for sure that Butch and Sundance enjoyed finery – deluxe hotels, tailored clothing, good wine and cigars. In comparison, Sego was a throwback to the Stone Age.

At the summit, we quickly unloaded, but not without a brief but alarming skirmish inside the packed trailer between my mare Sunday and one of the mules Kurt was also hauling.

We sat and demolished a packed lunch before striking out into unknown territory. Perched on the bluff, we gazed towards Green River. The sky was white. In the distance, a sea of brown, beige and orange hills floated on the horizon, below us a series of canyons slashed by evergreens promised interesting riding country. Altitude was up to 6,400 feet.

Kurt led down a gentle ridge paralleling Thompson Canyon towards Hell's Hole. His mules rapidly outdistanced our horses – their pace was phenomenal. Within minutes, they had disappeared into the thick undergrowth, leaving us floundering.

We struggled on thrashing through the foliage when suddenly a sheer drop of a thousand feet presented itself in the form of a canyon below. The horses began to baulk. Richard carefully traversed up a rocky slope, and we continued edging through the troublesome undergrowth. Kurt was waiting patiently on a ridge wondering what the fuss was about. It was certainly tough going for the horses – but the mules were unperturbed. I was impressed.

RICHARD:

Mules are better than horses for many duties. The US military successfully used mules for 125 years (until 1956) and considered them hardier than the horse, believing too that they were more agile, stronger, and could haul heavier loads over longer distances and more demanding terrain. They needed less grain, could subsist better on the vegetation available, were fast walkers with excellent recuperative powers and intelligent enough to recognize approaching danger – and avoid it.

So why, if we knew this much, were we on horses? Good question. Using mules was never considered because Joe had advised that for us horses were a better prospect. With hindsight and a reasonable time frame to allow for proper training in the handling of mules, yes, we might have used them.

Barbara's opinion was that she could control them easily, but I doubted that. Lacking physical strength, in a tight situation she would have her work cut out dealing with the packhorses. Simon was always cautious about the pack train. Whatever the opinions were, many times we heard that no one was ever willing to part with a decent mule – which meant the buyer always had to beware, and beginners like us could easily be had. So Joe was probably right.

SIMON:

We rested and checked the GPS. Kurt was impressed with the gadget, so Richard demonstrated its use. Richard's outstanding map reading skills had located many trails out of tight situations. He possessed a remarkable ability to pick a route through unyielding country apparently without the slightest difficulty. Three hours later, we crossed a lush valley floor, carpeted in magnificent grass, before scrambling over a tricky rock face to arrive at a tiny creek.

Bones promptly refused to cross. That was par for the course, and we were getting pretty pissed off with it. Kurt wisely took the cue and announced he was turning for home. We shook hands and parted company. I watched him and the mules rapidly disappear over a ridge for the long ride back.

RICHARD:

Alone once more, the fun and games began. We cursed, cajoled, dragged and finally spanked the stubborn Bones over a foot-wide stream. Half a mile further on, she lay down. This was tantamount to the old military definition of mutiny. She was throwing down her hat with a cry of: "I will soldier no more, you may do as you please!"

Barbara at once called for a halt and an immediate camp. I said we should carry on. Progress had been slow, the site was not secure and anyway we were blocking a dirt track. Also, I had planned to reach high ground before nightfall to ensure a good start the following morning. I got Bones to her feet and led her for another fifty yards, but she promptly sat down again. We stopped. Hobson's choice.

We camped in Corral Canyon, a beautiful grassy valley hemmed in by pine and deciduous trees. Altitude now registered 8,379 feet, which accounted for the decline in our pace. We turned the horses out to graze, ate supper silently and retired to our bedrolls. By midnight there was a commotion as the horses attempted to escape for no apparent reason. We left our warm bivvies to calm the horses. The entire routine had to be repeated fifteen minutes later. The temperature dropped alarmingly, and we were bitterly cold. I slept only intermittently.

Next morning, as we left the valley, I saw our second bear, which probably explained why the horses were so restless.

After a grindingly hard climb through dense forest, we reached the summit of Mormon Ridge. The view was stunning. Early morning sun blazed brightly across a glowing orange desert floor, then melted into the horizon. We stopped to take pictures, savour the moment and check the map.

The trailhead altitude eventually nudged 9,609 feet – the highest point of the trip. This really was the high country. Again we stopped to graze the horses on fine grass before resuming along the muddy track. Miles later, after heading down a grassy valley and traversing a long spur, we spied the end of Mormon Ridge dropping over a sheer ledge.

SIMON:

It was a foregone conclusion that a stony path would miraculously lead us down an escape trail to the canyon floor below. We congratulated ourselves in anticipation of a decent campsite later. Until Richard glanced at the parallel ridge and saw a plume of dust trailing a truck. Were we on the right ridge? We must be. Ted Ekker in Green River had said so. We trekked on, wondering, before halting dead in our tracks an hour later. The route ahead was totally blocked by vicious and impenetrable brush.

"The path's probably right there," I said, pointing ahead hopefully.

"I'm not so sure," said Richard tersely. "Maybe that truck was on the right track and we're not."

"There's bound to be a game trail down," I declared.

Our earlier optimism vanished into the thinner air. We stood impassively, keeping our malevolent thoughts to ourselves. Despite our apparently excellent brief, there was no trail, only a 1,500 foot drop into the forbidding canyon below. Bollocks! Our task now was to backtrack to where the trail had forked that morning. Exasperated, Barbara lit a cigarette and looked darkly at us.

"What now?" she queried, her tone both accusing and militant.

"A fucking long ride back almost to where we camped," I exclaimed.

Hostile looks. Silence. I stepped off Sunday and tried to find a path down but quickly gave up. We were stranded. The fiasco had cost us a day's riding. Richard fumed.

Like Robbers Roost, the Book Cliffs provided a safe haven for the Wild Bunch. If lawmen or posses ventured up here, they would get lost among the ridges and canyons as we had done. Unlike them, we did not also have to worry about being ambushed.

By May 1898, the authorities are under mounting pressure – from Wyoming banks, the powerful railroads and the express companies – to form a strike force similar to the Texas Rangers, with a mandate to capture or eliminate the outlaws.

On May 12, a posse led by Sheriff C.W. Allred rides out of Price. Well armed and prepared for a two-week sortie, their aim is to retrieve horses and cattle stolen from the Whitmore Ranch. Following the rustlers' route, they pick up a trail near Lower Crossing. Leading north towards Range Valley, they find the stolen livestock abandoned by the rustlers – the trail leads directly to Jim McPherson's ranch.

McPherson is called out for interrogation but he denies seeing the rustlers and is persuaded, possibly at gunpoint, to join the posse as a guide. Tracks change direction, heading for the hostile canyon country. Perfect for ambush, the precipitous and narrow trails are so hard to negotiate that it takes the posse four hours to ride three miles. Allred wisely decides to wait until morning rather than ride into a trap. A late camp is made near Florence Creek, within a mile of the outlaws.

On May 13, just before daylight, the posse resumes the chase. They spot the outlaws, spread out and advance quietly on foot. Creeping in, they see four men fast asleep in their bedrolls on a rock shelf protected by a deep ravine. The sleepers are swiftly surrounded and called upon to surrender. Two men jump up and put their hands in the air, the others go for their guns, and trade shots till their ammunition runs out. Turning to escape, they are cut down by a hail of gunfire and die instantly. Over fifty shots are fired.

First to be identified is Joe Walker. When Sheriff Allred turns over the body of the second man, he is sure it is Butch Cassidy. Great excitement. The posse's feelings run very high and some are all for cutting off the outlaws' heads and burying them where they lie, rather than hauling them all the way to town, but Jim McPherson successfully resists this proposal.

There follows a difficult forty-mile journey back to Thompson Springs, with Walker and Cassidy handcuffed and strapped across their saddles. Governor Heber Wells of Utah receives this telegram from deputy US Marshal Joe Bush:

"Came up with outlaws five this morning. Killed Joe Walker and Cassidy (sic), captured Lay and one man. Have prisoners and dead men here. Send message to my house please. Sheriff Allred and posse did nobly. JR Bush."

It seems the Butch Cassidy crisis is over.

But back in Price, the news spreads like wildfire. Rumours abound that there are doubts about the identities of the deceased outlaws. Townsfolk assemble to view the corpses, and Joe Walker is positively identified, the other still presumed to be Butch Cassidy. A swift inquest is held, using the testimony of Sheriffs Allred and Tuttle, which decides it is definitely Butch. The bodies are placed in coffins and buried next day.

When the captured accomplices eventually confirm that it isn't Butch Cassidy, but a Wyoming cowboy named Johnny Herring, there are some red faces. Sheriff John Ward from Evanston, Wyoming and Sheriff Doc Shores of Gunnison County, Colorado are summoned to an exhumation to confirm officially that the body is not that of

Cassidy. To add insult to injury, a rumoured $15,000 reward (a fortune by the standards of the day) is forfeited, and to cap it all, the two suspects who surrendered during the shootout have to be turned loose for lack of evidence.

It seems the Butch Cassidy crisis is not over. It is merely entering a new phase, a dangerous one for the outlaws. The powers that be are red-faced and hopping mad.

SIMON:

Drawing a veil over our sullen, resentful eighteen mile backtrack, once we had recovered and reached the previous morning's start point we cheered up at once. We rode on, delighted to be heading once again in the right direction. Opposite Flat Nose George Canyon, I told Richard who Flat Nose Currie was (no relation to Kid Curry, aka Harvey Logan), and how he was ambushed. He and one Tom Dilly had been rustling cattle. Flat Nose had based himself in a cave hideout in Rattlesnake Canyon just below Florence Creek. Dilly had been holding the stolen cattle nearby on a temporary basis.

April 17, 1900. Following a tip-off from Mr Fullerton, manager of the Webster Cattle Company, Sheriff Preece of Vernal and his posse are in hot pursuit of Tom Dilly. Preece, now reinforced by Sheriff Tyler of Moab and his posse, spots Flat Nose Currie and a running battle develops. Flat Nose quickly crosses the river on a raft and takes up a strategic position hidden in the rocks. Shots are exchanged, and the posses divide, moving in cautiously, shooting and calling on the fugitive to surrender. When fire is no longer returned, the posses close in and find Flat Nose dead.

An argument quickly breaks out about who has fired the fatal shot. Doc King, a member of Crip Tyler's posse, has fired a round at over 200 yards and achieved a freak headshot, perhaps off a ricochet. But Tyler claims that his bullet – which has passed through Currie's cartridge belt and come out in the middle of his back – has done the job.

George Currie, wanted dead or alive, has a $3,000 bounty on his head offered by the Union Pacific Railroad, which at this time is a sum of money worth arguing about. The corpse is strapped to the back of a mule, taken to Thompson and buried. Later, George's father arrives, disinters the body and takes it home for re-burial.

A month later, three men ride into the Webster City Cattle Company ranch. Next they are seen riding through Moab, travelling north. At Thompson Springs, they make enquiries as to the whereabouts of the Currie killing. They are plainly tracking the killers of Flat Nose. Who are they?

It gets murky, but Sheriff Tyler, Sam Jenkins, Mr. Fullerton, Deputy Sheriff Herbert Day, Sheriff Preece and Mert Wade track the mysterious trio into the Book Cliffs. They split up, and Tyler, Jenkins and Day proceed alone.

On the morning of May 27, 1900 they come upon a camp they believe to be Ute Indians. Tyler is heard to remark:

"Here are the Indians we assisted across the stream yesterday."

The Sheriffs slide down from their horses and walk towards the camp. Tyler says:

"Hello boys." These are his last words.

Unwittingly, the pair has walked straight into Kid Curry's camp – their rifles still in the scabbards on their saddles. They walk unarmed into a hail of bullets.

Deputy Sheriff Herbert Day says he is fifty yards away when he sees them run for their horses, hears the crackle of gunfire and witnesses the gruesome spectacle of his comrades being cut down. Day disappears unscathed into the brush. Tyler has been hit twice in the right side, Jenkins struck five times in the back below the shoulders, the bullets passing through his chest and almost cutting off his arm.

Day escapes and locates Preece, telling him of the killings. Sensation. Preece is reluctantly persuaded to head back to Moab for reinforcements before chasing after the killers. Tyler's and Jenkins' bodies are tied to mules, and the party backtracks, arriving in Thompson Springs two days later.

This prompts Governor Wells to cable his peers in Arizona, Colorado and Wyoming. Posses are immediately sent into the field to block all known trails in and out of Robbers Roost, Brown's Park and Hole-in-the-Wall. The authorities consider it impossible for the killers to escape their clutches, but the initial delays have enabled the outlaws to secure fresh horses and disappear.

Preece's posse rides an incredible hundred and twenty miles in twenty-four hours to Ouray, but while they sleep, their horses are stolen (by friends or wellwishers of the outlaws), and since no fresh mounts can be found, the chase is abandoned. The authorities are convinced the killers are Kid Curry, Butch Cassidy and Charlie Hanks. The best report of the incident is written up by the Moab Grand Valley Times in the issue of June 1, 1900.

Meanwhile, the outlaws ford the White River aiming for the town of Rangely, then cross the railroad tracks near Cisco and head south over the Colorado River about twelve miles below Green River Station. This connects up to the Horsethief Trail, and thence to the safety of Robbers Roost.

Posses are still out trying to head off the fugitives at Ouray. Men answering their descriptions are seen at the K Ranch, close to the Utah-Colorado line. Another posse rides out from Fort Duchesne to Rangely and scours the Badlands in the Bear River Country. Trails are nearly impossible to find. Also, the outlaws have drawn the posses dangerously deep into the ominous wasteland. The pursuers cover an average fifty miles per day, riding from dawn till dusk. But the trail of (is it?) Curry, Cassidy and Hanks peters out, and thus ends the greatest manhunt in the history of Utah.

SIMON:

Pursuing Butch and Sundance into such unforgiving lands was not easy. We endured many periods of monotony, but we were living the adventure and felt privileged to be doing so. We marvelled yet again at the geographical know-how of the outlaws.

Altitude dropped, alpine scenery melted, grass thinned and temperatures soared. We gazed towards Florence Creek, totally encompassed by a myriad of tight, interlocking tricky canyons within the McPherson Range. All the names had historical significance: Horse Canyon, Walker Point and Post Canyon.

The posses that chased the Wild Bunch had ridden into this desolate country and shown considerable nerve to do so. They were off their ground and vulnerable. You could almost feel – and share – their sense of foreboding, as if it were still hanging in the air a hundred years later, a kind of gut instinct that you were some place you shouldn't be at.

We arrived at an old abandoned homestead. It was four miles east of the Herring and Walker ambush site at Moonwater Springs. A cluster of broken down log buildings remained, nearly hidden by masses of brush and undergrowth. Richard searched in vain for water. The horses were in desperate need, having gone without since Mormon Ridge. We rode on and eventually endured a dry camp in the woods. Enough grazing was available, but our concerns about water were mounting once more.

I wanted to visit the gun-battle site, but it was just not possible. Deviations from the main stem of the Outlaw Trail were proving to be incompatible with our tight time scales. A round trip of eight miles scrabbling through rough country would take at best four hours. It was an added risk we did not need. I promised myself I would return.

The next morning we pinpointed Goat Spring. Down a steep ridge across two awkward re-entrants, it was impossible to access. Not for nothing was it called Goat Spring. We were leading the horses on foot, all very thirsty, and my new boots (a gift from Ted Ekker) were giving me seven kinds of hell. They had not been broken in, and the truth was they were too small anyway but mighty handsome. Vanity, all is vanity. The sun blasted mercilessly, and conditions were shite.

The major consolation, which made my day (but certainly not Barbara's!), was that we were following the trail the outlaws used after the double killing of Tyler and Jenkins.

We rode past the entrance for Mail Canyon. It was located on the dusty flats. We rested near Dry Creek, which lived up to its name, and we were getting distinctly worried. Then Richard miraculously nosed out a faint cow trail down a rocky entrant into a gully, where a hidden seep called Flat Rock Spring was bubbling out of the ground. Richard had done it yet again. The man was uncanny. The horses had been without water for nearly twenty-four hours.

RICHARD:

The horses crowded at the edge madly slaking their thirst. I was very glad to have found water. In this climate and terrain, any water source can dry up in high summer, and usually does. I was also delighted to quit the saddle after a demanding ten-hour stint. The camp was good despite the mosquitoes, a small price to pay (or so we thought), and we were pleased for the horses.

We sat down to enjoy the late afternoon. Presently, a small band of wild horses arrived to take water. They kept a wary eye on the human intruders. Simon returned the compliment, fearful lest our own horses would decide to clear off with them. Later, I took the canteens and walked ahead to confirm the watercourse, hoping it would yield feed along the trail.

Next morning, we made an early start. At Gray Knolls, the canyon walls shrank, and the landscape opened. Nearby were Desolation Canyon and Nutters Hole. Nine Mile Canyon collided with a small reservoir above the Horse Bench. Worryingly, the watercourse was sunk twenty feet below the valley floor and shrouded by dense undergrowth. Temperatures rose, conditions changed. It was a dustbowl. A sign denoted that the land was US Navy-owned. They were welcome to it.

Simon:

Near Big Pack Mountain, the terrain was a barren moonscape, bleached by the sun. Not a living creature walked or crawled. We were learning fast there was no good reason to be out here. With exquisite timing, Pancho threw a shoe, and Richard worked relentlessly in burning heat for over an hour to tack it on.

When we got going again, Hill Creek maintained its alien dreadfulness. When we came to a junction, the track seemed to turn back on itself and follow a canyon wall to nowhere. Hawkeye Richard had spotted a fertile patch sunk in a depression, so we forked right. Thick vegetation barred our path. We crashed through the low hanging undergrowth on horseback, trying to keep our own heads at least as low as those of our mounts or we could have been torn from the saddle. Eventually, we broke through to a landlocked oasis of barley grass. Saved!

Our camp opposite Wild Horse Bench proved to be the worst ever. We deliberated: ride or stay? Fear of no feed for the horses was decisive, so we let them graze at leisure while we settled for a siesta. At least, Richard and Barbara dozed under a tree; I kept one wary eye open for the horses. After the last debacle, I had promised myself we would never again be left stranded on foot.

By early evening, the mosquitoes had multiplied to a frightening extent. We slapped the marauders constantly, leaving bloody handprints on the horses' necks, backs and flanks. Eating dinner was impossible. We got bitten to blazes and covered up as best we could. The repellents were worse than useless. Though hobbled, the horses were clearly anxious to move out, but it was too late now to re-pack and locate an alternative site.

The mosquitoes were a nightmare, and unbelievably, there was no respite for twelve hours. Could they be working in shifts? Permanently zipped into our stifling bivvies we counted down the hours and minutes until dawn.

We then broke all previous records for a speedy morning departure. We sprayed the last of the repellents and inspected the horses' underbellies. They sported thousands of lumps. I counted three hundred bites on my massively swollen right arm. Yet despite all this, Richard had made a brilliant decision to stay. The barley grass was a lifesaver for the horses, especially as our hard feed was used up, so the horses had to forfeit their normal morning and evening rations supplement.

Once we got going the mosquitoes quickly subsided. They were probably driven off by the squadrons of sinister deerflies that took their place. Blackish with grey wings, they peeled off and homed in like Stukas. For forty-five minutes, these evil daylight raiders harried us all, including the horses, mercilessly.

At the confluence with Willow Creek a new obstacle presented itself: an iron-bridge. Minus railings, it spanned a forty-foot drop with no alternative crossing. Predictably, Bones flatly refused to cross. Yazz would not lead either. I headed the party on Sunday, and as Richard followed, Bones slammed on the brakes. Barbara and Pancho crossed without incident. Richard and I cajoled, cursed and hauled against Bones like a tug-of-war team – the stubborn mare using all her might to avoid stepping onto the bridge. We would have been there still if I had not eventually laid into her, lashing her haunches with my reins until she proceeded.

This was the negative aspect of horseback travel. Those moments were riddled with self-reproach, but it had to be done. Our expedition was severely testing, and once committed, we just had to stick to our route. Otherwise we might as well have done the entire trip by train.

RICHARD:

An hour later, a plume of dust aroused our hopes. A pickup appeared, and we flagged it down. The occupant, a driver in his thirties, expressed complete surprise that riders should be on the coalfields. We told him about our mission, and in return gleaned directions to Ouray. It was ten miles on with no store to re-supply. That meant two days of riding without hard feed to supplement the horses' diet.

Minutes later, an Indian Agency vehicle suddenly stopped. The first truck roared off, and as it did so, my heart sank. In the rear was a sack of grain. The second driver grinned and introduced himself as James. An attractive lady sat beside him.

"You guys riding to Ouray?"

"Yeah, we've come from Thompson," Simon replied.

"That's a long ways. Nobody comes from there on a horse – well not since the old times, anyway."

"We need feed for the horses," I cut in quickly.

"Stop at Jenks's place over the bridge. I'll call and advise you're on the way."

Minutes later, the first truck returned. The driver jumped out and introduced himself as Gary Dye.

"Hey, I thought about you guys and want to donate this." Gary heaved the sack of grain out of the pickup and tossed it onto the floor.

"I'm a Mormon and I've a big interest in Butch Cassidy." We laughed, shook hands warmly and parted.

The horses received a generous feed. Relieved at the minor miracle which had occurred, we pressed on.

Later, a car drew up alongside us.

"You guys should be in Vernal by now!" Ted Ekker barked.

Ted was taking a trip to research the Hole-in-the-Wall country with his charming wife Iona. He delved into an enormous cool-box and handed out Pepsis.

"We're on our way to the Outlaw Trail Centre first," Ted announced, and then added, "How did the ride work out on Mormon Ridge?"

"It didn't, Ted," I replied.

"What happened?"

"We got to the end of the bluff and there was no trail down, so we rode back for a day to connect onto the Wagon Road," I reported, while Ted scratched his head, absolutely sure that a trail led off the ridge.

SIMON:

We waved *adios* and remounted for Ouray. Every which way I scanned the range it looked identical – a veritable dustbowl devoid of flora and fauna. Aside from the mountain country in New Mexico and Arizona, we had ridden through high desert for the best part of 900 miles.

To give the horses some respite in the brutal heat, we alternated riding and walking, US Cavalry style. In the distance, I saw a gleam. The Ouray National Waterfowl Refuge sprawled ahead – a fabulous eight-mile oasis where water had been flooded to create a swamp with a vast array of bird-life, plus, of course, the friendly neighbourhood mosquitoes.

At the Jenks's place, we bought enough hay and re-filled our canteens with fresh water. Ouray was no town, merely a cluster of buildings. I counted seven residences, a barn, corrals and nothing else.

It was near here that Sheriff Preece and his weary posse had their horses stolen following the Tyler and Jenkins murders in May 1900. Preece managed to procure a mount locally and resumed the chase alone. He must have been one tough son-of-a-gun. I wondered what became of him in later life. What did lawmen do when they got past it? I thought of the aging Joel McCrea in Peckinpah's *Ride the High Country*. Preece rode the high country all right, and so had we.

When Kid Curry, Butch and (presumptively) Hanks were being pursued by the posses, their escape trails were either Nine Mile Canyon near Towave Reservoir or a network of tracks leading to Brown's Park. We were plumping for the latter. I don't know if Sheriff Preece made the same choice.

RICHARD:

Whilst the horses rested and munched their hay contentedly, Barbara announced that she would be stopping and refused to go further. I was taken aback. To stay here was madness, adjacent to a man-made lake teeming with mosquitoes.

"I'll be leaving in one hour, with or without you," I told her bluntly.

"I bet you would." She replied angrily.

"You're right," I said and walked away.

In my mind, I reviewed Barbara's failings as a team member to date, at the end of which I mentally wrote her off. I then watched curiously (and ungenerously) as she struggled to lift and hook a pannier onto a sawbuck saddle.

"This is how you're going to complete the ride on your own, then?" I asked.

Our relationship went even further downhill, but I could not forgive her continuous, open contempt for Simon. I wasn't that proud of my own negative attitudes to Simon, though mine were less damaging because they were less overt. God knows he could be a pain in the butt at times, and what he knew about horses wouldn't fill a book of stamps, but he was realising a dream, he had put his soul into it for several years and his single-minded commitment to success was infectious.

We loaded and rode silently for Pelican Lake and Leota. According to Percy Jenks, a restaurant there cooked incredible steaks, and my mouth watered already. Back on the tarmac, however, Pancho at once started favouring a leg. I checked twice and we proceeded. Again he picked up a hoof. Immediately Simon and I unpacked him and switched his duty to saddle horse. It didn't help, and our concern grew. I decided to remove the shoe I had tacked on earlier.

Barbara, still enraged with me, screamed out:

"He's got laminitis," she said, adding, "You've been feeding the horses too much grain."

"Don't be ridiculous," I said.

"I wouldn't say a damn word about feeding the horses, Barbara, if

I were you," Simon chipped in heatedly.

We stood around studying Pancho, and failed to notice two young lads had arrived on a quad bike. They saw our difficulty and offered us corrals and a telephone at their nearby family ranch. Jeremiah and Travis Batty threw in hay, piped water and summoned their father from Vernal.

Simon rang Ray Hunting, also of Vernal, our next port of call, and gave him a sitrep. The major worry was Rusty's Arab – if lame, he would be out. It was likely that two horses would need to be bought in Vernal. Then we had the logistical nightmare of transporting Pancho to Wyoming, plus the acute embarrassment of another spoiled horse to our credit.

Joe Batty appeared in an hour and suggested we stay overnight. Ray Hunting announced that he would arrive at six-thirty the next morning to haul Pancho and the packs into town. The generosity of these people was nothing short of magnificent. Although we missed out on that fine steak dinner at Leota, some great friends were made.

We hoped our ride would change for the better at Vernal too. Most of Simon's contacts were placed in northeastern Utah, Colorado, Wyoming and Montana. No doubt there would still be clashing personality problems, but I felt (for the first time) that maybe Barbara wouldn't finish the ride. More importantly, despite our differences, I fancied I detected the beginnings of a bond between Simon and me. Whatever else happened, I hoped he and I would be riding together onward to Canada.

THE OUTLAW STRIP &
BROWN'S PARK

"Boy, a few dark clouds appear on your horizon,
you just go all to pieces."
BUTCH CASSIDY

SIMON:

Northwest of Ouray was the location of a notorious outlaw refuge. Every bit as infamous as the Hole-in-the-Wall, the Outlaw Strip was the stuff of which legends are made. This was the real deal, the stand-alone refuge accurately stereotyped and portrayed in so many western movies. It sounded too good to be true.

The Outlaw Strip came into existence through the discovery of Gilsonite, a rare, black hydrocarbon used mainly for making paints and varnishes. It is found only in the Uinta Basin, and was first experimented with by mineralogist Samuel H. Gilson. Discovery dates are unknown, but it was sometime before Fort Duchesne was established. Indians had used this material for centuries to waterproof their baskets.

In partnership with Bert Seaboldt, the fort's post trader, Sam Gilson plans to start mining. Since they are on Ute land, they seek legal advice and determine they can only proceed if Congress acts to make the property public land.

In 1883, backed by powerful business and political leaders, a Congressional bill restores part of the Uintah Valley Indian reservation to the public domain. To this end, Fort Duchesne officers swear affidavits that the land is "utterly worthless to the tribes for any purpose."

Before the land can be transferred to the mining interests, every adult member of the Ute tribes has to sign a treaty. Knowing the Utes are suspicious (with good reason) of the treaty process, and will naturally baulk at signing away more land, Seaboldt volunteers to supply whisky at the signing. Major Adna Chaffee, the Fort's commanding officer, condones the action, which is a success. Each Ute Indian who signs is given free whisky. The soldiers expect trouble, but by the end of the first day, every single Ute is fast asleep.

The resultant shantytown is known as the Duchesne Strip or more familiarly, The Strip. It becomes a hotbed of all kinds of vice and corruption, and soon, in addition to saloons, gambling halls and brothels, it boasts a store, hotel, barber's shop, blacksmith, stage station and telegraph office. But drinking, gambling and whoring remain its twenty-four hour a day activities.

Fights are frequent, and some sixteen men are killed in gunfights, which makes The Strip more dangerous than Tombstone. It is a lawless refuge and a useful halfway house between Robbers Roost and Hole-in-the-Wall.

Neither the territorial Government nor the Uintah County peace officers can enforce the law here because the excluded land is not Indian-owned. A federal marshal has jurisdiction, but only if he is bold enough to risk his life.

Butch's buddy Elzy Lay owns a saloon, which is known as "The Strip's worst gambling-hell" and is particularly infamous for shoot-outs. Off-duty soldiers drink, then enter into confrontations with settlers, sometimes resulting in deaths. For twenty years, The Strip will periodically play host to Butch Cassidy, The Sundance Kid, Matt Warner and Dave Lant.

Elzy's spare time is spent counterfeiting. At one point, Sheriff John T. Pope rides in under instructions from the US district attorney to close down Elzy's operation. Pope takes an inventory of the saloon's stock and finds $2,000 in phoney money Elzy has failed to dispose of. What he does not find is Elzy.

By 1894, even the military are complaining to the United States Attorney in Utah. It makes no difference. Only when Fort Duchesne is finally abandoned by the Army in 1911, does support for the local businesses rapidly disappear, and The Strip becomes part of frontier history.

SIMON:

Naturally, I wanted to see the location. But despite The Strip being only five miles away, we deliberated. The round trip was five hours – over half a day's riding. The reality was that no single building remained as a testament to the outlaws' time, so we decided to ride on to Vernal.

Leota comprised a few houses set beside the road. We breakfasted at Peg's Café, then pressed on along the tarmac. By noon, the heat had returned with a vengeance and riding was monotonous. We had a horse-watering stop arranged, which turned out to be a splendid lunch for us with the Kossoff and Brown families.

Craig Kossoff also very kindly checked the horses' hooves and tacked on Yazz's loose shoes before we struck out to Vernal and a well-deserved four-day rest. Plans were to leave the horses with the Huntings and find a cheap hotel, then re-supply and make for Brown's Park, Colorado – another of the really major league hideouts, and the halfway point of our expedition!

We arrived early evening, and the Huntings at once invited us to stay. It was another enormous gesture. Four horses, three smelly humans and a load of dirty equipment dumped without ceremony on their doorstep. Nothing seemed to faze the Americans we were meeting. Later, Americana historian Doris Burton and colleagues from the Outlaw Trail History Association sponsored dinner. It was an evening of great camaraderie – like a family gathering.

"We didn't think you were coming," said one voice along the table.

"Doris got your letter saying you'd left and were riding through the Roost – we thought you wouldn't make it, and I still can't believe you have!" said Ray Hunting, our host, an ex-rancher and horse-breeder who had spent time in Brown's Park. We smiled and soaked up the atmosphere.

Ray was a throwback to the old West: affable, polite, but rugged. He quizzed us shrewdly, and why not? What were three English folk doing riding the Outlaw Trail? We responded as best we could, ate well and promised to meet for a barbecue the following evening at the Burtons'.

We had a great time in Vernal. Our appetites were gluttonous. Richard and I guzzled beer, doughnuts and candy – all the goodies unavailable on the trail (purely to restore lost body weight, you understand). We relaxed, believing that compared with what we had been through, Wyoming was sure to offer great riding conditions. Until Marilyn Hunting informed us that a ferocious heat wave was registering daily averages in the hundreds.

Our thoughts turned to crossing the Red Desert. A dilemma emerged: from which direction to approach Atlantic and South Pass Cities? Ride to Rock Springs and Farson along Pacific Creek, or across the Red Desert itself? Farson was off the Outlaw Trail. Jeffrey City cut mileage but missed the important towns of Lander, Riverton, Shoshoni and Copper Mountain. Decisions, decisions.

RICHARD:

This was tough country. It seemed that until South Pass, the Outlaw Trail was no place for a horse north of the Colorado line. We deliberated again. The stats read 990 miles in sixty riding days, or exactly 16.5 miles per day. Getting better.

I left Simon to figure out the history and was determined to reduce our pack weight. I re-supplied with more dried food, bought military mosquito nets, re-stocked insect repellent and managed to create a mix that stank of creosote. I was leaving nothing to chance for the Tongue River section to Miles City. I made ground stakes and spent a day assembling and oiling the new leathers of our pack gear shipped from the Denver Colorado Saddle Company. Ray had located a horse, the new equipment arrived and we were back to full strength – I was buzzing.

We met our new horse, Ditch, a four-year-old gelding of fifteen hands. He was a stocky brute weighing close to 1,200 pounds with dun coloring, black brindled legs, tail and mane. Ditch, clearly born in one, had a piratical look, with one eye brown and the other silver, and could only be caught with grain. Ray informed us casually that he had never been used as a packhorse either. Simon twitched. A pre-requisite had been a horse that would saddle and pack, but the packing was more important. A horse similar to Bones was our ideal. Mountain country was imminent, and we would immerse ourselves in the Wind Rivers in Wyoming. On no account did I want a "green" horse in the string holding us back and creating further anxiety.

Ray caught Ditch and blanketed up slowly and carefully. Pack-saddle and cinch ready, we placed the full panniers on his back and held our breath. Ditch tensed momentarily but did not explode into a bucking frenzy. Ray continued to walk him round, praising and continually rubbing his chest. I decided we would pack Ditch to break him into the task quickly.

Later that afternoon, we departed for the cinema. *Wild Wild West* was showing, and since we were reliving an element of it, we decided to check the movie out. I thought it was garbage, and Simon, our Western movie buff, agreed vehemently.

We took the Jones Hole road to Brown's Park. It was fifty miles distant. The land flattened and the lush grass began to subside. Mid-morning temperatures climbed to the mid-nineties. Our pace was predictably slow, as Ditch struggled to keep up with a hardened and trail-broken team. After two days, he had still not been accepted by the other horses. He was extremely reluctant and needed to be dragged along. A twelve hundred pound horse dragging on your arm was no fun. The constant pressure, compounded by rearwards lunging, kept my right arm ready to snap out of its socket.

SIMON:

July 4. Smiles returned briefly when Doris Burton arrived to catch us on candid camera for an article in the *Outlaw Trail Journal*, then on to the Nielson's Circle X Ranch.

The location was stunning. Beautiful, remote and sixteen miles from Vernal, ranch HQ was perched on a plateau overlooking Ashley National Forest and the Uinta Mountains. A superb barbecue had been laid on, and we were guests of honour. It had not occurred to us that it was Independence Day.

The Burtons were there amongst the Nielson family and friends, and yet again, we felt like minor celebrities and sat exchanging stories with these wonderful people. I suppose it was here that Richard and I began a series of red meat overdoses, tucking in to thick juicy chops, huge ribs, cheeseburgers and prime steak, with all the trimmings. With distended bellies, we drew close to the open pit fire as the balmy evening closed.

Troy Burton strummed a guitar whilst Doris accompanied on fiddle. They sang traditional cowboy songs and were gifted and highly entertaining players. It was a perfect setting.

I gazed into the flames, acknowledging that our life-way had changed dramatically from the daily grind of the twentieth century. Catching the spirit of the West, I felt I had been born in the wrong century. It had been an unrepeatable evening of camaraderie, and although we were virtual strangers, there was a strong sense of empathy, of synergy almost, as if they and we drew more from each other than was normally there. This was how Butch and Sundance had lived much of their lives, riding the trail and spending time with great people.

Next day, when Bob Nielson rode out with us on his splendid Tennessee Walker, it was a chance to compare this famous breed with our motley quarter-horses. Bob's fine chestnut blazed into the smooth, running gait that is the Walker's special characteristic – they can reach up to fifteen miles per hour. Like Kurt Olsen's mules, the Walker horse left us for dead as we trailed over a brook and up a steep gully into Chicken Coop Draw. For six miles, we twisted and turned whilst Bob impressed us with vast knowledge of flora, grasses, plants and their uses for humans and horses alike.

We climbed. The scenery roughened. Stunted trees and undergrowth invaded our path. The Uinta Mountains beckoned, the only range in America that runs east to west. The highest peak is 13,498 feet above sea level. Rolling hills interspersed with red, rocky outcrops melt below a pale blue sky. The ride was real outlaw stuff – following narrow gullies and *arroyos* and keeping off the skyline before exiting Chicken Coop onto the tarmac.

A famous landmark high on my want-to-see-again list was the exotically named Diamond Mountain.

Butch's early close associate Matt Warner has raised horses on Diamond Mountain. Warner says, "I was on the mountain from about the age of fifteen to twenty. Those five years was my schooling and graduation into outright outlawry, through the process of horse and cattle rustling."

Another friend of Butch's, rancher Charlie Crouse, makes his home here too. Butch rides into Crouse's looking for work in the summer of 1886. Crouse loves liquor, horses and gambling. He appreciates a young cowboy who knows how to handle horses, and hires Butch as horse breaker and racehorse jockey.

At the time, many ranchers located around Diamond Mountain make their living partly from regular ranching, partly from rustling. Charlie Crouse raises stock and expands his holdings into a sizeable horse ranch. Outlaws are welcomed. Word is that Crouse can be trusted to watch out for his shady guests if the law is nearby, and he is rewarded for this service.

Butch and Matt hide out in a cabin concealed up a canyon near a spring. A makeshift trail leads to this hideaway and is nearly impassable, masked by cottonwoods, box elders and a heavy growth of willows. Butch, Matt and Tom McCarty seek sanctuary here after the successful Telluride robbery in 1889.

Following his imprisonment in Wyoming in 1896, Butch leaves for Diamond Mountain and again moves into a cabin with Matt Warner. There he renews his friendship with Elzy Lay, who has also been working as a cowboy at the Bassett Ranch in Brown's Park. Butch stays there in the fall of 1889 before he and Elzy relocate to Little Hole, north of Vernal, and become involved in laundering counterfeit money from Canada.

RICHARD:

We had seen some pretty country on the early morning ride. Saying goodbye, Bob urged us to lose more weight from the panniers. It was impossible. One of the main weight factors was grain. The horses were consuming huge quantities of it. I had put my trust in Joe Armstrong's experience; to chop and change would have been folly. The horses were in good condition, still spirited, and Ray Hunting confirmed as much.

We set to riding. Temperature increased tremendously from noon and battered down on the grassy plateau. It was hugely uncomfortable. I doubt if the horses made two miles an hour. I checked the GPS – 7,000 feet. We watered the horses at Diamond Gulch and re-packed for Pot Creek.

SIMON:

Later, we passed the location where Matt Warner, Elzy Lay and Lew McCarty had robbed a peddler on his way to Brown's Park. The trio had plundered the unfortunate man's wagonload of clothing, tin-ware and jewelry before scattering any unwanted supplies. They finally took his money and turned him loose on foot for the long walk back to Vernal. That was a shoddy robbery, fellas!

Brown's Park is a kind of triangular No Man's Land which crosses the Utah-Colorado state lines and touches Wyoming. It runs along the Green River, wending through a deep canyon between Diamond Mountain and Cold Springs Mountain.

The Park is named after Baptiste Brown, a French Canadian trapper circa 1827. About ten years later, a fur trading post is built north of Lodore Canyon which operates successfully for three years or so. In the early 1840s, beaver become scarce, few trappers remain and the Park is virtually abandoned until around 1870 when a few settlers start to arrive.

Not long after, news comes in that a transcontinental railroad is being built across the desert sixty-five miles north. This creates a social change almost overnight. Brown's Park becomes a favourite wintering stopover for herds of cattle being trailed from Texas north to Wyoming. These immense herds are a magnet for organised rustlers, and the peaceful Brown's Park community of Indians and trappers becomes an outlaw rendezvous.

The Park becomes infested with out-of-work Texas cowboys. Ostensibly, they help passing trail herders by rounding up their stray stock, but actually they scatter the strays into Brown's Park to be fattened, re-branded and marketed later.

It seems that the small legitimate community and the rustlers get along fine provided both sides know how to behave. A case in point is Basset's Ranch. This is the focal point around which revolves much of Brown's Park's social life, and Butch and Sundance are always welcome there.

In 1896, a splendid Thanksgiving dinner is given for the Bassets and their neighbours, apparently hosted by Butch Cassidy, Elzy Lay and their friends, including one Harry Roudenbaugh (undoubtedly Longabaugh, aka Sundance), as a gesture of appreciation to the Park's residents. Thirty-five people attend; Butch, Elzy and Harry serve as waiters, while others help in the kitchen.

Later in 1896, Butch and Elzy rent a cabin in Maeser, a rural area encompassed by Vernal, near the parents of Maude Davis, Elzy's girlfriend. Butch and Elzy divide the cabin and move in their respective girlfriends. There is some uncertainty whether Butch's female companion is Etta Place or Ann Bassett from Brown's Park.

Uintah County Sheriff John Pope is alerted by sheriffs in Idaho that Butch and Elzy are wanted for a robbery in Montpelier. Pope knows both men, and when tip-offs indicate they are at the Davis's place, he rides out with a warrant, supported by four deputies. They surround the property, but Maude's brother Frank slips away, runs to the Jones cabin and reports the arrival of the posse to Elzy, who quickly gathers his belongings and rides off. Butch is busy in Vernal patronising the Overholt Saloon.

Pope is denied his quarry. He returns to town, and on passing the saloon, notices Albert Davis outside. They see one another, and Davis dashes inside, while Pope organizes his men to surround the building. Since Pope knows Butch, perhaps he does not move to storm the Overholt Saloon as swiftly as he might. Whatever happens, incredibly, Butch escapes again.

RICHARD:

Camp by the corrals was good. Liz King, Stan McMickel and family arrived late afternoon to hold another barbecue. Around the crackling campfire, we swapped yarns and told ghost stories whilst dispatching a huge feast of baked potatoes, delicious chicken, salad, trimmings, beer and ice cream. It almost defeated me, but Simon could eat for England.

Later, Stan and I jumped into the pickup truck for a quick recce down Crouse Canyon. I wanted an early start tomorrow and was concerned about the rocky trail. My worries were unfounded. On our return, a chill descended, and the party broke up. It had been another great night. Barbara quickly turned in, and our thoughts focused on the official halfway mark and our arrival at Colorado State – a double landmark. Simon and I huddled round the fire to keep warm then hit our bedrolls. I felt that Barbara was becoming even more remote.

SIMON:

We rode down Crouse Canyon, a two-mile gorge cutting its way through the craggy reddish-gray rock face. The trail descended along a loose gravel track threading gently round Diamond Mountain. Forty minutes later, we exited the narrow track where a creek cascaded over a rocky abyss into the Green River. Heading across the valley, we descended an awkward bluff onto the rough road and arrived at the infamous swinging bridge and the long anticipated halfway point of our ride.

The weight limit said three tons. The horses were unpredictable. Two loathed crossings and Ditch, yet untried, might be the same. The bridge span was around a hundred feet by nine feet wide. It was hemmed by high guardrails, useful to keep cattle and horses focused on going forward. Rather than risk riding over at once, I led Sunday over the wooden boards. The bridge remained firm. Barbara, riding Pancho, towed Ditch. Immediately, Richard proceeded with Yazz and Bones. The bridge began to sway marginally, not enough to warrant concern. The horses were unperturbed.

RICHARD:

On reaching the safety of terra firma in Colorado, we cheered. I hoped we would celebrate the milestone; drink a little alcohol together. It was not to be. There was no real bonding between us, nor any sharing either of the responsibilities or achievements.

The sun beat down relentlessly. There was no shade, so I constructed a lean-to shelter and produced lunch. When the time came to decamp, I asked Simon and Barbara to help, but they declined and went down to the river to relax. I was annoyed at their lack of consideration and blew my stack, complaining of their attitude to work.

"I'm sick of being treated like a servant," I told them bluntly.

Simon responded predictably:

"I'm relaxing in the cool by the river rather than sit in boiling heat."

We both flared, and Simon added:

"You're not in the army now, giving orders. And if you don't understand that, then you are not part of this concept."

I very nearly chucked him in the river. Barbara stood by lapping up our battle of words. It was insanity. Simon's provocative (and inaccurate) reference to my time in the Marines was pathetic.

We rapidly cooled our tempers, and apologised. Leaving at a snail's pace, we watered the horses at Warren Bottoms and aimed for Crook Camp. The valley was bare, apart from a luxurious patch of grass near a belt of cottonwoods. Heat was gruelling, altitude dropped from 8,000 to 5,500 feet, and conditions emulated earlier miseries through Arizona.

The Green River turned sharply round the edge of Diamond Mountain, leading into the gates of Lodore and on through the encouragingly-named Disaster Falls and Hell's Half Mile. We hugged the river west of Harry Hoy Bottoms and reined in at the Dickinson's line camp at Stirling Springs, right on the south slope of Cold Springs Mountain.

SIMON:

It had been ten hours in the saddle, which numbed the mind – and everything else. We retired to the mobile house and pored over maps to decide the route to the Vermilion Ranch in the morning. The choice was ride round Cold Springs Mountain and up Irish Canyon, a twenty-three mile trek, or traverse it using the rugged Matt Trail. The shortest route appealed on paper because six miles is a long way.

We quickly regretted the decision.

We rode through a pasture onto a rocky trail. Altitude was 5,445 feet before the ascent. The gradient climbed quickly enough to warrant stepping out of the saddle within two hundred yards. Richard led, Yazz and Bones in tow. We scrabbled up a ten-foot wide rocky trail flanked by firs. The horses stumbled on the loose shale, and we stopped every two hundred yards to catch our breath.

Behind, Diamond Mountain's blackened slopes created a magnificent backdrop. Clouds cast huge shadows across a beige-green valley floor. The trail was never-ending, and Barbara slowly fell behind with Pancho and Ditch. After an hour, I sat down to rest, holding Sunday. The mare hadn't even broken sweat. Richard disappeared and Barbara was out of sight. I wondered if Ditch was creating problems and waited for fifteen minutes. No shouts for help could be heard, so Sunday and I resumed the trek skywards. I talked to the mare, reminding her that I should be riding rather than walking, because cowboys and outlaws don't walk – they ride. She cocked an ear and gave me a look, as if to say:

"You wanted to save the six miles pal, so keep walking!"

Two hours later, I topped the ridge. Richard was dozing at the summit – 7,425 feet. Yazz and Bones were happily grazing on the luxuriant grass as if nothing had happened. Despite the cool morning, I felt like I had sweated off seven pounds. I consumed over half a gallon of water.

RICHARD:

"Barbara's way back down the trail," said Simon. "She was complaining of chest pains."

"Do you think that's a ruse?" I asked.

"Don't know. I walked to save Sunday, and I hope she's done likewise for Pancho."

"You sound more concerned about the horse."

"You're right – we can't afford any more horse trouble."

His dislike for her made him implacable, as unfeeling as stone.

I retraced my steps and found Barbara. She appeared suddenly riding out of the firs, ashen and exhausted, then mentioned chest pains, putting it down to asthma. Simon hinted later that she might have suffered a mild heart attack. He hoped not, since that would mean backtracking and delays. He is all heart, is Simon.

The hostility between my two companions was turning into a full time job. That's how it goes on an expedition when the team falls apart. The Matt Trail had tested us almost to destruction, opening up the cracks that were already there.

Matt Rash, after whom the trail is named, comes to Brown's Park in 1883. A Texas cowboy, he starts his ranch with stolen cattle run off from the Two Bar outfit on Little Snake River. At Summit Springs on the same mountain, another whose ranch is stocked with stolen cattle is Isom Dart, a black cowboy who wears – for the camera at any rate – two guns on his belly, butts facing inwards towards his navel for an improbable two-handed cross-draw. They are associated in the rustling business, although rumours persist that neither particularly likes the other.

They are both known to be good friends of the Bassett family, which provides a possible link to Butch, who returns, broke, to Brown's Park after his release from Wyoming's state penitentiary in 1896. He keeps out of sight and spends some time at the John Jarvie Place.

Plans are in hand to form a formidable new gang to be called the Train Robbers Syndicate. Sundance probably joins this large group – which already includes Harvey Logan, and Flat Nose Currie, sometime in 1896-1897.

Meanwhile, cattle rustlers are rapidly depleting the passing herds here, and no one is safe from their depredations. Farmers, haulers and other travellers all fall victim to banditry. When two part-time rustlers kill a sixteen-year-old boy in nearby Powder Springs, it is bad news. The perpetrators stop at a hideout close to the Wyoming line, between Baggs and Brown's Park. A posse rides in, led by Sheriff Charles Neiman of Routt County, Colorado, and a shoot-out occurs which results in the death of respected rancher Valentine Hoy.

This latest crop of killings prompts a concerted effort to break up the outlaws by the Governors of Colorado, Wyoming and Utah. Bounty hunters familiar with the area are encouraged to stay on the trail of the outlaws. Butch realizes Brown's Park is no longer a safe

*refuge, so he and Sundance (and probably their closest associates)
have prudently moved on by the time legendary bounty hunter Tom
Horn, hired in by the powerful cattle barons, kills both Matt Rash
and Isom Dart on Cold Springs Mountain. Brown's Park is to change
forever.*

RICHARD:

On top of Cold Springs Mountain, I picked a trail from Willow Springs.
We rode through prime pasture, but I misinterpreted directions, and
found I was ninety degrees out. We backtracked and entered the
head of Chokecherry Draw near a thicket, where we picked up a
faint trail. It led round a bluff through thick undergrowth. The slope
was too steep for the horses, so we traversed down into a stream and
headed up a narrow draw opposite Diamond Peak.

After seventeen miles of hard riding, we arrived at the Vermilion,
glad to unload with the seventh generation Dickinson family, who own
and operate a vast cow and calf spread. Simon had visited the family
in 1996 to research Brown's Park and experience the hard work of
ranching. The Dickinsons remain a throwback to the halcyon days of
the real west. They are proud of their heritage as committed ranchers,
and of the history that links them with the past of Brown's Park.

We sat at the dining table, the hub of any working ranch, and
talked history. Dick Dickinson explained that eleven miles east of the
Utah line is an important outlaw rendezvous: the dugout at the John
Jarvie homestead where Butch started to form his Train Robbers
Syndicate.

*By July 1897, Butch has assembled his Syndicate – hand-picked
members of various successful outlaw gangs specialising in banks,
payrolls and trains. The brief is to loot shipments of currency and
gold being transported by the Union Pacific Railroad.*

*News of the Syndicate leaks and comes to the attention of Union
Pacific. Disguised detectives infiltrate the outer circle, and the
indefatigable Charles Siringo poses as an outlaw, passes information
back to base, and sets back the Syndicate for at least a year. Later,
the gang's name changes to the Wild Bunch, perhaps because of their*

behaviour when in celebration mode.

Butch spends a winter in Rock Springs, Wyoming, a coal-mining town, as cowboys often travelled elsewhere to obtain reliable work in the colder months. Butch likely found it easier cutting and selling meat for William Gottsche. Perhaps the job gave him his famous moniker? Outlaw Matt Warner claims he and Tom McCarty gave the nickname after Cassidy had difficulty operating a rifle belonging to Warner. Others claim it came from a camp cook on a roundup, since those who hunted and provided meat were often referred to as 'Butches'.

SIMON:

Dick suggested we ride for Powder Springs, another hideout twenty-five miles northeast, astride the state lines of Colorado and Wyoming. Butch had built a cabin near the upper springs in a little meadow which provided feed for a number of saddle horses the year round. The lower springs two miles south lay in rolling terrain, a useful oasis on the border of a bleak country. The trail from the Vermilion would take us around Sugar Loaf Butte and along Shell Creek towards Racetrack Flats. From there, we could ride due north to Cow Creek reservoir and Bitter Creek. This was the likeliest route for Butch to use after hitting the Union Pacific train at Tipton.

RICHARD:

Should we ride for Rock Springs or Powder Springs? Again, decisions. Dick Dickinson suggested we scout the trails. Jumping into a pickup, we headed into the green undulating hills, interspersed with red, rocky outcrops. A light drizzle blew over the mountains. Powder Rim looked impressive, a series of draws and small interlocking canyons, perfect hideout country for outlaws.

We returned to pore over the maps, and totaled the mileage ridden from Mexico: 1,086 in sixty-five riding days, equating to 16.70 miles a day. Creeping up.

Barbara suddenly appeared – she had been avoiding us. To our amazement, she announced that a TV company wanted to meet her.

Strangely, the producer was not interested in the ride and just wanted an exclusive with her – minus us! We greeted the news with disbelief; it was yet another cynical attempt to promote her role.

Simon was furious. We scuppered any plans for her to link with the TV team on the trail on the grounds that we had not decided on our route. Our ride was turning into internal warfare, and policing Barbara became an important secondary objective.

SIMON:

Marc Dickinson offered new information regarding another trail leading to Powder Springs. On a roundup he had located old corrals in Dry Creek. It was near one of the lesser hideouts on a branch off the Outlaw Trail's main stem. Dry Creek is sandwiched between Vermilion Creek and Bluffs. A faint trail can be traced two miles south of the confluence of Vermilion and Shell Creeks.

Heading east, you ride onto the bluffs around Lookout Mountain before reaching Ace-in-the-Hole Draw. This formed part of the lower section of the escape trail that Butch and Sundance had taken after the Tipton train robbery. The Outlaw Trail's maze of criss-crossing tracks was incredible and almost impossible to follow.

We eventually took the Irish Canyon road north. Heading along a dust track, the range flattened, leaving us in a wide expanse of high desert. The lush greenery of Brown's Park quickly evaporated.

Richard led, towing Ditch behind Yazz, but the two horses hated one another. Yazz predictably tired of his space being invaded and kicked out, narrowly missing the hapless gelding. The lethal hooves cracked the side of a pannier, severely bruising Yazz's hock. He began limping immediately, forcing Richard to dismount and walk. What a start.

I took Ditch in hand, but Sunday, my mare, was equally displeased and frequently snapped. The early stages of trying to break Ditch into packing had a lasting negative effect. He became a halter puller all the way to Canada. Thankfully, my right arm has since returned to its normal length.

The heat rose as we neared the fringe of the Red Desert, which was sand and scrub, totally devoid of trees and grazing. The horses predictably slowed as the moisture was sucked from them. Barbara continued to complain vigorously about the ride and the logistics. Exasperated, I queried wearily:

"What did you expect?"

"A great deal more support and assistance."

Richard laughed in disbelief. Barbara scowled. She was concerned for herself, and much of the horses' welfare stuff seemed to be an attempt to disguise her own shortcomings. Furious, I rode Sunday headlong towards Pancho, nearly knocking her out of her saddle.

"You're fucking pompous!" I yelled. "Just get riding, or else quit!" Enough was enough. None of us came well out of bad-tempered scenes like that. Team spirit was extremely low.

We endured incredible heat for another fifteen miles. Unloading at the Mike Farley homestead on Coyote Creek, the horses were turned loose in a pasture and we sat to contemplate. I apologised to Barbara, reiterating the aim of the quest and the need to persevere. Richard marked off the maps. Seven miles remained to Wyoming. Our position was south of Rife's Rim some fifteen miles west of Kinney Rim.

RICHARD:

We settled in the shade. I judged this to be our last easy day's riding for a week. Tomorrow, the Red Desert would be upon us. Yet another desert – this would be the fourth. I wondered what else the Outlaw Trail held in store for us. My concern was to guarantee feed and water for the horses between the designated rendezvous sites. Ditch's lack of fitness was a problem. His pace would determine our progress. I set up the fire, and then debated the trail ahead with Simon. Butch and Sundance were drawing us into yet another hostile, challenging zone.

A Sting in the Tail

"Good. For a minute I thought we were in trouble."
Butch Cassidy

Richard:

Kinney Rim rose from the plains. The high escarpment stood blocking our path and a rough, white dirt track paved the way over a brownish landscape disappearing into a grey skyline. We crossed Granary Draw to Chicken Creek, a fifteen-mile plod through a flat, dusty valley devoid of flora. Riding was a grind and the murderous heat tortured us.

In camp earlier, the horses had refused water – by midday at Alkali Creek, they were gasping, only to find vile, stagnant liquid surrounded by very soft ground. They refused to approach it. Frustrated, we resigned ourselves to their going without until we reached the springs.

We started the arduous climb, stopping frequently to let the horses rest. Barbara soon fell behind with Pancho and Ditch. Near the summit, the Rim flattened. From our position, we could see cattle dotted in bunches, and bands of wild horses coming in to water at the springs.

Barbara caught up, requesting we cease for the day. Bones did her best to second the motion, which was defeated. Lacking grass and water, we had to continue in order to make safe camp. We traversed down the bluff and twenty minutes later reached Carson Springs.

We camped, hobbled the horses and relaxed. Feed was good, water ample. Completely treeless, we tried picketing with metal stakes.

Initially Bones sat down, refusing to eat, exhausted from the haul over Kinney Rim. Barbara was beside herself with worry, but before long the mare was back on her feet, rested and grazing with the others. The wild horses kept their distance, and Simon periodically scanned the valley with binoculars until nightfall, alert for any impending visit. A stud horse coming through camp would run our mares into his herd. Geldings would be chased off, or worse, killed in a leadership battle.

SIMON:

We woke to find the metal pickets had worked well. By nine-thirty, our scorching pace took us to the rendezvous at the Eversoles'. Hosts John and Debbie arrived moments later. We were invited in for brunch, where John expressed his interest in the outlaws and told us a forgotten hideout was located in the Haystacks. This was news.

Twenty-four miles north of Powder Springs and two miles south of the Overland Trail, the Haystacks connect into Skull Creek Rim and Powder Rim as a series of draws and gullies. It might have been a one-night stopover that Butch and Sundance used on their way to the Powder Springs camp. No trail led into the hideout. The outlaws' tracks had vanished. There were no references in the history books either. Only oral tradition, which didn't make it wrong.

We were close to the Little Snake River, an area which featured in Sundance's life. According to author and relative Donna Ernst, Sundance had been employed locally in 1896 and hired on at the Reader Ranch using the alias of Harry Alonzo.

RICHARD:

After an enjoyable break, it was back to riding. John and Debbie Eversole were concerned about us heading into the Red Desert. They phoned the Hays and arranged a rendezvous for us at Table Rock, bang on the Union Pacific line.

We hit the trail early afternoon, the worst possible time and in ferocious heat. Conditions became grim. The bond between the horses was shifting, much as it did with the humans. Yazz would now only allow Bones close by, and vice versa. Sunday did not tolerate Ditch following her, which meant Barbara had to string him behind Pancho. Barbara also had to ride Ditch on his days off from packing duty. Ditch's body was like a barrel and Barbara's Spanish saddle slipped repeatedly, making life hugely uncomfortable for her up to ten hours a day.

It was six when we watered the horses at Long Draw. We accessed the stream by unravelling a fence and led the thirsty horses down a steep, grassy bank. It had taken over three hours to cover seven miles.

The sun still blasted, and heat shimmered off the parched prairie. The pace was down to one mile an hour. It was quicker to walk alongside the horses than to ride. Six miles remained to the Hungry Hollow campsite. Our location was southwest of the Delaney Rim and the dirt road we were traversing was the Overland Trail. Soon the confluence of Bitter Creek and Red Wash should appear. Dusk was drawing in and our concerns increased.

The Eversoles stopped by on their return trip from Rock Springs. John had kindly checked the route we proposed to take to the Hay Ranch.

"There's no water for at least two days – maybe three," he warned. "You're in the peak month for high temperatures. Once you're at Mary's, re-think your route. Good luck."

The Red Desert was no place for horseback travel in July. I overshot our intended camp by two miles. Night was falling. We turned back and pitched camp in a draw with high walls, and fenced off the ends of the dried riverbed. The horses were hobbled and turned out to graze overnight. They were noisy in the night and I slept only fitfully.

At four, I was awake and dressing when suddenly an enormous fireball exploded into the sky a little way off, from the direction of our outfit.

SIMON:

It was futile trying to rest, and the horses hated camp. I decided to make coffee early and surprise Richard. There was ice on top of our bivvy bags, so I set up the stove, but the gas went out. Refilling the canister, I primed the pump to no avail. Working in the dark was awkward. My torch batteries had given out so I did the unthinkable and foolishly used a lighter.

The spark caught fuel vapours and a flame thirty feet high shot up, narrowly missing my hands and face. In the mêlée, I tipped the fuel canister over, catching the bushes on fire. With flammable liquid spilling everywhere, I had set the desert ablaze. It got worse. Grabbing a horse blanket I desperately tried to stifle the flames – and the blanket caught alight. Shit. I kicked sand furiously over the offending stove and brought the flames under control. Richard rushed to investigate.

"What's going on?"

"Stove went over and ignited the fuel. It's destroyed," I replied, guilty as hell. I apologised for my supreme carelessness. It had been a very close shave, for me and for our kit.

Richard looked round in wonder at the charred, blackened wreckage, and shook his head.

"Bad night," he said. "But the cabaret was spectacular."

It was July 11. We broke camp at six-ten, in record time. No stove, so no coffee and breakfast. Not for nothing was it called Hungry Hollow. We left for Table Rock, another landmark Wild Bunch site some ten miles distant. In a little over three hours riding, we hoped to rendezvous with rancher Leonard Hay.

The route ahead was the escape trail ridden by Butch Cassidy, The Sundance Kid and Harvey Logan (Kid Curry) after the Union Pacific train robbery in Tipton, Wyoming.

RICHARD:

We rode along a rough track past an oil well. Antelope abounded. Grazing was surprisingly good, but on arriving at the Delaney Rim, a high escarpment overlooking the Red Desert Basin, the terrain became flat, dusty and devoid of scenery. Four thousand square miles of inhospitable land, hot sand shimmering in the haze. I checked altitude – a surprising 7,200 feet. In the distance, we picked out the Table Rock Diner and rode for it, the last civilised stop-off point before crossing the Red Desert.

Down on the valley floor, junk and debris were scattered, an unpleasant reminder we were approaching so-called civilization. At the Table Rock Diner, we hobbled the horses and telephoned the Hays. Mary arrived two hours later in a pickup, and we chucked our gear in the back.

"You can ride over to the Bar X later and stay with Roy and Jacci," Mary announced, pointing to the site a mile yonder. It was a good offer and too hot to attempt anything else.

Mary roared off. We rested the horses beneath a cottonwood grove and waited for early evening. After the appalling heat subsided, we rode for the Bar X, and in less than an hour, the day was done. Roy and Jacci Barber welcomed and invited us to a barbecue, which we accepted gratefully, and mellowed out nicely in the early evening sun, quenching our thirst with iced tea. A few miles away lay a major Wild Bunch robbery site.

As I absorbed the growing strength of the link between our expedition and the long dead outlaws, I became increasingly interested in the history and began to connect to Butch and Sundance. Whilst supping tea, we talked about the local landmark. Two and a half miles from the Table Rock Ranch was the scene of the legendary Tipton robbery.

Wednesday, August 29, 1900. The Union Pacific Number 3 train out of Omaha is stopped by robbers on the slope of the Divide near Table Rock. The hold-up occurs about two thirty am and follows the familiar procedure of unhitching the engine, baggage and express cars. Woodcock, the same messenger as at the Wilcox robbery a year before, is ordered to open up – he refuses to comply until convinced that dynamite is being readied to blow the doors. It takes three charges to open the safe, and the massive explosion blows out the roof, sides and ends of the baggage car, along with the car next to it.

The robbery is credited to Butch Cassidy, accompanied by Harvey Logan and the Sundance Kid. The actual amount stolen is never verified, though later Express Messenger Ernest Woodcock informs the press that the haul was close to $55,000 – a fortune.

The outlaws escape in a southeast direction, and the train continues to Green River. A reward is offered of $1,000 for each outlaw, and three posses totaling forty men mount the chase.

Butch, Sundance and Logan make for the Delaney Rim. The Rock Springs Posse is rushed in by train and picks up their trail. Another is dispatched from Rawlins but is delayed. The ground being solid and grassy just south of the rim, the robbers' tracks become increasingly hard to follow. The terrain slows Sheriff Pete Swanson and his posse considerably. Later, Sheriff Hadsell, leading the Rawlins posse, catches up with Swanson, but by the afternoon, less than half the forty men remain in the chase – the half mounted on good horses.

Locally, they say that before the Tipton train robbery, Butch and Co rounded up wild horses, shod them, and remove the shoes from their own relay horses. After the hold-up, the gang turns loose the range horses, who promptly head back into the basin. At least one of the chasing posses rides after them, following the false trail in the wrong direction.

US Marshal Joe LeFors believes Butch and Sundance are heading for Baggs, Wyoming, with Kid Curry and two other unnamed accomplices. Baggs is another favourite hideout town two miles north of the Colorado line and easily accessible from Powder Springs. LeFors heads the tracking party while the posse itself is strung out for over two miles. He later writes:

"After passing Delaney Springs, I determined that we were following three men and one pack horse and were now heading straight across the Red Desert. The day was hot. Horses and men were suffering for water. The robbers had figured that by going past Soda Springs we would be set afoot, perhaps some of us would perish. I had no doubt this was part of their game."

LeFors is not a man to be put off by a red-hot, waterless desert. He wants those outlaws so bad he can taste it. He follows their tracks, and by sundown reaches Little Snake River above the Colorado line, an incredible 120 mile run. As he leads his horse down the north side of the river, he spots three men and a packhorse climbing the slope opposite.

"They were climbing the hills for a night ride. The next morning we determined they had stopped about a mile down the river, had something to eat and adjusted the pack. There was a big amount of paper there, torn off the express package, so they divided the money. I did not have any doubt they had seen us."

Simon:

If Butch was directing the flight to Brown's Park, the fastest route on a dead run after topping the Delaney Rim would be to aim for Kinney Rim. Water was available at Antelope Creek, Carlson Springs, Mike Farley Homestead and the Hiawatha Camp. The outlaws' choice was to ride southwest into Brown's Park or take a trail through Dry Creek to the Little Snake River. This took us four days of hard riding on horses at walking pace. I can't imagine the hardships the posse members and their mounts endured, or for that matter how the outlaws' packhorse survived.

On the chase, LeFors and Hadsell are down to a dozen men. Having had no sleep for twenty hours, as darkness descends they decide not to risk ambush but to camp and take up the pursuit next morning. LeFors locates the trail again after dawn.

Throughout the run, the tireless LeFors tries to increase speed and gain on the robbers – typically, the posse isn't seasoned and cannot maintain the fast pace. The trail leads south, which suggests that Butch will take that direction then cut back and lose the posse in the wilderness of Brown's Park. The posse covers another twenty miles and finds the robbers' grey packhorse virtually dead on its feet.

After following tracks for a further fifteen miles, the posse surrounds a thick grove of willows – perfect for an ambush. LeFors and two volunteers crawl on their knees and elbows whilst the remainder of the group split up and surround the grove. They find three used-up horses. No Butch, Sundance or Harvey Logan. A classic Wild Bunch manoeuvre has taken place: a pre-planned horse change. The exhausting chase, delays, hunger and spent horses mean that the posse members have had enough. They are through. The wily trio make a fast getaway to Brown's Park then split up, to meet up later and spend the money.

Richard:

Discussing Butch and Sundance's exploits was fascinating, but the reality of riding north promised to be a logistical nightmare. Being cautious, I wanted to gather information about the three-day ride to South Pass before risking the horses. There were deep concerns about the lack of feed, water, corrals and even trees. Diamond Mountain rancher Bob Nielson had twice expressed doubt about our ability to cross the Red Desert without mishap, and John Eversole echoed his opinion.

"You can't ride round it," Simon pointed out, "and we're not altering the trail in any direction either." Trying to defy the laws of nature and local knowledge was grossly imprudent. We deliberated, then Roy and Jacci brought us back down to earth.

"You won't get through and you'll get trouble with the wild horses. The ride will be over. It's not possible with no water, feed or ranchers' assistance."

So we spent the evening lazing in the garden, talking and drinking. The Barbers were good people who cared about what we were doing, and probably as much or more about the welfare of our horses. After watching the sun sink, we retired to our bedrolls in the storage shed, thoughts cascading.

Maybe we could ride to Jeffrey City on a north-northeast bearing and cut through the Green Mountains? It might reduce mileage.

October, or thereabouts, 1899. Butch Cassidy's attorney Douglas Preston and Union Pacific representatives are set to meet at the Lost Soldier Stage Station in Jeffrey City. The aim is to strike a deal with the railroad as a preliminary to obtaining a pardon for Butch, who has approached Judge OW Powers soliciting his support for an amnesty request to Utah Governor Heber Wells in return for a promise to go straight. Preston is unfortunately delayed, and the meeting never takes place. Butch is furious and leaves a note:

"Damn you, Preston, you double-crossed me. I waited all day but you didn't show up. Tell the UP to go to hell. And you can go with them."

Butch's next strike is against the Union Pacific at Tipton.

SIMON:

The route to Jeffrey City was a shortcut to reach Lost Cabin country and Hole-in-the-wall. As the historian, I would rule against it, because it avoided passing through South Pass and Atlantic Cities, Lander and the *Quién Sabe* hideout on Copper Mountain. These were important places on the Outlaw Trail's main stem. We would get a plan together in the morning.

Over breakfast, Jacci announced that John and Debbie Eversole were due to arrive. After private communications, they were lifting us to Oregon Buttes. Our plans had been made for us.

With mixed feelings initially, we took the Bar X road on exit 152 of Interstate 80. From Wamsutter, not a scrap of feed was available. The basin was a burning yellow void. A man could go mad riding through it on horseback. No water, corrals or even trees. Nothing lived here. *Nada*.

We looped over Alkali Basin through three miles of sand dunes to the Pinnacles. The Bar X and Oregon Buttes road converged. It was a Godforsaken land, and as we trailed alongside the Continental Divide for eight miles, I was mighty relieved we hadn't tried something really stupid.

John shut the truck down at Oregon Buttes, an oasis with two huge water reservoirs. Debbie provided a superb picnic, and we ate like kings. Another twelve miles remained to the Sweetwater Ranch.

Mary Hay's spread was remote and close to the Wind River Mountain range. Snow lingered on the peaks. The location was roughly twenty miles from the mining town of South Pass and the Oregon Trail. Five miles west of the Sweetwater Ranch lay Pacific Springs.

We spent a delightful afternoon resting. Mary had a wonderful location, and like many Westerners was holding out, running cattle and leasing more land. Dinner that evening was fresh trout caught from the river, and we talked passionately about the life-way and the romance of the West. Mary Hay was a throwback to the pioneers: tough, resourceful and determined.

We rode out and crossed the Sweetwater River. Riding was easy, as we connected to a dirt track that led into South Pass City. Splendidly restored, many of the buildings are original. A post office, saloon, hotel, general store, jail and blacksmith's forge are set amongst manicured lawns and divided by a main street half a mile long. Boardwalks connect the narrow buildings. Everything was so small.

We let the horses graze while we grabbed coffee. Thousands of people passed through this historic town between 1841 and 1869, their last post before the jump-off to Salt Lake Valley and the Oregon and Californian territories.

Next stop was to visit local blacksmith Steve Green to obtain directions to the Mercantile Bar in Atlantic City. I had met Steve briefly three years earlier and threatened that I might be back on a horse. Steve suggested we ask for a character by the name of JD who might be inclined to help us.

We traversed a gravel road over undulating hills. Three miles later, Atlantic City revealed itself, comfortably nestled in a small valley. Houses were Spartan. Roads were dirt tracks. Time had almost stood still. We heard a familiar clip-clop. Another horseman appeared, and we asked for directions. JD was behind us! I wheeled Sunday, helloed and made the connection from Steve Green. Minutes later, we had unloaded, put the horses up and invited JD and his wife Patti for drinks.

Atlantic City had boomed, boasting general stores, hotels, saloons, livery stables, restaurants, a cigar store, dancehall and two breweries. It was discovered in 1869 by miners on a busman's holiday from South Pass City, and two thousand populated the gulch. Ten years later, most moved, leaving a handful of prospectors. Some buildings date to the nineteenth century. The Mercantile, built in 1893, was originally the Giessler store. A false-fronted building typical of the era, it looked very well preserved.

We strode along wooden boardwalks soaking up the atmosphere, and dived into the Mercantile's cool, inviting interior. It was appropriately decked with old pictures and Western memorabilia, its best feature being the splendid original wooden bar and oval mirror behind it.

As we sampled the bar's wares, I wondered if Butch and Sundance had patronised Atlantic City's saloons. Eugene Amoretti (Butch's banker) had a mercantile business in South Pass with a store in Atlantic City, which was strategically placed between two hideouts. Maybe the duo had slaked their thirst here? It was good to think so, and to have another small libation on the strength of it.

We checked the horses, fed them more grain and returned to

the Mercantile for another round, or maybe two, and a late dinner. Barbara remained alone – distant. Later still, at the bar we struck up conversation with a few locals, with whom naturally we exchanged a courteous round or so of refreshments. On a small stage, a trio of musicians was strumming guitars. I failed to recognize any of the tunes. I was drunk. Or, to use the clinically more correct term, pissed as arseholes.

Richard and I were making up for lost ground. A bond was forging, and we were trying to capture the spirit of the past, visiting old bars and hangouts, imagining we were outlaws reincarnated. Not many historic places have survived on the Outlaw Trail, and we made the most of this one.

We eventually weaved unsteadily back to our cabin, pleased to have made such a sizeable dent in the barkeeper's stock, though I feared that with the morning might come just a hint of remorse. I visualised myself slumped uselessly in the saddle. Like the scene in *Cat Ballou* when on the morning of the big shootout, we find the gunman on whom all depends (Oscar-winning Lee Marvin) on his horse, both rider and mount propped up against the wall, both unconscious, and both drunk as skunks.

Crashed out on the bed, my thoughts wandered sleepily, and I recalled a vivid and, I often think, slightly spooky dream:

Through the mists of my mind somehow I've joined Redford and Newman. They are Butch and Sundance. Have I crept into George Roy Hill's movie? Inside the cabin on the ridge top, we are pinned down by rifle fire. Bullets ricochet off the cedar logs. Newman, as Butch, turns to me, pistol in hand, asks, "You okay, Kid?"

Before I can answer, Redford, as Sundance, says, "Better get busy."

He reaches into his coat pocket and hands me a fistful of cartridges. A forty-five is in my hand. Footsteps are closing in outside. I prepare to chamber the cylinder, but to my horror, the cartridges are all different sizes – some are empty shells, others bent out of shape. The gunfire reaches a crescendo. The door crashes open, and I realize this is the end.

Then I woke up, grateful to do so.

As I crawled painfully out of bed, I became aware that my brief visit to Atlantic City had a sting in the tail, perhaps literally. Because something was firmly attached to or embedded in my penis: a tiny, red scorpion-like insect clung like a limpet. What showed, I judged, to be a quarter-inch in length. I had dark thoughts – how large could it be? I gently pulled on the tailpiece. It moved. I prodded again, and it duly responded. This bastard is alive and it's eating my dick!

I didn't want Richard to come out of the shower and find me cock firmly in hand, but I squeezed the base of the lump – hard. Hey presto, it popped and squished, quite dead. I inspected the tiny wound and was fairly satisfied that the honourable member would survive until its next thousand-mile service. I dressed and packed cautiously, no sudden movements, trying the while to remember what I had read about tick fever.

We exited Atlantic City in a fragile silence, heading for the old railroad gauge. Nauseous, my skull being trepanned without benefit of anaesthetic, with a sore dick and a mouth like a vulture's armpit, I rode towards my lofty destiny wishing man could train horses to walk on tiptoe.

QUIÉN SABE?

"Etta's thinking of maybe leaving."
THE SUNDANCE KID

SIMON:

The gravel railroad grade gave way to silver barked mountain ash. In the distance, the Wind Rivers beckoned. After two hours following the track, we arrived at the gates of the Shoshone National Forest. Altitude had risen to 8,000 feet and the horses were slow. It was a welcome change from the high desert country. A hard-packed dirt road cut through a glorious lush meadow then disappeared out of sight. Beyond, Roaring Fork Mountain towered; a splendid alpine backdrop.

The road meandered through the forest. A smell of pine needles permeated the air; the only sound was the shuffling of the horse's hooves. We continued on autopilot, only pausing to gaze across the vast, dark blue millpond of Louis Lake. It was total tranquillity.

At the Little Popo Agie Basin, the trees closed tightly and the increased gradient required us to dismount. Richard seemed to be on a forced march with Yazz and Pancho. I followed with Sunday whilst Barbara trailed with Bones and the reluctant Ditch. The gelding was terrified of Bones's lethal temper and hung back, continually testing Barbara's patience to the limit.

RICHARD:

We headed through Burnt Gulch. It wasn't burnt, but the valley was stripped naked of its trees. The silence was broken when we heard the telltale noise of a V8 engine burbling. Soon a truck slowed and crept within yards of Sunday's butt. Seconds later a voice cried out, "Where are you guys headed?"

We plodded on. Without stopping or turning, I casually replied, "Canada."

"We're having a barbecue for you at Frye Lake!"

It was JD and Patti laughing their heads off. They had driven specially from Atlantic City to host dinner in the wilderness. Such goodwill is America at its very best.

With enough daylight to set picket lines, we quickly prepared camp, turned the horses loose to graze and settled down to a mouth-watering feast of elk steaks, potatoes and vegetables. Camp was the last pitch by the lakeside, a splendid location perfect for watching the dying rays shimmer on the water as the sun set slowly over the snowcapped Atlantic Peak. We popped beers and gorged ourselves, chatting of the trail ahead, grateful to dine in such salubrious surroundings.

Throughout, Barbara's aloofness was noticeable. She distanced herself purposely, only speaking when necessary, and confirming my suspicion that maybe the trip was getting too much for her. JD and Patti departed cordially, and Simon and I sat huddled near the roaring fire, grateful for warmth. The mercury had already fallen to zero. We passed the pot between us for our customary late evening coffee. Then we turned in.

SIMON

We woke with ice on our sleeping bags and departed fast. The track wound through the forest and dumped us on a bluff overlooking Sinks Canyon. By the time we reached the valley floor, the sun was burning through the haze. We crossed the metal bridge over the Middle Popo Agie River, and traffic appeared like magic. Sinks Canyon is a State Park.

Then six miles of uninteresting riding, passing scattered houses flanking the road. It began to drizzle as we reached the beautifully restored houses on the outskirts of town. We reined in, and when our horses momentarily checked a young lady driving by, on impulse

I produced my list of contacts and cheekily asked if she knew any of them. Bingo! The third name down was her Dad, Gary Barney, an important attorney. From then on everything ran smoothly: Dad's palatial office in the centre of Lander, the ranch, then the barn where we were to camp.

Butch makes a number of visits to Lander around 1889. Using the moniker George Cassidy, he and a cowboy named Al Hainer both work on the EA Ranch owned by banker Eugene Amoretti. The two cowboys buy property on the Horse Creek in Dubois, intending to go into the horse business. Dubois lies seventy-five miles northwest of Lander in the Upper Wind River area.

During this period, Butch also spends time with the Meeks family, meeting young Henry Wilbur "Bub" Meeks who later rides with him during a short career as an outlaw.

Well-known and well-liked in Lander, old timers tell of an incident when Butch and friends startle the town. According to reports, Butch hitches four unbroken horses to an old stage coach, fills it with rouged women and lets her rip, banging his six-shooters to the shrieks of the female passengers. He also likes to gamble and is seen frequently playing faro and monte.

Lander becomes one of Butch's favourite hangouts. On the run after the Teluride bank robbery, he and Matt Warner nearly get caught in a saloon when a local cowboy announces that the law is searching for strangers. Butch and Matt down their drinks and leave quickly. Their departure is noticed, and a chase ensues. They lose the posse by riding for the Lander cut-off, an old Indian track which has become part of the Oregon Trail. It passes near Marbleton and over the Salt Range to Star Valley.

Star Valley is a Mormon settlement which in winter is virtually inaccessible, and no posse is likely to pursue riders there. Butch uses it on at least two more occasions for handy escapes.

First, there is Montpelier, Idaho, hemmed in by forests and perfectly isolated. On 13 August 1896 Butch, Elzy Lay and Bub Meeks ride into town with a packhorse and hitch in front of the bank. They step inside, drawing their guns and ushering in with them several bystanders.

A cashier is directed to hand over money bills and a sack of gold coins. The three leave the bank, load the booty, mount their horses and depart at speed. At the edge of town they turn up Montpelier Canyon towards the Wyoming line, fifteen miles away.

The alarm is raised, and a posse, led by Sheriff Jeff Davis and Deputy Mike Malone, rides in hot pursuit. At Montpelier Canyon, nerves fray and pace slows. Posse members drop out and the two lawmen race on alone. Reports of gunfire are heard. The posse believes Sheriff and Deputy have been ambushed, so they hurriedly return to town, badly shaken. Word spreads that the two lawmen have been killed.

Meanwhile Davis and Malone discover a stash of relay horses. Realising the robbers have planned well, they quickly return to town to organize a real posse. Locals believe the robbers are led by Tom McCarty and have crossed the Wyoming line for Star Valley, where he has been known to operate.

The law divides its forces. One posse pursues the outlaws, another takes a shortcut, hoping to reach Star Valley first and trap them there. Butch switches horses, leaves the main trail and takes to the rocks. Before hitting soft ground, he slips moccasins over the horses' hooves (an old Indian trick) to avoid leaving tracks. The chase is over. Butch escapes, the bank lies about its losses and the audit reveals over $16,500 has been taken. Neat work and a job well done.

The second robbery takes place in Winnemucca, Nevada four years later. The outlaws familiarize themselves thoroughly with the town and surrounding area. On 19 September 1900, Sundance, Harvey Logan and Will Carver hitch their horses in an alley next to the First National Bank, enter the front door with pistols drawn and go through the usual procedures.

Logan kicks in an office door behind the counter, pulls a knife and threatens head cashier Nixon and horse buyer WS Johnson with instant death. Instructing Nixon to open the vault and remove its three bags of gold coins, the bandits steal a total of $32,640 – very big money – before ushering the bank staff outside. They run to their horses and hightail it down Second Street towards the Golconda Road.

A posse is organised and pursuit begins. Butch has a fresh relay of horses waiting thirty miles east of Winnemucca, but he has forgotten that the Southern Pacific Rail Road parallels the escape route for five miles. Aided by a train crew, Deputy Sheriff George Rose gives chase and closes the gap, firing from the engine cab, but the distance is too great and no hits are recorded.

Telegraph operators wire Golconda, alerting the authorities, but they underestimate the speed at which the outlaws are travelling. Further telegrams are sent out calling for assistance to join the chase from as far afield as Boise, Idaho and Vale, Oregon.

Butch switches horses, believing he is safe. He hasn't bargained for such a determined pursuit. A posse is seen heading their way. Butch, Sundance, Logan and Carver hurriedly ride towards the Owyhee River, feinting to head for the Junipers, a remote, almost inaccessible, wilderness region spanning the Nevada-Idaho state lines.

A second posse joins the chase, hoping to cut off the bandits before they reach the river. The outlaws make a clean getaway, and the posse retrieves for its efforts one abandoned horse. The authorities maintain the manhunt for another week but give up chasing wild rumours. Big rewards totaling over $10,000 – a pension for life – are posted for the capture of Sundance, Logan and Carver.

SIMON:

Time in Lander was good for Butch, but it turned sour for us on departure, July 16. Riverton was twenty-six miles distant. Mileage ridden: 1,255 in seventy-two days; the averages were looking good at 17.43 miles per day. But our weighing scales were playing up. This delayed final packing. Richard, up since four, was urging haste as I retrieved the horses, totally caked in mud from a very wet pasture.

"Have you weighed and finished?"

"Not quite."

"Why not?"

"I'm waiting for the brushes – the scales are misreading."

"Get a move on," Richard replied, more aggressively than was necessary.

"Shout at Barbara – I'm almost ready," I snapped back.

Richard pounced. Pushing me backwards against the barn door and jamming his forearm under my neck, he raved:

"Get a fucking move on, you idle bastard!"

I said, "You militaristic bullyboy turd, your basic training is showing: 'If it moves, salute it, if it doesn't move, paint it white. And if it answers back, thump it.'" But I said it all privately, to myself.

Out loud, quite out of character, I meekly suggested that Richard make Barbara feed the horses, since she was contributing nothing to the expedition. Wrong move. More verbals. Richard's temper was volcanic. Barbara stepped out of the combat zone. Richard reminded me I was a "little shit." I wondered whether we had gone too far and the ride would end right here. A long silence followed, then I said, "Fall out with me and I'll use every contact I've got to get you back on a plane home. Everything was packed, the horses were filthy and I wasn't risking them getting sore backs for the sake of a minute's delay."

Another silence.

"Sorry, I just lost it," Richard acknowledged, so quietly it was almost a whisper.

The tension evaporated. No ill feeling remained. A heat-of-the-moment clash; these things happen.

The trail to Riverton was dull as ditch water. We rode to the City auction corrals. The place was deserted. I dismounted and walked to a house and helloed, hoping someone was home.

"Wanna put the horses up?" said a friendly lady padding down the path to meet us.

"Will it be okay? No one's around," I replied, worried we needed permission, adding, "The manager is Ritchie Venzer – are you certain he won't mind us stopping over?"

"He's my husband!" came the reply. Fawn graciously opened the facility. A character called Bill appeared, jumped into a truck, reversed it through the network of corrals and forked a huge quantity of feed. Within half an hour, our party was ensconced in the El Rancho Hotel.

RICHARD:

We spent our day off on Main Street and sampled an eat-all-you-can restaurant. Barbara was conspicuous by her absence. Simon and I planned ahead. We notified Gene Vieh at Hole-in-the-Wall and the

Thorens at Copper Mountain of our location.

Copper Mountain was promising to be a gruelling thirty-four mile haul. Our concern was a limited water supply. There were few settlements, and horrendous temperatures were guaranteed over the next week. With the horses in mind, we could not afford to miscalculate on mileage.

"Good to know Barbara's bought herself another water bottle," Simon said, adding sarcastically, "It won't be too hot, maybe the low hundreds – no matter how much she hogs the water, she's sure to collapse."

"I think she intends to leave us soon anyway," I replied, airing my hunch.

"You're joking. We can't be that lucky."

"Where's the most likely place that she could bale out from?"

"Hole-in-the-Wall. Look, if you know something I don't, then let's hear it," Simon demanded, clearly relishing the idea.

Barbara had no cast-iron intention to leave that I knew of. It was just beginning to look more likely.

Later, over coffees, the three of us discussed the Montana sections. Simon informed us gleefully that the Missouri Breaks section was uncharted territory, and from Sheridan to Miles City it promised to be an awful slog. He was twisting the knife in the wound, and Barbara's face at once showed anguish and stress.

Her leaving the expedition might create one problem – money, since she owed me. The benefits were greater: one less horse to care for and maintain (probably Pancho) and less gear to haul. I reckoned we could lose weight-load to the extent of one canvas "H" pack and a set of panniers, keeping them empty so we could double up on grain if necessary.

SIMON:

Riverton was uneventful, and we pulled out. On Main Street, I rode to the bank and restocked with cash before heading onto the old railroad grade to Shoshoni.

Mosquito swarms appeared. We sprayed insect repellent generously to no avail, so we retrieved the military mosquito nets. Worn like a skullcap, with a hat jammed on top, the netting was shoulder length. Humans looked like prats and fared quite well, but not the horses. We repeatedly doused them, yet still the mosquitoes dived in. This abortive activity didn't abate till we reached Hidden Valley, where the railroad grade suddenly vanished into a huge sandy wash.

I unravelled a fence and we led the horses down a bank into the wash. It avoided the high drop into Muskrat Creek, but meant pressing the packhorses up an awkward, steep sandy bank on the other side, a feat they achieved with much encouragement (and some abuse) from us.

Within half a mile, the ditch petered out and so did the mosquitoes. This section was dull riding in frightful heat and conditions. A track led through a steep cut and onto a wooden railway bridge, and the outskirts of Shoshoni loomed. It was late afternoon when we reined in at a smallholding, hoping to put the horses up.

"No, I'm sorry. I don't want your horses near ours. No offence. It's just that health wise they mightn't be clear," stated Tim Thompson, a short blond-haired man with a moustache.

"Which way did you come into town, by the way?"

"Over the bridge using the old railroad grade."

I pointed to the way we came.

"Sheee-it. That place is riddled with snakes – see any ridin' through?"

"Nope, but can we buy hay?" I asked.

I opened my wallet and at once noticed a huge gap, right where my MBNA gold card was supposed to be. Now, I am meticulous about cards. I quickly checked my pommel bag and pockets, but as I thought, no sign. My obvious panic prompted Tim to ask if I was OK.

"I've misplaced a credit card – I may have lost it in Riverton," I said as calmly as I could, which was not very. Sweat was breaking out.

"That's the last place you want that to happen. We'll call the police. Where did you use it?" Tim asked, showing genuine concern.

"In the bank on Main," I replied, my heart sinking.

We returned to the corrals. Incredibly, a police patrol car arrived right on cue. The officer rang to see if it had been handed in at the station. I waited.

"No one's reported it. Expect the worst, bud."

I wanted to take the Winchester and shoot myself. This was the cash-converting card – the one with an enormous limit, the only card we had that guaranteed the financial backing to reach Canada. Barbara and Richard were out of money.

Tim called Norwest Bank, but it had just closed. I then rang MBNA in Chester. A young lady calmly suggested that she would deposit a lump sum into my bank account, rendering my debit card fully operative with funds to back it, and immediately cancel the lost plastic. Brilliant! Out of trouble on the finances, but whoever held that card was probably enjoying its ten thousand pound spending limit.

That night, the mosquitoes returned on a thousand-bomber raid. The only respite was by zipping into our bivvy bags to endure appalling humidity and heat.

RICHARD:

Simon created quite a drama over the loss of his card. Tim Thompson agreed to drive him back to Riverton and retrieve it if possible. Barbara and I strung Sunday and loaded the gear into Tim's pickup with an arrangement to meet later on the trail between Shoshoni and the Quién Sabe. We had an uneventful ride across bleak country to Bonneville. I had taken a bearing and was making for the Birdseye Road, which led to Copper Mountain. It was hot again, and we rode in silence.

SIMON:

Leaving the riders, Tim and I hopped in the truck and departed. The bank had left a message. The machine had swallowed the card and the bank had cut it in half. I was ecstatic, and we drove to the local restaurant for a celebratory breakfast, which we shared with a dedicated treasure hunter who was relentlessly searching for a Wild Bunch cache in the Owl Creek Mountains. According to legend, gold coins had been buried in a cave following a Union Pacific train robbery in Wyoming. I made my own views plain:

"There isn't any hidden bullion. Those guys spent or gave away every damn dime they ever robbed."

We left to re-join the others. The truck made easy work. Richard and Barbara were already on Route 189 opposite Boysen State Park. The land was flat and arid, reminding me of the Red Desert. Altitude nudged 5,000 feet. To our west lay the Owl Creek Mountains.

"Find your card then?" Richard asked casually.

"Nope. Nor did anyone else." I related the outcome.

We shook Tim's hand and thanked him for going out of his way to help us.

"Well, if you guys ride up this way again, stop by. We'll have room for you next time!"

Bill and Fran Thoren met us leading up the foothills to their secluded ranch. It was thanks to Wild Bunch historian and writer Dan Buck that we were invited to stay. A huge cottonwood shaded an old bunkhouse. The backdrop to the century-old cabin was the interlocking spurs of Copper Mountain.

We turned the horses out into a fabulous pasture and marvelled at such an idyllic location. This was the Quién Sabe. Sixteen miles northeast of Shoshoni it stretched from Poison Creek, north up Hoodoo and Tough Creeks over the mountain to Jones Creek. It has been in Bill Thoren's family since 1907.

The first to settle at Copper Mountain are Mexicans. These vaqueros use the hidden valleys and canyons to hold stolen horses and cattle until the wealthy cattle barons drive them off.

Around 1883, three Englishmen establish a partnership headquarters on the Hoodoo Creek. When asked the name of the operation, the hired Mexican hands at the ranch reply, "Quién sabe?" "Who knows?" The name is adopted.

The outlaw period here probably starts post-1886 when Tom Osborne stays on at the spread as owner after the English have sold out. Tom and Butch are already friends when Tom gets into big trouble. He befriends a drifter named Thorn, who soon discovers Osborne cannot read, and so dupes him out of title to the ranch by filing a claim in Lander, deeding property and livestock away. When Tom realizes his mistake, he finds Thorn in Lanigan's Saloon. He walks over and shoots him dead. Convicted for a term of fifteen years in the penitentiary, the false claim is nevertheless cancelled, and Tom hands the *Quién Sabe* Ranch over to Butch Cassidy. As early as 1892, Butch is already heading for trouble. He unwisely buys three horses without a bill of sale from a young rustler named Billy Nutcher. Butch and Al Hainer are named as suspects when a witness sees the horses in Butch's possession.

At the time, the ranchers are making enormous efforts to rid the range of horse thieves. A major sweep begins in the Badlands of South Dakota, across Wyoming to the Idaho border. Butch and Hainer are spotted near the town of Auburn, and Deputy Sheriff Bob Calverly and stockman John Chapman, accompanied by local law officers, arrive and find Hainer working at a sawmill on the property. He is promptly arrested and tied to a tree.

The lawmen manage to apprehend Butch in the bunkhouse after he attempts to go for his gun. It is a close call. Calverly has thrown down at the same moment; his pistol misfires, but when it does fire a bullet, it strikes Butch a glancing blow on his forehead, enabling the officers to subdue him.

Butch and Hainer are jailed at Evanston and then Lander, where they spend two months languishing in the Fremont County hoosegow. After much legal wrangling, they are released on bail for a year as the court grants a continuance. Butch travels, then returns to stand trial on January 20, 1893. Witnesses are not available to testify, but requests for further stays are denied, and a court is convened. Remarkably, the jury acquits Butch and Hainer.

Unhappily for Butch, three days earlier, a new complaint has been sworn out that another horse has been stolen. Butch and Hainer are charged with a separate crime, resulting in a new trial. Eventually, Butch is found guilty of stealing a five-dollar horse, and is sentenced to two years' hard labour. It could have been ten. Hainer is acquitted, having done a deal. Butch waves goodbye to his freedom on July 15, 1894 and enters the gates of Wyoming's State Penitentiary.

RICHARD:

We enjoyed the brief stop at the *Quién Sabe* but were back in the saddle the following morning. Taking a rough track off Copper Mountain leading through rolling hills and interlocking arroyos, we rode down a steep draw. Over a bluff, a cattle trail meandered through the shallow foothills.

Below Cedar Ridge, we crossed the Badwater Road and followed a fence over undulating sandy hills for seven miles. The heat and conditions were brutal. Finally, at Long Butte we rejoined the Badwater Road and stopped at a smelly gas well to let the horses nibble on grass.

It was impossible to camp here. The horses had already slowed considerably, but I decided to press on. We rode along a billiard-cue-straight, dusty track and could see the foothills of the Bighorn Mountains looming. The country was desolate, parched and devoid of life. Wyoming started to grip us in her heat wave.

We arrived at the tiny settlement of Lysite, which comprised a few houses set in the shade of enormous cottonwoods. Whenever we stopped, it was my habit to purchase provisions as required – usually snacks, drinks, breakfast items or lunch for the team. I had exhausted $5,000 cash from Mexico to this point. My disbelief and disappointment were boundless when Barbara went into the store and bought for herself alone – a second blatant display of selfishness following the water incident before Robbers Roost. I was starting to see Barbara through Simon's eyes.

SIMON:

We rode three miles to a tiny township called Lost Cabin, established near Lysite in 1900 by a wealthy rancher. We were to meet Zane Fross, its official custodian.

Lost Cabin is a useful horse relay station for the Wild Bunch. Ideally located between the Hole-in-the-Wall and Quién Sabe, a southerly route leads directly to Powder Springs on the Wyoming-Colorado line. During the summer of 1897, a veritable reign of terror takes place in the newly formed Bighorn County between Basin City and Hole-in-the-Wall.

A gang led by Tom O'Day, a former cowpuncher, is stealing cattle. O'Day makes his home here and is still listed as a resident in 1910 following release from prison in Deadwood for bank robbery (1898) and from Laramie for horse theft (1908).

In 1891, Butch is nearly caught rustling too. With Matt Warner and Tom McCarty, he loads up packhorses with essentials, then rides north to Ten Sleep and east to the Powder River picking up strays.

Rustling in and around Johnson County is at its peak. The Wyoming cattle barons have given up relying on the local law to solve their problems. They hire Frank Canton, a ruthless gunfighter, and some ugly killings follow. In July, Major Frank Wolcott, manager of the Tolland Cattle Company's VR Ranch, is given a remit and funds to declare war on all rustlers. To this end, he produces a death list of seventy names, one of which is Butch Cassidy.

Butch and his buddies are gathering cattle in the region and keeping a watchful eye out. They have no interest in what is basically a local power struggle, but they have a very close shave just north of Lost Cabin. They are removing their saddles to rest when Butch spies riders carrying Winchesters heading in their direction. They race for their lives and the chase continues until sundown, when Butch suggests they split into the timbers near the Wind River. They all get away.

RICHARD:

Zane Fross was welcoming and hospitable, but it was a disappointment to learn that Lost Cabin, which had sounded so intriguing, effectively no longer existed. Instead, we discussed the difficult business of locating water for the horses on our next leg. I was keen to recce the route ahead to find Jackpot Reservoir, our intended next camp. I was told the Jackpot had been dry for five years! The run in to Hole-in-the-Wall was beginning to look very uncomfortable. Compounding this, we were a vital USGS map short and could only estimate mileage.

We saddled up for the twenty-one mile ride. It was frustrating to have to circle east before heading north, but the more direct route involved a faint trail through interlocking draws and *arroyos*. I would have chosen it on fresh horses without packs and with good maps, but as we were, it wasn't worth the risk.

SIMON:

The road was a poor-quality tarmac surface flanked by dust and sparse vegetation. The altitude was increasing at Red Creek when we suddenly spotted a cattle watering hole. The horses scrambled down a bank towards the muddy water. Richard took Yazz and Bones, and I followed with Sunday. Barbara waited with Pancho and Ditch until the others had their fill. The edge of the pool was extremely soft and we were careful with the horses.

Then Pancho and Ditch came charging eagerly down the slope. Richard called to warn Barbara there was a risk of them getting caught in the mire. Too late. Ditch lunged forward, yanked the rope out of Barbara's hand and suddenly found himself almost up to his chest in thick mud and sinking steadily. He panicked for a few seconds, then seemed to succumb to the conditions. A sinkhole is a death trap for a horse.

"Get that damned horse up and out of there!" Richard roared.

We abandoned the other horses and rushed to haul Ditch out of the mess. He had given up struggling and lay on his side.

"He's going under," Richard shouted.

I ran to Sunday to get my lariat, in the hope of throwing a line over him. If not, it meant wading in and trying to get a rope around his chest. Barbara stood rooted to the spot and looked on mortified. Ditch woke up as we wrenched on his lead rope. If he did not get on to his feet, he was a goner. Richard tugged furiously and I joined the fray, yelling expletives. We managed to turn Ditch's head towards us and the edge of the sinkhole, hoping he would lunge and strike terra firma. Prayers were answered, and he scrambled out of the mire totally caked in thick mud.

RICHARD:

It was another mighty close call. Barbara was very shaken after the incident. I felt she had been momentarily transported back to the death of Imasizzlin'lady in the Book Cliffs.

We rode in grim silence under thick, grey clouds. A thunderstorm looked imminent, and soon rain splattered, the temperature cooled and a sharp wind whipped up. In the distance, we spied Arminto and got there just before the heavens opened. I elected to walk to the hamlet in search of drinking water.

Barbara and Simon prepared camp, then tried to catch Ditch and groom him to get the mud off. I knew this would be difficult – Ditch hated being brushed. I reappeared with an older gentleman I had met on yesterday's recce. He filled our canteens and generously donated a carton of cold beer. Later, Simon and I watched the sun sink slowly over the southern end of the Bighorns. We enjoyed a relaxed evening, then laid out our sleeping bags inside the stockade and polished off the beers.

SIMON:

"The horses have eaten a vast quantity of grain," Richard pointed out, "but they've left nearly all their hay."

"You know what that means," I said, "So what's the mileage tomorrow?"

"Late twenties – early thirties," said Richard, suggesting a monumental trek.

I said nothing when Richard decided to inform rancher Gene Vieh that we would arrive at the Willow Creek the following evening. By tacit agreement, we did not level with Barbara over our mileage plans to avoid her total demoralization. She would be convinced the horses were not up to it. An additional eight miles equated to three hours' riding, worth it to Richard and me, both keen to have more time at the famous Hole-in-the-Wall.

We hit our bedrolls slightly drunk, knowing the next day would be a tough one. The last thing I said to Richard, in a quiet undertone, was, "Do you really think she's going to pull out of the trip?"

He paused for a moment, considering. He was obviously reviewing the events since the outlaw hideout at Copper Mountain, because he shrugged and replied in only two words:

"*Quién sabe?*" Who knows?

HOLE-IN-THE-WALL

*"Y' know, every time I see Hole-in-the-Wall again
it's like seeing it fresh, for the very first time."*
BUTCH CASSIDY

SIMON:

Pleasantly cool, the sun's rays streamed through the stockade,
promising a scorcher for later.

"We need to get going, it's a long day to make Hole-in-the-Wall,"
said Richard.

The horses were already fed, camp remarkably tidy. I dressed and
tied my bedroll, gathered personal belongings, tacked up and pulled
out – that quick. A narrow dirt track led to Deadman Butte and the
start of the winding Red Wall. Richard and I were both a little high on
thoughts of the impending rendezvous with the Armstrong and Vieh
families. This was to be a big moment. Much had happened since we
waved *adios* to Joe and Rusty near Joseph City, Arizona.

Barbara forced the conversation:

"How many miles?"

"Twenty-sixish," I replied evasively.

The maps promised thirty-four and then some. If daily riding
averages were hovering around seventeen miles per day, that meant a
two-day ride. I was in denial.

"Well don't you know?" she demanded.

I ignored the brusque question.

Barbara shot me a dark glance. Richard also gave her an evasive reply. The matter was now closed, and Barbara angry with the pair of us. We rode on silently. The horses padded along on autopilot with the exception of Ditch, who, like Barbara, was having the makings of a very bad day.

RICHARD:

Buffalo Creek Road was another hard-packed dirt track. We rounded a curve and the majestic Red Wall came into view. Massive sandstone bluffs reminiscent of the Grand Canyon jutted into the green-carpeted valley.

Barbara had already distanced herself from us since the earlier conversation. Slowing her pace, she chided Ditch, continually cursing him and lashing out with the lead rope. Heat rose, tempers frayed and the wily gelding gave her a hard time.

Simon was requested to "ride herd" on Ditch, but was reluctant to contravene their mutual non-co-operation pact. To obviate the misery, I switched Bones for Ditch. Much to Barbara's chagrin, Simon now chased and chivvied Ditch relentlessly on my behalf, just to rub salt in the wound. Hauling the gelding was hard, un-enjoyable riding, but it was some compensation that we were finally leaving high desert for grass country.

Hours later, we rode into the Shepperson Ranch, a vast 100,000 acre spread. The family simultaneously poured out from house, barn and store shed, interested to know what riders were in their yard. I asked if we could water the horses.

"Where you headed?"

"Willow Creek Ranch."

"Step down – unload your gear. Come and have some iced tea," barked Bob Shepperson, an archetypal grizzled rancher.

SIMON:

We gratefully unloaded and turned the horses loose. An hour later, a fine lunch of sausage and potatoes was served by Mrs. Shepperson, and we ate greedily. Bob broke the clattering of cutlery:

"Better make a call. Git your gear hauled, you cain't make it with them packs today. It's around twenty-two miles from Arminto Stockade to here."

Oops. Now the mileage tally was out of the bag. Barbara shot a black look at Richard. We proclaimed our intention to ride off later that afternoon, regardless, hoping to be at Butch Cassidy's favourite hideout by six. I daresay if a pistol had been to hand, Barbara might have used it on the pair of us.

"Well, you've got a ways to go yet," Bob said, then proceeded to expand on the Tipton train robbery.

"Robbers came this way – found old jewelry on the ranch."

"Did you contact historical societies or archivists?" I asked at once.

"Nope," Bob replied bluntly.

It stopped the conversation dead. Gold coins that the outlaws removed would be worth big money today – if only for their intrinsic value. Jewelry had been taken at Tipton too. This was unusual. Normally, Butch didn't interfere with passengers. Doing so was risky in the narrow confines of a railway carriage, with many passengers armed – and besides, public goodwill (or absence of ill-will) was a useful asset, not to be squandered.

Two days after the holdup, a general manager of the Union Pacific Railroad confirmed to Denver newspapers that the outlaws had taken three money packages and "two packages of cheap jewelry." Did Bob have some goodies hidden away? We left the Sheppersons at three o'clock and never found out.

The heat was intolerable. The mercury clocked ninety-five in the shade and was slowly rising – to match Barbara's temper.

The range opened out and through an immense pasture an old truck burbled alongside us before stopping – it was Ord Buckingham, foreman of the Willow Creek. The Buckinghams had ranched for six generations in central Wyoming. Ord was the genuine article, the real deal. We shook hands. His style and demeanour had not changed a bit. He eyed us up, not quite sure if we were lunatics, greenhorns or true range riders.

Ord's uniform had not altered either: beat-up Stetson, worn boots, faded Wranglers. If Ord were to change, Hole-in-the-Wall would too. In his slow, deliberate drawl, he casually informed us that another eight miles remained. On tired horses, this was a marathon.

Nudging the hundreds at 6,000 feet was exhausting work for the horses. Turning off Thirty-Three Mile Road onto Willow Creek Road, we started climbing Roughlock Hill. I felt a needle of excitement. Somehow it felt like we were coming home.

We topped a ridge and rested, absorbing Natrona County's expansive range. Hills and swales gently rolled. A green carpet merged into the blue horizon. The Red Wall swerved from its easterly course and headed north. In the distance, a row of cottonwoods shaded ranch buildings. Horses were grazing contentedly. I could taste elation.

"We're almost there," I announced, punching the air.

We cut down a steep draw before heading across a pasture towards the sheep-shearing sheds. Nothing had altered since my last visit in 1998. I could see that Rusty Armstrong was already walking out to meet us from the old bunkhouse. We had made it – a distance of 1,395 miles from Mexico. Rusty was thrilled to see us, and I felt we had achieved something special by riding thus far. I stepped off Sunday and Rusty and I hugged, relieved to see one another.

RICHARD:

Arrival was an emotional experience for me too. Hole-in-the-Wall held a special place in my mind's eye since Simon had pointed it out to me on the map, in London. Until now, it had seemed an unattainable point of the journey. I understood the concerns of Joe and Rusty Armstrong, their fears that perhaps we wouldn't make it.

Gene Vieh and his wife Sammye were the new owners of the Willow Creek, happy to have acquired the historic ranch and committed to securing its future. Originally from Atlanta, Georgia, they extended characteristic Southern hospitality.

We settled in the original 1890s bunkhouse for a late meal. Hewn out of old cedar logs and restored to former glories, the structure sat beneath the shade of cottonwoods surrounded by corrals, a paddock and two enormous pastures. Beyond the living area, a kitchen with a huge stove led to three further bedrooms and two bathrooms. We ate and watched the dwindling sun's rays cascade onto the Red Wall. For the first time in a long time, I felt totally relaxed.

It was an easy decision to extend our stopover. We planned a total of four days to rest and contemplate the journey ahead. It was great to relax and absorb history. I loved the place and the people, and helped re-shoe the horses with Umberto, Gene's Mexican hand who was an expert trick-roper. I learned to throw a loop too.

While plotting our course, Gene informed us that many landowners had adopted a locked gate stance, not taking kindly to trespassing. No permission to cross meant no riding. Gene promised to have our packs shipped ahead. This, he hoped, would be the start of a continuous relay. Persuasive bargaining with neighbours and locals meant the ride to Buffalo wouldn't have to be abandoned. The hard part was over, or so we thought.

On Monday, July 26, Barbara quit, just like that. It was her fourth and final declaration of withdrawal. Simon and I had already discussed privately our response to such an announcement: our acceptance would be final. For months, there had been a hole in the team. Barbara felt the ride had been the most miserable part of her life. On arrival, she broke down in tears. She said she could protect the horses no longer and had to leave.

I expressed my disappointment, but very cautiously. Her responsibilities for horse welfare had been upheld only with her mouth – she had not done the job. She protested that neither of us had taken notice of her advice and that we had marginalised her. In fact, it was difficult to recall a single positive suggestion she had made to offset her continuous undermining of Simon. The simple truth was she didn't enjoy the ride and disliked Simon with a passion.

SIMON:

It seemed too good to be true, and I still harboured the suspicion that Barbara might try to secure horses *and* beat us to the border, scooping the concept and the book deal as she had been threatening all along. By quitting, she was in breach of that deal, but I was crazy not to have everything in writing, as Richard regularly pointed out.

But her departure promised Richard and me freedom of thought and action, and release from continuous tension. I was also glad I had out-ridden the rider. Richard and I drove to Kaycee, the nearest settlement, to celebrate the news quietly.

Kaycee is named for John Nolan's ranch brand. Rustler and fringe Wild Buncher Tom O'Day partners Nolan in a saloon business there. The KC Ranch is where the Johnson County War of 1892 finally ignites. It is a brutal conflict between the cattle barons who form the Wyoming Stock Growers Association and anyone who gets in their way, be they rustlers or innocent homesteaders.

Shootings and lynchings by Frank Canton and others have heated emotions. Butch Cassidy nearly rides straight into the conflict when he quits the Wind River country in the spring of 1890 to ride to Hole-in-the-Wall. Among the outlaws already located in the valley when Butch arrives are Tom O'Day, Flat Nose Currie, Walt Punteney and Nate Champion.

Butch settles, taking a squatter's claim on the Blue Creek, but his stay is a short one. When word gets out that he is on the cattle barons' death list, he quickly sells his stake to Jim Stubbs, a respected settler. The powder keg finally explodes when an army of invaders, including fifty hired Texas gunfighters, surrounds a cabin at Nolan's Ranch and lays siege to it. Nick Rae is shot and fatally wounded and the cabin fired.

Nate Champion becomes a frontier hero by holding out all day – and keeping a log of events. He is finally forced out by the fire and cut down in a hail of gunfire. On his bloodstained vest (allegedly, he has twenty-eight bullets in him), the killers pin a card reading, "Cattle thieves, beware!" Butch departs swiftly to escape a similar fate.

RICHARD:

Today, Kaycee is a quiet town with a post office, general store, a delightful museum full of interesting frontier artifacts – well worth the visit – a garage and two mandatory bars flanking a rough tarmac road. It also boasts a splendid rodeo. Almost opposite the derelict taxidermists, a sign marks the site where Champion and Rae were killed. We checked into the Hole-in-the-Wall saloon and popped a few beers before heading back.

Thoughts turned to the trail ahead. Two riders meant I could dramatically thin down our equipment. One set of panniers would carry a hundred and fifty pounds of grain, if needed, equating to six twenty-five pound feeds. Those rations would last the horses three days. The "H" pack (weighing thirty pounds) carried bedrolls and human and equine medical kits. The remaindered gear was left, including stove and fuel. Where possible we would pre-dump the panniers and string two spare horses. Personal effects were carried in our saddlebags. Four horses gave a saddle and pack animal for each rider, so Pancho could remain with Rusty. The Arab had been a truly great horse, the best all-rounder in the *remuda*.

We visited with Carole and Ord Buckingham for afternoon tea and collected some of the best advice we had heard on the trip thus far. Ord suggested we ride early, finishing by noon. Cover a week's mileage in four days, then give the horses three days' complete rest. On the trail, we should alternate walking and trotting, ensuring the horses were very heavily grained twice a day and rotating their duties where possible. To real Westerners, this was obvious and even elementary, but it revolutionised the trip ahead.

It was hard to leave Willow Creek. Sammye Vieh and Sara Whalley spoiled us. The food alone was worth the ride from Mexico. On July 29, Barbara bade us farewell with a crowd watching. It was her birthday, and it felt strange that she wasn't riding out. I remember feeling sorry. On a more upbeat note, I had also just learned that my new grandson had been born in Las Vegas, Nevada.

When we set off, I rode Yazz and towed Bones – Simon saddled Sunday and strung Ditch. Within the hour, the ride took on a different feel. We began to cement the friendship that exists between us today.

SIMON:

For me, Barbara's leaving created no problems. After saddling up and checking our outfits, Richard walked over to me, grinned and extended his hand.

"We've a third of the way to go, we're on our own, so let's make it a good one."

As we gently trotted the horses, my mind drifted to the distant past.

At 2.18 am on Friday, June 2, 1899, Union Pacific Overland Flyer Number One is flagged down by an emergency flare between the settlements of LeRoy and Wilcox, Wyoming. Thinking a bridge might be out, engineer WR Jones stops the train. A masked robber leaps onto the footplate, points a gun at Jones and orders him to pull up near Como Ridge. When he reacts too slowly, he is buffaloed with a six-gun. The outlaws set to work and shout to the mail clerks to open up. After fifteen minutes, shots are fired, and moments later, a dynamite explosion nearly rocks the car off the tracks. Now the bridge is really out. The robbers point out that the next charge will blow up the mail-car – the doors are opened swiftly and the clerks emerge.

Whilst the captives are being lined up alongside the car, a headlight is seen approaching. When questioned, the crew volunteers that the second section of the train is carrying soldiers. This might be true or it might be just quick-witted opportunism. The robbers dare not risk it. At once, they set dynamite onto the doors of the express baggage-car and blow them. Woodcock the messenger is stunned in the explosion but not seriously hurt. The remainder of the charges are used to open the safes. After scooping the contents, they head for their horses and make off with $8,000. Not their record haul by a long way, but enough to keep the participants in modest comfort for nearly a year or (more their style) in the lap of luxury for two or three months.

The gang splits up. Hard rain makes their trails difficult to follow, and the picture is confused. Reports of sightings pour in from all sorts of unlikely places, and within twenty-four hours, there are a hundred men out from Laramie, Casper and Lander hoping to catch the robbers.

One group of outlaws takes a northerly direction towards Hole-in-the-Wall, and a sizeable force of law officers and Union Pacific detectives gather in Casper ready to mount a chase. Another promising report says that three suspicious strangers are occupying a cabin six miles northwest of Casper itself, and a posse consisting of Converse County Sheriff Josiah Hazen, Natrona County Sheriff Oscar Hiestand and nine others is quickly formed. Sheriff Hazen eventually catches up with three of the outlaws – probably the same three – near Horse Ranch, Wyoming. The posse closes in, and a gun battle begins. Hazen is fatally wounded, taking a bullet to the stomach, and is rushed by wagon to Casper. He loses much blood on the way and dies the following day.

The robbery sees the introduction by the outlaws of a formidable new weapon: smokeless powder. When you are firing from cover, only the tell-tale puffs of gunsmoke reveal your position. If you make no smoke, your adversaries have nothing to shoot at.

After the shooting of Sheriff Hazen, the three outlaws involved immediately head north through Castle Creek, where they pick up fresh supplies and horses before riding towards Thermopolis. On June 15, 1899, the State Militia is hard on the trail, chasing a massive $18,000 dollar reward for the capture of these fugitives, who are named as Flat Nose George Currie and two accomplices.

The robber group, which heads north, probably camps near Mayoworth on a ranch owned by Albert Brock. Fred Hans, a professional man-hunter, calls the escape of this group "the most remarkable flight in the criminal history of the West."

Veteran stock detective Joe LeFors is tracking these northbound robbers. He picks up their trail near Hole-in-the-Wall. With some circling and doubling back, the chase continues for nearly two hundred miles to the north end of EK Mountain.

The outlaws cross the Owl Creeks using a well-hidden trail up a side canyon and drop down into the Wind River Basin by way of Mexican Pass. Once across, they make their way directly to the isolated Muddy Creek Road ranch owned by Emery Burnaugh. Later, the Burnaughs recall that the outlaw party actually numbers five, including Butch Cassidy. The outlaws conceal themselves in a natural cave in a sandstone outcrop near the ranch, and they are supplied by the Burnaugh family. It is very likely that one of the outlaws, identity still contested, is badly wounded during the chase and finds a lonely grave above the cave.

LeFors writes of the chase:

"I knew from the start that the Hole-in-the-Wall locals would not give us any information – they could if they wanted to, but they were friends or at least allies of the lawless bunch. We pushed our horses at a fast trot, and sometimes we hit a good gallop, making around eight or nine miles an hour and kept up that gait without much change, *because I could trail about as fast as the horses could hold out."*

LeFors feels progress is dogged from the outset. After meeting Lander law officer Arthur Sparhawk, Frank Wheeler (UP's chief special agent in charge of the posse) suggests trailing the robbers through Wind River Canyon. LeFors knows better. The pair disagrees, so Joe reluctantly defers. He states, "The posse pulled out for the canyon. I stayed back, as I had no more trailing to do. They were onto a bad lead. I was positive those fellows would not go to a place where they could not possibly hide or escape from a posse. Not one track of anything did we find and our chase was ended. Many times since I have wondered if the whole thing was not planned to keep me from riding onto the robbers and having a fight."

Joe LeFors provides a unique insight. Why is the chase effectively hampered? Perhaps it is simply self-preservation on the part of the lawmen. For certain, there are very few hardened lawmen and bounty hunters ready to tough it out face-to-face with these feared bandits.

Initially, there is confusion and disagreement about who was in on the robbery. One trio is identified as Flat Nose George Currie and the Roberts brothers (aka Harvey and Lonny Logan). Regarding the others, speculation and rumour are rife, though no one doubts that Butch and Sundance are deeply involved.

SIMON:

We rode on through lush pasture. Fluffy white clouds drifted overhead punctuated by clear, blue sky. Buffalo Creek entered the valley to Hole-in-the-Wall. I pointed out the geological formation to Richard where the sandstone divide turns. A faint game-trail leads up an awkward rocky slope to a "V" notch in the Red Wall. Discovered by the outlaw fraternity years earlier, it was used to drive stolen stock to a corral where an ash grove presides at the bend in the Buffalo Creek. Tracking east to west, anyone coming to the Red Wall would believe it was impossible to penetrate. Once safely inside, the rustlers made use of the beautiful grassy valley.

Shorty Wheelwright, a former army scout who worked for General George Crook in 1876, is one of the first to find Hole-in-the-Wall.

Frank and Jesse James come here too, as do many other Civil War deserters. Rustlers Flat Nose Currie, Black Henry Smith, Walt Punteney and Tom O'Day learn that by moving a large triangular gypsum boulder across the notch in the wall's cleft, pursuers are unable to detect a trail because the red sandstone leaves no mark.

Hole-in-the-Wall remains the most famous hideout of all time. Two miles west from the "V" notch, Butch and Sundance locate in a prime spot. Good water, abundance of game and plenty of feed for horses easily enables them to hold out.

The hideout becomes famous as an impregnable fortress. To disprove this, the feared Joe LeFors plans to lead an expedition of twenty men directly into Hole-in-the-Wall to round up stolen livestock. The outlaws boldly retort that they will repel any invasion.

On July 23, 1897, the two forces meet in a narrow canyon. Eyewitnesses say they pass within an arm's length of one another, both sides riding slowly with rifles to hand. The only rustlers in sight are Al and Bob Smith. When they have ridden some distance past the cowmen, Bob Smith steps off his horse. This action is interpreted as a hostile move, and Bob Devine dismounts, takes aim and shoots Bob Smith from behind his horse. A fusillade ensues, and around a hundred shots are fired. Both Devine and his son are injured in the gun battle, which leaves Bob Smith dying in the powder haze.

After Devine returns to Buffalo with a large number of cattle, Sheriff Al Sproul of Buffalo rides in two days later, despite similar warnings, and drives a herd of five hundred and fifty stolen livestock back to Casper.

For Butch, the writing is on the wall. His legendary hideout has been breached twice in a matter of days. The rustlers become wary and decide to travel.

SIMON:

I handed my binoculars to Richard. The Red Wall kinked to the left and swerved right, heading north, in line with the Bighorns. In the corner, I could make out two triangular rocks – one white, one orange. Running into the cleft at the base of the wall was an arroyo and a rough, rocky track.

"There it is," I proclaimed proudly.

"That's Hole-in-the-Wall?" Richard queried in surprise.

"Yep. You just rode over fourteen hundred miles to see a rocky slope in the middle of nowhere."

"No holes?"

"Just a wall – the trail goes up the rocky slope and bears right up onto that ledge. I guess Butch and Sundance made it up that way," I pointed to the dangerous trail.

We gazed at the sandstone cliff. It was tempting to try to ride up the rockslide to the summit, but after months on the trail, we knew better than to take needless risks with the horses – we didn't know the precise trail, and if a horse panicked, we knew another mount could be lost.

Crossing the valley, we arrived at a junction where a sign points to the Outlaw Cave. The hideout is located on the South River Slope of Middle Fork of Powder River, eight miles from the famed outlaw town site on Buffalo Creek.

"So we're not going to check the Cave then?" Richard asked.

"Love to, but it'll take a whole day," I replied.

"Have you seen it?"

"Nope. It's a hike down some cliffs and a river crossing – some say it's goat's work."

At the Richendifer place, I switched horses. Ditch was a continual pain in my arm. It was easier to ride him. We crossed a lush pasture to Castle Rock where three of the outlaws had switched horses following the Wilcox robbery. Over Middle Fork, we soon arrived at the Blue Creek. It was beautiful country. Red sandstone walls and rock faces, lush pasture, cottonwood trees and tranquillity.

Riding on, oblivious to impending danger, we paced down a slope and started to cross a dry creek drainage. Suddenly, without warning, our horses lurched and the ground seemed to rise under us. The horses stopped abruptly, and our stirrups were resting on the baked mud surface.

In sync we yelled, "Shit, quicksand!" and leaped off our horses. We scrambled out of the mud and hauled on reins and ropes. For a moment, they remained standing up to their girths, then, to our relief, they lurched out pretty easily, but it was yet another near-run thing.

RICHARD:

Relieved at our good fortune, we brushed ourselves down, remounted and continued. The track ran past a sort of rundown hillbilly ranch through a pasture to re-join a new tarmac road connecting Barnum to Kaycee. We jogged into Brock Road and arrived at the Triple E Ranch, tucked neatly under the shadows of Gardner Mountain.

Brock and Paula Hanson welcomed us in and announced that supper was imminent. Our hosts relieved us of our boots and firearms. It was clear Brock fancied Simon's Winchester; he hefted it, felt the weight, then tested the lever action and – snap – aimed it past me at the window, all in one slick movement. As I took in that Brock was assuming an unloaded rifle, and had unwittingly jacked a live round into the chamber, I barked a quick warning and, tensed for the crash-zipp of glass and bullet, ducked swiftly out of the line of fire, something I hadn't had to do for many years. Simon's and my reactions left Brock in no doubt about the situation, and he jerked the lever back to safety.

Order restored, our dinner conversation quickly turned to outlaw history.

"Tell us some interesting tales of the Wild Bunch," Simon prompted.

"Flat Nose George Currie tended the old Post Office in Mayoworth and was reputed to be a fine man. You'll ride past the site tomorrow," Paula informed us proudly.

"Have you any interesting stories handed down in your family?"

"Our family's opinion of Kid Curry was that he was okay, but the Sundance Kid was pretty mean," said Paula.

Simon smiled, then asked if that information had been passed on to Donna Ernst, grandniece of the Sundance Kid.

"Yes," Paula replied bluntly.

"Must have confounded the historians. Sundance was deemed far more affable than Harvey Logan."

"Of course, they were all over this country," Brock chimed in. "After Wilcox, they gave LeFors the shake. He was hated in these parts – he was mean and tricky too."

"Especially when he stitched up Tom Horn," I agreed, feeling comfortable in a conversation which would have been meaningless to me such a short time before.

The Hansons were congenial hosts. They explained they were having to work ever harder to maintain their family's ranching tradition. Brock reported that the cattle business in Wyoming was tough and prices were down, a sad story we had heard before.

Dinner over, we walked across the pasture. The horses were grazing contentedly on lush grass. It was a cool night – stars shone brilliantly in a clear sky. We eventually bedded down in a wooden cabin. Partially hidden down a steep draw and screened by trees, it was close to a tiny stream. Brock had informed us earlier that a lawman was ambushed here.

Lying comfortably in my bunk bed, I hoped his ghost wouldn't return to interrupt my sleep. I finally drifted off thinking Wyoming was becoming a breeze. We were having a great time.

THE BIGHORNS

"We do nice work."
BUTCH CASSIDY

The initial confusion about who was involved in the Wilcox train robbery gives way over time to some coherent probabilities. At least six outlaws are present at the actual robbery. With Butch and Elzy Lay as master planners and perhaps back-up, most likely Harvey Logan, Sundance, Flat Nose Currie, Lonnie Logan, Will Carver and Ben Kilpatrick (the Tall Texan) handle the main action, and Camillo Hanks, Bill Cruzan and Bill Jones may well be involved in the escape phase – it has to be a big, very well organised team, maybe the best ever.

When the gang splits up after the robbery, there are a great many false alarms and reported sightings of "riders." To throw off the hounding posses (literally, since Doctor Fulton's famous pack of Nebraska bloodhounds captures a lot of the headlines, if little else), the original northbound group turns due west then deftly doubles back to Billy Hill's ranch on the Red Fork of Powder River. Removing two saddles and three of Hill's finest mounts, they cross the Bighorns, thereby ridding themselves of the posse, which about-turns after a fifteen mile chase along steep trails made more hazardous by snow.

Three other riders head for Brown's Park. It seems they remain hidden in an aspen grove after the robbery, three miles from the scene. Once out of hiding, sporting new suits and clean faces, they pose as cattle buyers and ride off in a buckboard for a later rendezvous. The nerve and panache of this trio strongly suggests Elzy Lay, Butch and Sundance.

The last two are seen later with others celebrating at Linwood, on the Utah-Wyoming border. Witnesses say that Sundance sports a magnificent gold-braided vest with shiny brass buttons, and one of the other gang members wears a sober grey suit with a conservative brown vest.

Once the hubbub dies down, three of the robbers ride west to the Wind Rivers and head for Dubois – there, a short chase ensues by Fremont County officers. Stopping at Will Boyd's ranch at Crow Creek these three double back over the Owl Creek Mountains and are next seen in Thermopolis, apparently honouring the community in grand style reminiscent of the 1897 Baggs, Wyoming celebration. Again, very much the style of Butch and Sundance.

SIMON:

We rode out from the Hansons' due north along the escape route. As the horses walked steadily on, we soaked up the stunning scenery of the Bighorn Mountains. Their snow-capped peaks towering above, grass in the valley was lush, red, rocky outcrops glowed in the sun, the air was cool and refreshing. I glanced to the ridge line wondering if any hidden trails remained undiscovered along the backbone of this range, particularly the highpoints where most people would never dream of taking a horse. It was more than likely, but we were not about to find out.

Riding through a splendid pasture, we connected with the old stagecoach road, just a rough dirt track that wound through a pretty miniature gorge. As we topped a ridge, a trail came in from the west. This was Dull Knife Pass, and it curved around EK Mountain.

We then joined a road which has an old outlaw post office on it. An hour later, we came past the site, a solitary tall cottonwood tree fenced in, adjacent to some springs on the straight towards the settlement of Mayoworth. Posing as an outlaw, man-hunter Charles Siringo had learned that Butch and Sundance kept in regular contact with other members of the Wild Bunch through a series of what in the espionage world are called dead letter drops, established along the Outlaw Trail. Thankfully, nobody has chopped the tree down for firewood.

We alternated jogging and walking for mile upon mile, at a pace which the horses could more than keep up all day. Sunday wanted Ditch behind her, but Ditch refused to comply, fearing a kicking. To obviate a lengthened right arm, I ran them in span formation and kept the pair challenging for the lead. Riding long in the saddle at the sitting trot soon became hugely enjoyable. Stirrups at full length, we leaned forward to take the weight off the horses' backs. When walking, we sat well back into the saddle, our butts pushed into the cantle, legs outstretched, and we could ride comfortably for eleven hours a day, seven days a week if necessary.

My state of mind on this trip had never been more relaxed. Horse work was the pinnacle of travel. Only forking a Harley-Davidson could come remotely close.

We walked on to the friendly sound of creaking saddle leather, delighting in our surroundings. At Horn Creek Reservoir, a superb view presented itself of the Bighorn Mountains' formidable wall running north. Blackened slopes looked daunting, confirming suspicions that crossing here was impossible. We followed Greub Road, a hard-packed, shale surface which swept through deep grass over rolling foothills. Altitude at ground level was 5,500 feet; the peaks rose to 8,100 feet. We stopped briefly to catch a breeze, check the map and scan ahead. Irrigated pastures ahead indicated smallholdings.

We reined in at Meadow Bank Ranch. Affable hosts Sally and Wally Ramsbottom informed us that the Denver Post was tracking us fervently. Apparently, journalist Jack Cox was preparing a thirty-year anniversary overview of the Hill/Goldman film. He had already rung the Outlaw Trail History Centre in Vernal to research for the piece, and learned that English riders were on the trail to Canada.

I called Jack, who didn't waste time, and we arranged to meet in Sheridan. It was exciting news. Enjoying our own enjoyment of minor celebrity status, our hosts generously called us in for a splendid gourmet dinner, and we ate like proverbial lords. We learned that the Ramsbottoms were close relatives of the Sheppersons and were reminded that despite riding such remote country, word had always gone ahead by telephone. People already knew who we were, expected us to pass through and were mostly ready to offer hospitality and help. Even without telephones, that kind of friendly bush telegraph had operated surprisingly well for the Wild Bunch too, who benefited from horse relays, food, shelter and flat denials to following lawmen.

We departed the following morning. Heavy, mist-laden grey clouds hung heavy over the mountains, and drizzle gently doused us. The Bighorns were totally encompassed, and for three hours we jogged and walked, making good mileage to Billy Creek.

After some uneventful riding, we reined in at the historic TA Ranch. While I was unhinging a gate, Ditch leapt across the cattle grid. Richard and I were speechless. This impatient and unruly horse cleared a six-foot gap in one bound. His action hadn't gone unnoticed. Earl Madsen, working nearby walked over and introduced himself thus:

"That's a dishonest horse you got there," he said, pointing at Ditch, now happily munching on grass.

"He's very resourceful when it suits," I replied.

We walked to a grove of trees and turned the horses into a paddock. Earl guided us for an impromptu tour of the TA. Beautifully restored to the highest standards, it retained many original pieces of furniture from the nineteenth century. The cabin we passed on entry once belonged to notorious gunman and bounty hunter Frank Canton.

"Canton was involved in the Johnson County War of 1892," said Earl. We nodded agreement. We got told a lot of things we knew already on that trip, but to say so was not only bad manners, it might turn off a tap just about to pour liquid gold.

The cattlemen's war, the so-called invasion, concludes dramatically at the TA ranch. The Wyoming Stock Growers Association are holed up with their hired gunfighters in the big barn which still sports the bullet holes. Roles are reversed when angry homesteaders – supported by townsfolk and local law – surround and outnumber the invaders, who have retreated inside and barricaded the building. Luckily for the latter, three Troops of the Sixth Cavalry arrive from Fort McKinney in the nick of time to raise the siege and prevent the otherwise inevitable carnage.

Frank Canton, like Tom Horn, is a somewhat shadowy figure who works mostly under cover. Around 1899, he decides to become a professional bounty hunter. He is motivated by the need for money but also hopes the notoriety gained will help re-establish him in the US Marshal Service. After the much publicised Union Pacific train robbery at Wilcox, Canton's timing is immaculate. The reward of $18,000 acts like a magnet. It is an enormous sum of money by the standards of the day.

The Pinkerton Detective Agency, through James McParland, contacts Canton, stating that the reward money holds good but that no further inducements can be offered. Canton immediately writes to his old friend T. Jeff Carr, one of the Super-Posse detectives already engaged by Union Pacific. Carr confirms that no warrants have been issued, that the reward money still stands, and that another character, "Tom Hale or Horn," has been looking for the robbers for some time. If Carr is telling the truth, Butch and Sundance are at greater risk than they think. LeFors, Horn and now Canton, an unnerving trio of ruthless lawmen and dedicated bounty hunters, are all pursuing the outlaws single-mindedly and relentlessly – on a competitive winner-takes-all basis.

It is a test of nerve, ingenuity and stamina for Butch and Sundance to escape certain death when Canton finds an informer who agrees to lead him to Flat Nose Currie. Butch flees for the safer climes of New Mexico whilst Currie keeps continually on the move through Wyoming, Montana and Utah. The hunt ends for Flat Nose when he is shot and killed by a posse in the Book Cliffs.

A self-confessed and convicted armed robber and an accused back-shooting assassin, Canton has been called a "Jekyll and Hyde of the Plains," equally ruthless working either side of the law. Happily for Butch and Sundance, Canton drops out of their picture when he decides his prospects are now poor and goes to Alaska early in 1898.

RICHARD:

We prepared for a lazy early evening. Ebullient Western writer Jerry Sinkovec bowled up bearing a multitude of accoutrements and baggage – including a gift for Simon, a dashing looking wide-brimmed Akubra hat to replace his beloved Stetson, now lost and much mourned by its bereaved owner.

Wyoming was being very generous to us, even by the handsome

standards of rural America. This, plus the pony express riding technique (not to mention the absence of a certain disturbing influence) made this by far the happiest leg of the trip so far. Water and feed were no problem so long as we rode from ranch to ranch, and we had hardly packed since Riverton, enjoying the faster riding and covering greater distances without working the horses so hard. Packing, although an art and certainly not a dying one, is interesting and rewarding, but after fourteen hundred miles of desert, mountain and canyon riding, we were very cheerful about doing less of it when the opportunity arose.

As we waved goodbye, Earl warned us to keep a closer eye on Ditch. Along Route 196, flanking Interstate 90, we rode through rolling green hills. Temperature was near perfect, around the late seventies. In Buffalo, locals seemed surprised to see us jog into the historic cowboy town, despite their local paper having announced our imminent arrival.

Buffalo was a charming, unspoiled, largely nineteenth-century town with many old buildings and a refreshing scarcity of modernity. If you breathed in hard you could almost smell the history. Buffalo had been the commercial centre for the Hole-in-the-Wall country and indeed depended on rustler trade, though no bar or hotel today claims that Butch or Sundance slept here.

We settled down for ten minutes to allow the horses to graze. A familiar voice helloed from the sidewalk. It was Jerry Sinkovec, walking towards us with a number of holsters and guns cradled in his arms and an impressive camera slung around his neck.

"Let's get a few shots with these on. Hold on, I'll just check them and make sure they're not loaded." stated Jerry, as we became weighted down with iron. We were walking arsenals, and I sincerely hoped the local police wouldn't catch us playing bandits for the camera. Horsemen in town waving guns would definitely call for armed response units, police helicopters, the lot.

SIMON:

Rock Creek Ranch was set in a beautiful meadow five miles north of town. Glen Means eyed us cautiously. He looked like a rancher used to the harsh rigours of outdoor life. Wife Sue made a fuss of the horses. Duly called in for beers, we were introduced to friends David and Bonnie Osmundsen.

Again, hospitality was lavished on the new Butch and Sundance – more beers, the invitation to stay and later, thick juicy steaks with all the usual trimmings. A delightful evening melted away in a haze of mild drunkenness and gluttony. This time around, the richest rewards of riding the outlaw trail were perfectly legal, perhaps even compulsory.

We slept like babies and awoke late. The tantalising smells of sizzling bacon and percolated coffee heralded a serious breakfast before gathering up the horses. Good weather had returned, and by nine we were already riding the fifteen miles to the Rafter Y Ranch. Earlier, I had often complained we had no solid routine, but we were making up for it now, and running like Swiss Railways.

Meandering along a small track, we soon arrived at the dreaded Interstate Highway. Hemmed in by ditches, fences and cattle-grids, cars and trucks thundered past buffeting us with their slipstream. It was far too dangerous to take the horses along that route. I wanted to ride close to the De Smet Lake. Using the underpass we turned off the highway and became hamstrung by a forest of fences, which reintroduced us after a gap to the joys (and delays) of unravelling barbed wire.

RICHARD:

If that wasn't enough, we soon became stranded by a deep invisible arroyo in a pasture. At first, I couldn't get Yazz and his accomplice Bones to slide down the hard mud bank, but eventually, once Simon led the way with Sunday and Ditch, my two followed meek as you like. We had just wasted valuable time and topped up our blood pressure.

After safely connecting with Monument Road, we relaxed, thinking it would be a formality to proceed to Lake De Smet and turn off for Kearny. Until we came to a gate sporting a shiny new heavy-duty padlock, which clearly signalled an about turn and a long, ignominious retreat.

"I don't think I can cope with this shit," said Simon, with vivid memories of nightmare fence riding.

But before I could answer, a pickup drove slowly up behind us, stopped, and a burly individual stepped out. Braced for an officious tirade about private land and trespass, to our surprise the gate was gladly opened, with a cheerful reassurance that there were no further padlocks ahead.

At Kearny, we rode for Piney River. The Lake De Smet region was extremely fertile. Snow-capped Black Tooth Mountain and Cloud Peak towered over delightful houses tucked in the rolling golden hills. We continued over a bluff and were presented with the glorious blue waters of the lake shimmering under a fabulous bright sky. The same lake had flooded the back road, closing our path ahead. The water was far too deep to consider crossing with the horses. Choices were backtracking or taking a risk by riding over an awkward bluff.

"Now what?" asked Simon.

"Over the top," said I.

"You think we'll make it?"

"You can ride back if you want."

We dithered, we swore, and finally we thought, Sod it, and led the horses scrambling up the steep bank. Safely at the summit, we snaked down the ridge and skirted the floodplain into a fortunately shallow marsh – another anxious moment. We edged carefully through a grove of trees, and after a few minor hassles, not much over an hour later, we were comfortably relaxing at the Rafter Y Ranch owned by the charming Goodwin family.

Rafter Y is 140 miles west of the small township of Sundance, Wyoming, from whence Harry Longabaugh takes his famous sobriquet. Harry is heading for Montana in search of ranch work, and reaching the Triple V ranch in Sundance, on February 27, 1887, he steals a horse, saddle and gun from a ranch hand then rides directly for Miles City, Montana. Unfortunately, the Triple V is run by John Clay. As president of the Wyoming Stock Growers Association, he has immense clout.

Therefore, Sheriff James Ryan trails Harry extra zealously and finally arrests him in Miles. But instead of taking his prisoner directly back to Sundance, he boards a train to St Paul, Minnesota. Harry, with the assistance of an accomplice (who might just be Butch Cassidy), picks the locks of his shackles and handcuffs and jumps off the moving train while the Sheriff is attending to the needs of nature.

Foolishly, instead of clearing off for Hole-in-the-Wall, Harry returns to the Miles City area and is re-captured near the N Bar Ranch on Powder River by Sheriff Eph K Davis and Stock Inspector W Smith. There is no second escape – although Harry comes close when lodged in the Custer County jail. He manages to defeat the locks again and makes for the window, but Sheriff Davis pulls a gun and the game is up.

Harry is taken to Sundance by buckboard. Confined in the new jail, he is held on grand larceny charges. Sentenced to eighteen months, he makes repeated escape attempts and again nearly succeeds. On February 4, 1889, one day before his scheduled release, Harry is granted a full pardon. The Sundance Gazette writes on February 8: "The term of 'Kid' Longabaugh expired on Tuesday morning, and the young man at once hid himself to the Hills, taking the coach for Deadwood." Next time Harry is heard of, a couple of months later, he has become the Sundance Kid.

SIMON:

We departed for Sheridan. The trail took us through rolling green hills overshadowed by the Bighorns. Dome Peak dominated the horizon at 9,200 feet. We passed close to the famous Bozeman Trail and the historic site of the short-lived Fort Phil Kearny.

Forts Phil Kearny and CF Smith are built by the Army in 1866 in an unsuccessful bid to keep the Bozeman Trail open for would-be gold miners to cross land already treatied to the Lakota Sioux. The construction of these Forts signals the beginning of Red Cloud's War, and the tough old Sioux chief refuses to sign the Fort Laramie peace treaty twenty months later unless the Forts are abandoned. He gets his way.

The brief lives of these ill-fated Forts are filled with drama: constant shortages of troops, weapons and supplies, continual hit-

and-run raids on wood and forage parties by the Indians, the epic Hayfield and Wagon Box fights – which make military history by demonstrating the ability of repeating rifles with good fields of fire to balance huge odds. There is too, quite early on, the epic four-day ride for help by civilian guide John "Portugee" Phillips, and the reason for it – the infamous Fetterman massacre, when eighty soldiers under an over-confident commander are first decoyed (strictly against orders) into an ambush, then destroyed to the last man.

This triumphant coup for the Sioux also marks the tactical coming-of-age of the young Oglala warchief Crazy Horse, who leads the Fetterman decoy party, then ten years later is the key figure in the even greater destruction of Custer's command at the Little Bighorn.

RICHARD:

We jogged the horses through the sleepy settlements of Story and Banner – a smattering of houses surrounded by trees. Summer sun had turned the grass yellow. Irrigated fields splashed deep green under the white cumulus clouds drifting across the bright blue sky, and the distant hills looked black from being covered by pine trees.

The delightful Sue Means flagged us down and produced a fine packed lunch. We were being spoiled rotten and had to remind ourselves that the Outlaw Trail would rudely awaken us again. At the miniscule settlement of Bighorn, a character pulled in and introduced himself as Steve Kobold. Blond and stocky and in his early thirties, Steve was a highly recommended farrier we were hoping to meet later.

"I'll be along tomorrow to sort the horses out with new and alternative shoes."

We were intrigued.

After riding through the charming, leafy suburbs of Sheridan, we reined in at the Wilson's Animal Sanctuary. Money was extremely tight so we opted to sleep under the stars and shower in the YMCA opposite. Our planned day off was a busy one. Maps were required for the Tongue River section, along with re-supply of grain and foodstuffs, shoeing, visiting the local press plus an interview with Jack Cox of the Denver Post.

Doctor John Wilson ambled over to introduce himself, and we were instructed to make ourselves at home. Twenty minutes later, after cleaning up, we found the famous Mint Bar on Main Street. Simon and I were reluctant to pass up such an opportunity to slake our thirst. We finally managed to exit the welcoming water hole after three hours solid work at the bar, bantering – and in Simon's case, bullshitting – with the colourful locals, in the course of which I learned that we were not that far from a hard-to-find Butch and Sundance hideout in an isolated wilderness called the Cook Stove Basin.

To reach Cook Stove Basin, the outlaws ride out of the Hole-in-the-Wall to Ten Sleep, passing through Manderson and Greybull, trailing along the Bighorn River to the extreme northeast reach of the Bighorn Mountains.

Overlooking the Bighorn Canyon, the outlaws have an excellent base with fine grass, water and an abundance of game. There is a cabin in the basin built by another rustler, Sam Garvin. Horse thieves use this area during the 1880s and Kid Curry has a hideout across the gorge in the Prior Mountains. The outlaws ford the river at Chain Canyon, named for the barricade of chains the rustlers have suspended from bolts driven into the canyon's rock walls. Following the Wilcox robbery, Butch heads here for a short stay then rides north out of Prior Gap to Laurel, Montana, to hole up at Harvey Logan's Hideaway Coulee, located deep in the awkward Missouri Breaks country of Blaine County.

SIMON:

I was woken at four in the morning by a dog howling pitifully. Richard was still feeling no pain after the anaesthetic self-administered at the Mint Bar the previous evening, but I spent three hours nursing malevolent thoughts about man's best friend, taking time off only to complete our statistics, which made an impressive 1,514 miles in eighty-four riding days, or a whisker over eighteen miles per day.

Later that morning, we met Denver Post journalist Jack Cox, who over a liquid lunch expanded on his commemorative piece on the

Hill and Goldman movie. Jack intended to feature us in a September issue alongside Butch and Sundance and also actors Newman and Redford. We did our best to conceal our gratified smirks.

Back at the sanctuary, Dr Wilson had inspected our horses. We asked for an honest appraisal. John pronounced them to be in outstanding condition considering the journey they had endured. We breathed a sigh of relief.

A monumental horseshoeing job began at five-thirty that afternoon when Steve Kobold arrived. Steve had major plans. New shoes all round for our bunch. Apparently, special borium studs were to be welded onto the standard horseshoes. This necessitated heating the shoes in pairs until white-hot, then applying four blobs of a silvery compound, which in turn became hard as titanium when cooled.

"These will last for a year, but those studs will smash anything," warned Steve darkly. "If you've got kickers in the bunch, make sure they stay well apart."

In other words, the hooves of Yazz and Bones were now even more lethal weapons, which would kick the living shit out of any human or equine being that dared to invade their space. We would have to be doubly alert.

The impending route to Miles City led us back into remote country. We were informed, "You're on your own until Miles." The locals predicted a four or five day ride. There were no towns on the maps, just hamlets and remote outposts. We were looking at nothing more than old names. We reflected then brightened; remembering the nice lady in Buffalo had mentioned a family lived in Birney. And there was a possible stopover in Decker. It wasn't all bad.

"So what are we in for on this leg?" Richard queried.

"I don't know," I replied, trying not to remember where I had read that the southeast corner of Montana is a barren dust bowl plagued by droughts, insects and harsh conditions.

LICKING THE TONGUE

"Why are we killing ourselves? It's night…"
BUTCH CASSIDY

SIMON:

At 6.30 am on August 5, we left Wilson's Animal Sanctuary feeling pretty hyped up. Maybe it was the prospect of this next Tongue River leg being another endurance test. It was conveniently overcast, and we hoped for respite from the boiling heat of Wyoming. The horses walked well on their new shoes, the borium studs keeping the plates half an inch off the tarmac. Once on Main Street, the Sheridan Press ambushed us, took photos and announced we were to be featured on the front page. Great news!

We made our way towards Decker, a small settlement just into Montana that breaks the journey between Sheridan and Miles City. Along the way, we pass close to the Interstate 90 to Billings, on which the traffic streams by the site of the Little Bighorn battlefield. There on June 25, 1876, Custer and two-thirds of his vaunted Seventh Cavalry were wiped out by the biggest assembly of the Sioux tribes and their allies ever seen.

Gently rolling yellow hills stretched for miles, occasionally flecked by green tree clusters in the distance. Our enjoyment was marred when Richard announced that Bones might be slightly lame. We hoped it was just a slight tenderness following yesterday evening's shoeing. Later, the heat returned with renewed vigour, and it became most uncomfortable.

Nearly 150 miles to the east of us was the small town of Belle Fourche, South Dakota.

On June 28, 1897, the Butte County Bank in Belle Fourche, South Dakota, is in funds. The town has just come to the end of a lavish two day reunion of Civil War Veterans. Large sums of money have been pouring into the community, and much of it has now been deposited in the bank by local stores and other businesses.

Just before ten a.m. four riders dismount and hitch their horses at the bank's side entrance while two more wait across the street. Three of the four are Harvey Logan, Flat Nose Currie and the Sundance Kid – the fourth, Tom O'Day, holds the horses. The trio enters, and the robbery begins with the conventional instruction for everyone to raise their hands.

Head Cashier Arthur Marble bravely but unwisely reaches for a pistol under the counter, levels the gun, points it at Harvey Logan and pulls the trigger. It misfires – lucky Harvey. Logan turns to shoot but refrains when Marble lays down his weapon and raises both hands – lucky Arthur.

Flat Nose orders the customers to put their money in a sack, and one of them steps forward and drops in his takings. Meanwhile, nearby storeowner Alanson Giles happens to look out of his window and sees customers with their hands raised, so he races outside shouting, "They're robbing the bank!

Currie hears the shout and fires a shot through the glass door. This is the signal for the two robbers left outside to pull their guns and start shooting into the air to convince townsfolk it is only a couple of drunk cowboys playing pranks.

The sudden burst of gunfire spooks the horses, and as five of the outlaws jump onto their mounts for a fast exit, Tom O'Day's horse breaks free and joins the others on a dead run down Sixth Street. The escaping robbers check momentarily but don't hang about – they depart at speed, not slowed down at all by the weight of their haul, which is precisely $97.

Tom's loose horse is promptly shot. Tom himself attempts to escape on a nearby mule, but it won't do his bidding. Next, he ducks into an outhouse between Sebastian's Saloon and a printing office, but when *he comes out, he is stopped and held at gunpoint.*

Witnesses confirm that Tom has ridden into town with the bandits, yet when he is searched, he is found to have bullets but no gun. It is a nice try, but digging the dirt on the outhouse floor reveals a hidden pistol and bullets. He is taken into custody and held overnight. The Belle Fourche jail has recently been damaged in a fire so, ironically, Tom O'Day spends the night locked up in the bank vault.

Next day, he is transferred to a jail in Deadwood, South Dakota. It is almost certainly the jail in which Jack McCall was held a generation earlier, when he spoiled a good poker hand for James Butler (Wild Bill) Hickock by shooting the legendary holder in the back of the head.

Meanwhile, the other robbers head southwest into Wyoming for the Triple V Ranch. Hard on their heels is a posse led by Butte County Sheriff George Fuller, who gets close enough to shoot Sundance's horse. Despite which, and despite being surrounded in a timber tract by a huge posse of a hundred men, somehow, the outlaws slip away, some to Montana, some to the safety of Hole-in-the-Wall.

The Belle Fourche robbery is a botched affair with none of the meticulous planning and execution which are the hallmarks of Butch Cassidy or Elzy Lay. Harvey Logan nearly gets himself shot in the back, Tom O'Day is promptly jailed and Sundance has his horse shot out from under him. And all for $97 split six ways.

RICHARD:

We rode undisturbed and arrived at the Larsen place. Decker, Montana was nothing more than a handful of houses and ranches located between Sheridan and Miles City. The Larsens impressed us. They operated their ranch as a rawhide outfit – that is, doing things the old way, with horses. We were fed a very hearty late lunch, after which they suggested we stay overnight.

We mellowed out in the parlour and promptly fell asleep for the rest of the afternoon. Charlie Larsen woke us to point out we must make an early start – apparently, the daytime temperature tomorrow was going to rocket into the hundreds.

Southeast Montana was vast. We happily followed the river and used the invaluable GPS to mark off mileage. Altitude had fallen to around 3,000 feet, and the horizon was totally flat.

We headed off across the CX Ranchlands. Tall grass abounded, dotted with rocky outcrops, and we could see the faint outline of a bluff on the horizon. But all was not well with Sunday. As Simon led the ride, I saw that the mare's hind quarters displayed unmistakeable signs of an upset gut, and she soon began to groan loudly. I was alarmed but we were forced to ride on. At the pre-arranged rendezvous, we stopped for a rest, and by then Sunday's symptoms looked unnervingly like the onset of colic.

"I vote we ride for four hours," I said reluctantly. "The next ranch is about thirty-five miles away."

"Let's get on. We're not going to make big distance with the mare like that," said Simon. He accepted the inevitable but told me later he expected to have to walk both Sunday and Ditch for most of that time. But by ten to four, we were still riding along a single lane gravel road that follows the Tongue River.

Simon:

I developed what I think WWII fighter pilots called a Messerschmidt twitch: head rotating, eyes constantly peeled for the swarm of mosquitoes that might any moment come at us out of the sun. Gradually the scenery changed from the bleached yellow grass of Wyoming to a rich green. Within a further hour, the temperature suddenly dipped and rain began to spatter. We threw on the battered yellow slickers, superstitiously hoping to ward off the cloudburst. It worked: after three uneventful hours, we had completed nine dry miles. Sunday did a magnificent job bearing my weight, but, fearful of her condition, all I wanted was for her to rest with a decent feed as soon as possible.

We camped in old corrals opposite the Mulgrave Ranch. Turning the horses out to graze, I washed Sunday's hind end by the riverbank, keeping a wary eye on the others whilst Richard prepared dinner. I hoped the mare would improve before the twenty-two mile ride tomorrow. She remained motionless and refused to eat or drink. Later, when I grained up the horses, Sunday avoided the hard feed.

Like humans after a heavy night, nothing would go down.

I secured the horses in the corrals and laid out my bivvy. It was back to being regular outlaws in the bush. Much as I had enjoyed living high on the hog, I wasn't sorry to be back experiencing the Outlaw Trail the hard way, mixing the life styles as I knew Butch and Sundance had also done.

That afternoon, we had passed close to the site where allegedly Butch Cassidy was captured for the second time in his outlaw life. The location was the Isaac Kye Spring north of Decker, the year probably 1898.

Butch is on his way to rendezvous with Kid Curry at Miles City. He rests overnight with a friend who requests a favour: to take a message to another settler on the Ryegrass Creek. Butch stops there for a quick drink and is surprised by Deputy Sheriff Morgan who has tracked him carefully from Sheridan, Wyoming – a hundred miles distant.

Butch is trussed on his horse for the return. Eventually, Morgan decides his prisoner is safe and removes Butch's handcuffs. At Big Spring, it is Morgan's turn to water his horse, and in doing so, he bends over to release the bit from its mouth. Butch edges closer and seizes Morgan's pistol, reversing the situation. Morgan, now at gunpoint, has his hands tied behind his back, and is instructed to head for Sheridan on foot. Butch drives the Deputy's horse back over the trail knowing there is a ranch some five miles down the road. Again, Butch is very lucky to escape.

SIMON:

After a quiet night in the bush, we broke camp. Sunday seemed to have improved, and I was mighty relieved. The other bonus was no mosquitoes. The gravel road petered out and became a hard-packed dirt track. This country once belonged to the Lakota Sioux, who in 1876 fought with entirely unexpected tenacity and skill to defend it. George Crook, later the wisest of the Indian-fighting Generals, was badly outfought here at the Rosebud against Sioux and some Cheyennes, though he was not outnumbered. This was just eight days before Custer was taught an even more severe (and terminal) lesson at the Little Bighorn close by.

The exciting history drifting through my mind was dispelled as riding conditions, heat and dust steadily worsened. The horses slowed dramatically and, as promised by Charlie Larsen, the temperature rose to the late nineties. Next up for consideration was night riding, something we had vowed never to do.

The Montana sky was bright blue and stretched endlessly. At midday, we stopped briefly to water the horses, then pressed on. It was hard going.

Ditch, when lively, could always be relied on to break the monotony. As a ranch came into sight, a bunch of horses raced out to meet us, then wheeled and galloped back towards their corral. This was the signal, and Ditch took it right on cue. A mighty tug wrenched the rope clean out of my hand, and he raced off after the others with the panniers bumping, crashing and clattering. I cringed. Another expensive disaster was waiting to happen.

I turned Sunday and trotted into the ranch hoping to retrieve Ditch quickly. He saw my game and swerved as I attempted to snatch the rope. Weaving in and out of buildings, narrowly missing lethal machinery, the horses positively enjoyed the vigorous chase round the yard. Eventually, I stepped off in despair, so Ditch hurtled out of the gate, where Richard caught him effortlessly. Never a dull moment.

RICHARD:

We rode without incident until we arrived at the tiny settlement of Birney. Here it was my turn to endure horse trouble coaxing an extremely reluctant Bones to cross the bridge.

Birney was a one-horse township boasting a school, a post office and a dirt-track Main Street flanked by old wooden houses sheltering under cottonwood trees. We quietly rode through, wondering if anyone would notice us. Within minutes, we were hailed in for a cool beer and a friendly chat with interested locals.

The Bones Brothers spread was another two miles east into the foothills. After Simon had coped with yet another escape attempt by Ditch, the Aldersons made us very welcome. Ranching here hadn't changed since the turn of the century.

"Tomorrow will be ninety-eight, going into the hundreds," remarked Irv Alderson, a huge, rugged man.

"Tough on the horses, too, so rest then head out in the evening."

We were shown to a splendid log bungalow.

Late the following afternoon, well rested and cherishing the memory of a light-hearted dip in the Tongue River, we saddled up and rode out. It was still remarkably light and warm at seven-thirty, but I was slightly concerned – we possessed no lights, not even stirrup reflectors. Any passing night traffic would not expect riders in so remote an area.

As the light ebbed, we gradually acquired our night vision. The chill penetrated, and I regretted not bringing my dustcoat. The horses were at ease for five hours, the moon shone and we rode on, hooves muffled by the sandy track, shuffling along eerily like a ghost column. At 0100 hours, I fought off the first wave of drowsiness. Normally we were in our bedrolls by ten.

We rode like clockwork, letting the horses have their heads. We lost track of time. Hours later, in the pre-dawn glow, silhouetted buildings appeared on the outskirts of Ashland. The tally of twenty-seven miles had been completed with no fuss. I decided we would night ride to Miles City if the heat continued.

SIMON:

We reined in at White Moon Park. Burgers for breakfast were rapidly demolished, and we set about camping. I drew the short straw to watch the horses whilst Richard caught up on shuteye. Typically, the best grazing was close to the road, and the horses made for it. I spent three hours chasing them back onto the park, fearful of early, fast-moving vehicles.

When Richard woke later, I tried to sleep. It was useless; my body clock was totally out of sync. With some kind help from a very friendly Don Bixby, out for his morning stroll, we tracked down the sole and unexpected source of grain: the local Amish community.

Then, left to our own devices, the heat increased to ridiculous proportions, and we dozed beneath the shade of the trees to kill time.

We delayed our departure until nine p.m. There was much traffic until the seven-mile marker; thereafter, not a single car passed us until morning.

Night riding had its own special character: minimum communication, hard to judge anything, impossible to gauge mileage. The horses plodded along and we swayed to their motion, semi-conscious much of the time. At four a.m., we reined in at the Bull Ranch – it looked deserted. We were exhausted. After we lied almost comatose on the floor for an hour holding the horses, Don Bixby arrived with our gear, by arrangement, then very decently elected to drive to the next spread six miles ahead. The bush telegraph, old-style. But for us, another two hours of riding was necessary.

We continued on autopilot. Virtually falling out of the saddle with fatigue, we trudged onward; the dirt track splitting baked golden-brown fields before pitching outside the Sixes Ranch. Impromptu camp was adjacent to the road. We turned the horses into a pasture, quickly strung a flysheet lest the rains come, then acute tiredness hit. We urgently needed sleep before the final stretch of night riding.

Later, I walked up to ranch HQ and begged fresh water to top up our canteens. It was an opportunity to learn what to expect further along the trail. Ominously, I was informed there were no ranch houses until just south of Miles City.

Gazing across the range, my thoughts turned to the latter-day homesteaders. This was *Grapes of Wrath* country, the harsh and fragile farmlands which so readily became bankrupting dustbowls in the Great Depression and were immortalised by Steinbeck, John Ford and Henry Fonda.

We caught the horses, packed and were riding by eight. Next stop was the Brandenburg Gate. It was cooler and large bands of grey cloud drifted over the bleak plains. Dark came quickly and temperature plummeted, signs of an unfriendly weather change. As the impending storm stole up on us, so did tiredness.

Hours later, without warning, my saddle slipped, making Sunday spook. The action jolted me back to sharper senses – I'd been half-dozing. The mare drifted towards a ditch, stumbled and lost her footing. I leapt clear and yelled for Richard. Grabbing the saddle to stop it sliding under her belly, I also kept a tight hold on Ditch in case he tried to make one of his runs.

Richard wheeled and took the gelding. Sunday was a tremendous horse and waited patiently for me to unhitch pommel and saddlebags, canteens and rifle. I rapidly re-saddled, cinched and re-fixed my outfit just in time for the long-threatened rain to descend.

The heavens burst. A vicious wind lashed us mercilessly and rain drove in. We no longer had any suitable wet weather clothing (the old battered yellow slickers had long ceased to offer adequate protection). For over two hours, my denims bravely held off the worst of the elements. But inevitably, at a certain saturation point, a small trickle of water ran down my back, became a flood and within seconds it was as if I were standing naked under a waterfall. Cold penetrated my bones; the wind howled.

Thankfully, a tailwind kept the horses moving. Energy drained as we rode on blindly to Miles. I called out to Richard, or thought I did. Maybe I was hallucinating. We pounded on relentlessly, sodden, cold, exhausted and deeply dejected.

I pressed Sunday and caught up with Richard who was huddled over the pommel of his saddle.

"You soaked through?" I shouted over the howling wind.

"Yeah, what about you?"

"Freezing – have been for hours," I replied, seeking a comforting remark.

"Get out of the saddle, walk to raise your body temperature – keep functioning, we can't stop," Richard instructed firmly.

For the next hour, I trailed and staggered along, flanked by my trusty horses.

"There's a light over there – to our left," I yelled with hope an hour later.

"I see nothing," replied Richard, cutting the conversation dead.

We continued in undiluted misery. Who would go walking in a shitty thunderstorm in the early hours? Two British idiots pretending to be Butch and Sundance, that's who! For all the desert riding and endless heat endured from Mexico, freezing conditions on the way to Monument Valley and the spectacular thunderstorm near Green River, the ride between Ashland and Garland, Montana topped the league.

Moments like these made me consider the robustness of Butch and Sundance. They too would have endured appalling weather. They were outlaws on the dodge, not fair-weather riders. I re-conditioned my mind. Stop thinking like a tenderfoot, I told myself. Crap weather was simply another unpleasant reality of horseback exploring.

On a positive note, I like to believe the horses stayed close to us for comfort and security. Despite our earlier chastisement of Barbara for horse petting, both Richard and I had finally succumbed and bonded totally with our mounts.

Later, I felt a new surface underfoot. Tarmac! We had measured the map and knew this was the seventeen-mile marker. Hope stirred at the thought of stopping, but it was still dark and raining heavily. There was no opportunity to rest. Two hours crept by, then I spied a solitary yellow light burning through the mist. It shone like a beacon. I made out the shape of a barn and called out to Richard. We stopped and backed up twenty yards. A cluster of mailboxes could be seen on a gate.

"Let's check it out. We've done enough for tonight, and the horses are tired,'" I pleaded.

"What does it say?"

"Triangle T Ranch."

"We'll take a look, but it seems deserted."

"It's five in the morning, someone should be up soon," I begged.

Within seconds, the chill abated. The power of the mind is extraordinary. Wringing wet clothes and cowboy boots full of water made no impact as we squelched up the muddy drive and parked the horses in a barn. We hung blankets, saddles, tack and clothing up to dry, then we grained the horses. We were discussing what to do about what was technically a serious breach of Western etiquette when suddenly a woman appeared from nowhere. We froze guiltily. What would she do? Attack or retreat? Hysterics or summon the Rottweilers?

"Hi – I've got to get my car out. Mind if you move the horses?" this admirable lady requested nonchalantly.

Richard and I were stunned. Was this an everyday event in Montana? Two armed strangers and four horses in your barn at five in the morning? In this weather, apparently so. In England, the fan would have slung shit as far as the moon.

"Of course," I replied, adding belatedly but as courteously as I could, "We've come from Ashland and got caught in the thunderstorm – may we dry out in here please?"

"Sure. I'll tell my mother so she doesn't get a shock," replied Robyn Baker, a short lady with black hair and glasses.

We formally introduced ourselves and explained that we had ridden up from Mexico.

"You'd better stay and clean up. My mother will be around soon."

The car drove off. Turning the horses out into a corral, we began to inspect the sodden equipment. Half an hour later, another lady appeared.

"I'm Marilyn Fortune, Robyn's mother. Heard you got caught in the storm. Best take you to the line camp and get cleaned up. There's a boot dryer there too – place is used for hunters."

At fifty-something (I guess), Marilyn was typical of the best of the old-style ranching matriarchs. She had seen and done it all. Our arrival never fazed her for a moment. She was a forthright but charming lady who epitomised the Code of the West.

The line camp was a huge mobile home set in a pasture with its own gravel driveway. We de-camped and re-camped, removed our soaking clothes to the laundry room and showered. We felt civilised.

"I'll keep an eye on the horses – you rest. Be back later," called Marilyn.

No shuteye for three consecutive nights made us oversleep. Richard woke me four hours later.

"Laundry's gone."

"We're not leaving in a hurry then are we?" I replied.

"We didn't feed the horses either," Richard pointed out.

"They were turned loose next to a hay stack."

No self-respecting rider steps off his horse without seeing to their welfare – fresh water and ample hay are the minimum.

Later, we returned to HQ to meet Robyn Baker properly. The aroma of hot coffee, bacon and omelette was welcoming. Splendid ranch fare was set down. Unashamedly, we devoured a huge plateful of food and seconds. Conversation turned to the storm and our travels. It had been a gruelling ride from Decker. I apologised to Richard for fading so badly, but we agreed one of us had to give out first. Just as we finished the meal and contemplated our next move, shattering news was delivered:

"We checked the horses over. They look good but are a little tired. But the black is lame. We trailered him into Miles City for a second opinion," Marilyn reported.

In the dark, it would have been impossible for us to perceive a problem. Yazz was a warrior horse, but this was a serious worry.

"When we left yesterday he was fine," I pleaded.

"He may have bruised his hoof on a stone; the road's not that good," Marilyn replied matter-of-factly.

"How bad is he?" Richard queried.

"He might need a few days rest. Cal Davidson, our vet, removed a shoe and bandaged his hoof."

RICHARD:

Simon and I exchanged glances. We were down to three horses. I wondered whether the new shoes had been nailed on too tight – unlikely, since Steve Kobold was highly regarded as an excellent farrier.

Yazz was heading for a temporary rest, and I hoped he could be trail-headed and meet us later. Meanwhile, we would have to continue with just Bones, Sunday and Ditch. Later, Simon rang Bruce and Sandie Lockie, relatives of Zane and Ginger Fross at Lost Cabin, Wyoming to finalize a stopover in Miles City. This had possibilities for some fun, and I wanted to hit a few bars before crossing the Missouri Breaks. Miles was the last sizeable town before Canada.

We stayed a second night at the Triangle T. The hospitality and care had been second to none. Folk were becoming increasingly interested in our following Butch and Sundance's footsteps. We realised that many ranchers had disregarded or just taken for granted the outlaw trail history. A lot of nonsense has been written about Butch and Sundance, but the people we met had a definite empathy with our mission, rekindling through and with us their interest in the Old West, and a slice of their own history. If Simon and I occasionally breathed life back into some old, taken-for-granted dying embers, we felt privileged to do so.

It pained me deeply that Yazz looked like not completing the ride. Before setting out, we had confirmation he had punctured a hoof, although not badly. It might be possible to use him later, perhaps in a fortnight's time; however, there could be a risk of ruining the horse. I retired, checked dates (August 12) and our statistics – 1,653 miles in ninety days, averaging 18.36 per day. Tomorrow's mileage, calculated at twenty-three, made the Tongue River section a brutal 162 miles long.

We rode out on Bones and Ditch. Sunday and the packs were being expressed into Miles City later. Unbelievably, the weather forecast was hot, a total contrast to the last two days of exceedingly wet weather. Back on tarmac, we passed smallholdings scattered along the roadside. The flat yellow-brown country had been devoid of rain for over two months, and the grass verges sloshed with water.

We trotted along the barrow pit to save the horses' hooves and cannon bones from pounding the tarmac. Blue sky was dotted with small, white, puffy clouds against the burnt yellow and beige landscape. North of the junction where highways 232 and 59 meet, we forked left and calculated our journey into town to be ten miles. Bones and Ditch had nothing to spare, so Simon and I walked the remainder of the way.

Miles City reminded us of Lander: neat gardens, quiet, charming suburbs and pretty wooden houses that had been around since the turn of the century. We sat down for a short break, and moments later, a truck pulled over. Out stepped Bruce Lockie, who introduced himself and reported that the horses were booked into the Livestock Commission Yard.

We rode over the tracks, crossed the iron bridge (dating from 1897) which spanned the Tongue. I wondered if Butch and Sundance ever used the bridge and the livestock pens. The horses would be here for four days resting.

We retired to the Lockie's fine residence and related our travels over a barbecue. Bruce and Sandie advised that the "Breaks" section posed problems: difficulty picking up the trail northwest of town and vast lines of barbed wire. Bruce agreed to phone ranchers ahead and check on travel conditions. A second problem was that the Missouri

River had been dammed to create Fort Peck Lake Recreational Area – another Lake Powell-type concept.

Simon's original plan was to cross at Rocky Point where the outlaws did, but no ferries operated. We knew exactly where the trail led, but there was no opportunity to re-supply until Malta once we left Miles City. And we were relying on one packhorse to carry provisions when we needed two. Locals disliked our intended route to Sand Springs, a four-day ride away. The reason was no water fit for human consumption. If we drank from springs or rivers they said we would be squatting instead of riding.

SIMON:

Cal Davidson, Miles City's vet, confirmed that Yazz could not resume the ride. We had hoped a special shoe could be fitted, sealing the hoof to keep it clean, dry and infection free. Richard took the bad news remarkably well.

Then Cal told us the local brand inspector needed to see our horse papers. Ours had passed their dump by date the minute we left Arizona. Now it was too late to worry. It all depended on the attitude of the local officials. Maybe these things arranged themselves with a shrug and a smile, Italian style. Or maybe it would be the bureaucratic stereotype: rules are rules, and must be obeyed. In which case, the trip was over, the cup dashed from our lips.

Feeling tense, we confessed our sins of omission to Cal, who immediately said that he would do Coggins Tests and handle the brand inspections. It transpired the brand inspector's office was next door!

Relieved, we left to meet our Triangle T hostess Marilyn Fortune who, knowing our situation, had kindly arranged breakfast with the inspector himself. Gary Anderson looked very tall and upright, the picture of no nonsense probity. We took a table, and I meekly handed over our out-of-date paperwork, explaining as confidently as I could that we had carried them from Mexico.

Gary nodded, smiled then sifted through ownership papers, brand inspections, horse registrations and bills of sale.

Coffees were poured and the first of the food arrived. Gary

continued scrutinising the documents. We momentarily lost our tongues and appetites. The papers were as much use as a bunch of used bus tickets.

Gary looked up at us gravely and paused. Our hearts went pitter pat. Then he smiled:

"Well, these papers ain't much use, but we'll get you boys on the road as soon as!"

RICHARD:

Back in business. Miles City and the Lockie's generous hospitality had been superb. High time to celebrate. Unfortunately for me, a state fair had emptied the old cow town of all its sparkle, including the female talent. I dragged Simon to check all the bars – they were empty. The quiet was unbelievable. I'd ridden nearly two thousand miles and was ready for alcohol, women and a good time, in any order you like. We bellied up inside an old saloon. The old wooden bar looked like it had played host for over a century. We popped a couple of beers. We were close to the end of our trail.

"Zortman, then Malta, and that's it – we're home and dry!" Simon proclaimed. We touched beers and drank to that.

I gazed into the big, old mirror behind the bar and wondered how much history it had reflected right here. We relaxed and mellowed out pleasurably in the smoky confines of Miles City's finest before stepping out into the cool night.

BADLANDS &
MISSOURI BREAKS

"Come on, you guys!"
BUTCH & SUNDANCE

SIMON:

It was August 18. We had zero funds and we were down to three horses. More horse trouble would jeopardise our Canadian finish, and thus our entire project. We were under severe pressure. Ending the 2,000 mile ride on lousy bicycles was not part of our plans.

We tramped through thick mud, hastily packing kit for the tough section ahead. Yazz was loaded into a trailer bound for the Triangle T Ranch. Richard bade him adios. We felt bad. We brushed aside our feelings and swung into the saddle for the thirty-one mile ride to Angela – though Bones, who had followed Yazz blindly, pulled back at the moment of departure. Soon, we were clip-clopping down a buzzing Main Street and were caught on camera by the local newspaper.

The route for Butch and Sundance was to follow South Sunday Creek, heading northwest across the plains to Button Butte, a key landmark, before taking a rough trail to Rocky Point. Today, South Sunday Creek is inaccessible due to a mass of fencing. Instead, we opted to ride along North Sunday Creek paralleling the road to Angela. It was legitimate and it led the outlaws to Wolf Point.

Sundance worked here for the renowned N Bar N Ranch on the Little

Dry Creek. The outfit ran cattle on the open range between Wolf Point and Rock Creek to Miles City. In 1886 Sundance, then still known as Harry Longabaugh, signed on to a cattle drive along the route from Texas to Montana. Harry had ridden north to find work, learning that the N Bar N ran around 50,000 head of cattle and employed 150 people. Interestingly, the Curry Brothers were working for the MacNamaro-Marlow outfit near Big Sandy, handling their horses on a share basis. Harry, later as Sundance, and Harvey Curry, who became Kid Curry, first met here in Montana.

The Yellowstone was a wide, dirty brown, fast-flowing river. We crossed the bridge, trekking slowly up the long incline. Cars and trucks rattled past, ever closer to the horses. Travelling here was dangerous.

The land flattened, and brilliant yellow-gold fields stretched endlessly. A black, single-lane tarmac road cut a neat swathe paving our trail towards the horizon. It was a pretty picture with no fences to spoil the landscape. A smattering of white clouds drifted aimlessly across the pale blue sky.

Riding Bones, Richard pulled ahead. Fearing the mare's fierce temper, Ditch held back. Sunday, in a span formation with him, tried to race and snapped frequently to force Ditch behind. I hung on doggedly to both.

An hour later, a truck passed and pulled over. A rancher in his early sixties closely watched the horses' paces.

"Hi, I'm Artie Larson – that grey's maybe slightly lame," he announced, pointing to Sunday.

"Which leg?" I replied, absolutely mortified.

"Difficult to tell – saw her favouring the fore. I'll be passing again in an hour – we'll take a closer look then." Artie roared off towards Miles City. So used was I to the outgoing Western style, the concept of a con-man-slash-car-thief never entered my mind. Ditch was refusing to jog, and Richard had pulled ahead and disappeared. I sat back in the saddle ready for a long, uncomfortable day.

At the eighteen-mile marker, Artie returned with trailer.

"Load her up. I'll take her to my ranch at Hillside. You'll be there tomorrow. No sense in working her," he instructed.

"Thanks," I replied. "When you pass my partner, tell him what's happening."

I watched my mare depart. It was unbelievable. First Yazz, and now Sunday. Both saddle horses seemingly were out. Two horses remained. I was depressed by the implications.

We continued up a long gradient. Ditch, perhaps feeling lonely, whinnied incessantly. I checked my watch: five-thirty, and nine hours' riding done. I saw buildings, farm machinery and a solitary horse grazing. Richard had already been relaxing for nearly an hour.

"Thought you weren't coming."

"Yeah? Sunday looked lame. Guy called Artie Larson hauled her to his place at Hillside. He's expecting us tomorrow."

We rode out early for the seventeen-mile rendezvous. It was refreshingly cool.

"Bones might have sore feet," Richard remarked.

"Shit. You're kidding – are you certain?"

"It's that or something else. I can't detect it yet, but she's not quite right."

"If Sunday's out, looks like we'll be two up on Ditch," I replied.

It was unbelievable. No hoof problems had occurred with any of the horses until the Triangle T. Granted, the horses had come a long way. No wonder Butch and Sundance frequently switched horses when they were not pushing a large string.

We made exceptional time walking and jogging through an expanse of unfenced country and arrived at eleven a.m. I saw Sunday in the corrals alone. We stepped down.

"The grey is fine," announced Artie, striding out of an office next to the horse barn. "Wanna beer?"

It would have been rude to refuse, so we forced ourselves.

"We're with you," I replied, shaking hands.

Bones and Ditch rejoined the mare. We sat in the cool office sipping beer and discussing the last shoeing. Were the studs too long? Were the shoes too tight? Was it just that the horses were plain footsore? Artie realised we were very concerned, for which ailment the prescription was more beers produced from a fridge bulging with horse remedies. As we worked our way steadily through its contents, getting slightly tipsy in the process, I wondered if we had consumed anything marked with a skull and crossbones.

"Well, you've come a long ways," said Artie. "Food is served; let's go get some." Mrs Larson had prepared lunch, and we were forthwith invited to stay overnight in a mobile home. Remarkable people.

Discussions focused on the route ahead. We would ride to the west fork of Thompson Creek and on to Jim Williams' place at Spring Coulee. Butch and Sundance's Wild Bunch ran close to the Sunday Creeks, but it was guesswork precisely where. Much would have depended on the reason for their passage: re-supply with friendly ranchers, fast riding for escape or cautiously taking the remotest track to the next hideout.

Originally, our route involved following the Little Porcupine Creek around Crown Butte, crossing McGinnis and Big Dry Creeks, and turning west of Sand Springs near O'Day Butte. McGinnis and O'Day were outlaw names, and we believed this to be the top of their run in to the Missouri River crossing at Rocky Point.

The talk turned to land usage, ranching and (inevitably) what the Democrats had gotten wrong. Artie was dismissive of politicians:

"They're all fucked up. Take Clinton: he's redefined sex and drugs – he don't come and he don't inhale. Must be the only man on God's earth who does neither."

Artie paced up and down the office throwing more beers, changing subjects rapidly and peppering his speech with expletives. It was highly entertaining. By four-thirty, we were in danger of being seriously over-lubricated.

"Your bay mare might have a very slight bow in the tendon," Artie threw in.

Despite being mildly drunk, Artie's comment struck a chord. Bones was not our horse. I began to be concerned about having to inform Tom Klumker, but more beers and a fine evening meal effectively numbed the worry. We went to bed pissed. And the Larsons? They were absolutely first class.

RICHARD:

The following morning after breakfast, we assisted at a round-up. It was a hugely enjoyable first for me. Sunday, Simon's mare, was an ex-ranch horse and knew the drill. She relished chasing strays, weaving in and out and riding herd on steer intent on escaping the corrals. This activity seemed to compare pretty favourably with sitting astride a horse and riding mindlessly across America.

It was seventeen miles to the Williams's place on Christenson Creek. The land was changing from endless yellows and greens to a familiar rougher and rockier terrain. The colours brought back memories of the high desert in Utah. Mule deer and antelope bounded from our path as we edged closer to more remote country.

Bones was favouring a foreleg, and I regularly checked whether she was heating up, a symptom which spelled imminent trouble. Through the rolling hills, I wondered when our rendezvous would present itself. Simon often glassed the horizon and reported nothing. After four hours of riding, we topped a ridge. The Williams's Ranch lay in a shallow depression. Jim appeared from a building, said hello, helped settle the horses, then we settled down for a clean up and a beer.

That evening, Jim's friend Tom Horn hosted us for dinner. The original Horn was the infamous Government scout, muleteer, stock detective and bounty hunter. Over a superb chicken dinner, the latter-day Tom hinted that he might be a distant relative. Bells rang with Simon, who enthusiastically reeled off historical facts about this shadowy character and his highly dubious end.

Tom Horn is employed by the cattle bosses as a range detective in the Iron Mountain country near Bosler, Wyoming. Perhaps on orders from his employers, Horn becomes involved in a local feud. As part of his job (as he sees it), Horn prepares to dispatch one of the protagonists, but tragically, the target's horse, hat and slicker have been borrowed by his fourteen-year-old son.

Mistaken identity seals the fate of the boy, or so the story goes, and Tom Horn is accused of the murder on the basis of circumstantial evidence. Suspiciously, fellow man-hunter (and competitor) Joe LeFors is the man instrumental in Horn's very dubious entrapment and conviction.

Members of the Wild Bunch are believed to be planning a jailbreak. The threat is taken seriously, and extra guards are drafted in to keep watch. Locally, odds are given that Butch Cassidy will set Tom free.

Horn even wakes to see a message written in the snow outside his cell window. It reads, "Keep Your Nerve." Tom waits, Butch never comes, and the execution takes place on November 20, 1903.

SIMON:

Next day, we rode for five miles before a ridge blocked our path. We cautiously picked our way over the grassy bluff. A faint track led to the Beecher place. Following Little Dry Creek, altitude hovered between 3,000 and 3,500 feet. The low, rolling hills stretched for miles. Sparsely populated Montana promised a thin scattering of ranches until we reached the Missouri River. Richard was being strangely reticent about the routing until eventually I queried brusquely, "Where the hell are we?"

"Keep guessing; you might have a nice surprise later."

"Thanks," I said ironically. "I look forward to a decent bed and a steak dinner."

"You may be lucky yet."

The banter was comfortable, and we continued through low hills, sticking religiously to the dirt road. Two hours later, Richard stopped at a fork and grinned.

"Well?" I asked.

"Which way then?"

I pointed north. It was getting late. We topped another ridge and continued down a draw. A ranch appeared. So did two dogs barking their heads off. They bounded over to meet us. Moments later, a back door opened. I wondered whether our invasion would be repelled by a gun-toting farmer.

"Step off those horses! Got your call – didn't know whether you'd be ridin' through. We don't see many horsemen passing through these parts," said the man.

"You must be Gus Glasscock?" I replied neutrally. We had learned that even if we arrived recommended, we mustn't assume hospitality until invited.

"Pretty remote here," I commented.

"We like it. Moved out of Texas. Still has the feel of the Old West. How does beef sound to you guys?"

Richard winked at me. Accommodation and steak as promised!

In the kitchen, Karen, Gus's wife, was cooking up a serious dinner. Steak was on tap of killer proportions. We devoured a plate load with all the trimmings; the meat feasts were becoming legendary.

The talk turned to the subject of isolation, but it never affected everyday living despite Lewiston being one hundred miles away. The Glasscocks revered their lifestyle and shared many Westerners' belief that the only way to get here was to be born here. We slept like babies.

When we got back to business in the morning, a grinding thirty-mile trek loomed. Within minutes, a pickup appeared, stopped and flagged us. Two cowboys bowled over, grinning. Bill Brown introduced himself, told us how to find his ranch, and said he would see us later.

As we jogged along a dirt track for three hours, the wind gusted incessantly. Dreaded fences appeared, and we contemplated uneasily a day of line riding and reduced mileage. Richard was on a bearing and wasn't changing direction.

Soon our path was hemmed, and we cursed. There were no gates for miles. Shit! Using my Leatherman, I prised staples from the posts, and we slackened the barbed wire, Richard standing on it and both of us holding our breath as all three horses stepped delicately through. Relief. We repeated the process twice more then crashed through a cornfield. Down a draw we disappeared, passed a deserted property and connected onto Route 200.

We stopped at a remote post office and store denoted as Sand Springs. It was closed. Out of luck, we devoured a tin of sardines whilst the horses grazed contentedly. After that, everything ran like clockwork, and four hours later, we reined in at the LO Bar Ranch.

Bill Brown, a slight rancher in his sixties, inspected Bones. The bay mare had been out of sorts for three days. She wasn't lame, nor did she have any visible sign of injury, but something was wrong.

"Reckon you can get to Canada with two horses?" Bill quizzed.

"We'll have to somehow. What's up?" I replied, knowing no funds were available for replacement.

"She might get a bowed tendon if you carry on. There's something, but it's impossible to say what. Best leave her with me and be sure," advised Bill.

Sunday and Ditch would have to bear us to the border.

We were shown to the bunkhouse. A trip to Curry Coulee was planned for tomorrow to see a Kid Curry hideout I'd not heard of. The Browns also mentioned that a character called Joe Gibson would advise us through the Breaks and the Weingart place. We pored over BLM maps.

Returning from Jordan after dinner, the dark, starlit Montana night sky suddenly changed colour. A greenish luminance attracted our attention. Swirling columns flickered and grew brighter. The sky was alive. We looked at the heavens. Bands split, dancing, cascading, wavered then diminished. The spectacle lasted a few minutes, and we gaped in awe. It was my first sighting of the *aurora borealis*, and we retired well pleased with such a rare experience.

When Joe Gibson arrived, he reminded me of Whisky Pete: unshaven, long, drooping moustache and decked out in Wrangler jeans and boots. We pulled out for Sand Springs. The ride took us across country to a place called Benzien. At least, I think it was a place. It certainly wasn't a town!

Joe eventually drove down a gradient bumping to the edge of a bluff where the heat hit us full on. It was over a hundred. We stood at the edge and gazed. Joe pointed out Curry Coulee draining out of Little Squaw Creek. Interlocking hills and spurs overlapped, juniper trees dotted the slopes and the grass was bleached brown.

"Did the Kid have a cabin?" I asked.

"Sure."

"Does it still exist?"

"I think so – it's real hard to find. I'm not certain anyone knows the location," Joe replied pensively.

Richard and I both had a look round – part of the fun of following Butch and Sundance was trying to find secret hideouts. We tried to think like outlaws. Where would we build a cabin? It didn't take us long to realise the odds against our finding anything were of lottery-winning proportions. So nothing new for the history books.

August 24. Bones remained at the LO Bar. It was illogical to risk a permanent injury. The mare had done an astonishing job from Alma, New Mexico and deserved rest. She had been our best packhorse, but was clearly tired. We would collect her and the remaining gear on our return from Canada.

We resumed our travels. I rode Ditch, leaving Sunday for Richard, who was lighter.

An overcast morning gave way to relentless heat as we reached the Missouri Breaks. Temperature was now one hundred degrees, altitude had dropped to 2,700 feet and the undulating hills became interspersed with rocky outcrops, steep slopes and deep draws. The horses were hot and sweaty.

At Calf Creek, a series of coulees forced us to tack laterally over continuous swales. Taking a direct line was impossible for the horses, and we resigned ourselves to a long day weaving around obstacles, including fences.

Finally, we arrived at Stocker Coulee. Across the flats ranch, buildings appeared, and the leathery-looking Chuck Rich welcomed us. Brothers Art and Ed had returned to the family seat and brought their wives for the annual reunion. The ladies had prepared a late lunch, and we joined them. The heat was nothing short of brutal, and we were in no hurry to resume riding. We were much happier polishing off glasses of iced tea and double helpings of salad.

At six p.m., we departed. The Rich brothers led us to a shortcut for the Harris's place on Musselshell River. Soon, we found ourselves riding up and down more steep coulees. Sunday and Ditch competed vigorously with the other horses. An hour later, our guides departed. Deer were plentiful, then dusk began closing in, and we urged the horses onward.

Richard checked the map and announced we were virtually on the Blood Creek. Despite the gathering darkness, our presence had not gone unnoticed. As we rejoined the dirt track, a truck drove to meet us. I found it uncanny. Newlyweds Bill and Vicky Harris invited us in. Hospitality-wise, Montana was taking the gold medal. It was embarrassing, but we needed the Code of the West more than ever. Cash was low and our horses were very tired.

RICHARD:

Next day, we crossed the Musselshell River in the gravelly shallows, wary of sinking into sand. Unbelievably, a fence impeded us and necessitated careful negotiation along a path no more than a foot wide overhanging the river. It would have been impossible with packhorses. We followed a dirt track and topped a ridge. The Musselshell Valley was pretty country – golden grass burnt by the sun, flecked with junipers and firs.

Further north, the land flattened again. Looming out of the haze on the horizon were the Little Rocky Mountains, some forty miles distant. These were the "island" mountains, and according to Simon, Butch and Sundance only had to keep them in their sights to reach the tiny mining town of Landusky, a significant town in Wild Bunch history.

I could feel our adventure beginning to ebb away. Months earlier, the ride had been in jeopardy, and now, suddenly we were within eleven days riding of Canada. I had enjoyed the stark beauty of America, and also meeting some wonderful people. Following Barbara's departure, we had developed a level of amiable banter not too dissimilar from that projected by Butch and Sundance in the classic movie. Well, maybe not as witty, but close.

We passed Horse Camp on Crooked Creek, where the Horse Camp Trail connects with the Skyline Trail. These were just names on the map until Simon explained their significance. Apparently, the Wild Bunch used the Skyline Trail to reach Button Butte. This hump on the range was a useful marker that led due north to Rocky Point where Butch and the gang used to cross the Missouri River.

The outlaws' quickest route to Rocky Point was a trail leading round Sandstrom Coulee to Haines Ridge. We were unable to cross the Missouri here since the ferry no longer operated, and we knew it was suicidal to attempt swimming horses across.

Kid Curry saves his partner's life when they try swimming cattle over the Missouri for the Circle C Ranch. Jim Thornhill's horse gives out in the middle of the river. Thornhill is no swimmer. Curry swims his horse and manages to grab hold of the half-drowned Thornhill and pull him across the saddle horn to safety. Curry himself bales out, hangs onto a steer's tail and eventually they both manage to get ashore. In later years, Thornhill remarks: "Curry couldn't swim a lick, either."

At this time (around 1885), Rocky Point has long been more than just a ferry crossing. The trading post is a hangout for wolfers and whisky peddlers. It boasts a small saloon and a hotel that serves meals. As early as the 1870s, Rocky Point already enjoys a tough reputation, and a decade later, at the height of the steamboat era, gangs of horse-thieves make it a rendezvous.

SIMON:

We had a great night under the stars. Once the moon was up, it was uncannily light, almost as bright as early daylight. Thoughts wandered to Kid Curry and The Sundance Kid, who spent more time than the others in Montana.

On or around September 18, 1879, Sundance and Walt Punteney meet up with Kid Curry and probably Tom O'Day. They travel to Red Lodge, Montana to carry out a bank robbery. Their plans are thwarted when an optimistic attempt to bribe a local town marshal fails. Instead, they are recognised and reported. They make their escape empty-handed.

A posse is formed, headed up by Sheriff John Dunn. The outlaws are pursued through Big Timber, past the Murphy Ranch where Sundance once worked and on to Widow Ranch near Painted Robe. The posse arrives in Lavina, Montana, a small, sleepy town in remote country.

Sundance is blissfully unaware of being pursued. The outlaws make camp for the night at a spring on the Musselshell River, possibly on the way to Hideaway Coulee. While Curry tends his horse, the posse suddenly appears, and panic ensues.

Punteney jumps behind the edge of a small bluff. Sundance makes a rush for his horse and springs into the saddle. According to one version, he draws his Winchester and slides Indian fashion down the far side of the horse from the posse. But the animal falls, breaking its neck. Sundance scrambles to join Punteney behind the bluff, but they are forced to surrender.

Curry races away on his horse, and the posse fires shots which hit the animal three times, though it runs another mile before dropping dead. One of the bullets passes through the horse's neck and hits

Curry in the wrist, causing an injury that for the rest of his life is used to identify him. Curry is caught, and all the outlaws are taken by stagecoach to Billings then Deadwood, South Dakota. On October 31, 1897, they overpower their captors in the Bull Pen and escape. Curry and Sundance head back to Montana, but Punteney and Tom O'Day are captured near Spearfish. They are retried and then released for lack of evidence.

RICHARD:

The night was incredibly light and mild. We quickly packed and were on the road at 5.55 a.m. I followed the Musselshell Trail on a bearing to Mobridge. The usual drill was to alternate jogging and walking. We used a dirt track to Crossover Reservoir and made good time through an uninspiring landscape. We watered the horses and pressed on towards the 191. The Judith and Little Rocky Mountains were the only landmarks to rely on. I re-checked our location, suddenly realising I had taken a wrong fork and added to our mileage.

Over a rise, the road plummeted, disappearing round a curve some two miles distant. We led the horses down to the valley below, entering the Charles M. Russell National Wildlife Refuge. Passing Mobridge, we headed straight for the James Kipp Recreation Centre. Strictly speaking, horses were not allowed in such places. Simon went off to bullshit a ranger, apparently successfully, since we hobbled the horses to graze for the remainder of the day.

Later, Dave Rummel, another of Simon's contacts, arrived with wife Brenda and family in tow. Dave was distantly related to the notorious John Wesley Hardin, who shared with Wild Bill Hickock the reputation of being the most deadly pistoleer of them all. Both ended up shot dead – but from behind.

We fired up a fine barbecue and planned for the final section. Tomorrow, once across the Missouri River, our stop was at the tiny mining town of Zortman. A day off here was necessary to plan the run-in to Canada and the return to Sand Springs for Bones. I quickly checked our stats: 1,887 miles completed in one hundred riding days, just under nineteen miles per day. In the short time remaining, could we possibly hit the elusive twenty miles a day?

LAST OF THE BANDIT RIDERS

"Let's get it done…"
THE SUNDANCE KID

SIMON:

We broke camp early and walked over the Fred Robinson Bridge. Grey clouds had obliterated the Little Rockies peaks, and the good weather looked set to change imminently to something more foreboding. We made a creditable twenty-four miles in five hours, but it was dull riding. Rain hit us right on the turn-off at CK Creek, and within the hour, we were ensconced at our next port of call: the Storli residence, again arranged by Bush Telegraph.

Tracking Butch and Sundance in Montana was becoming more difficult – they left fewer known tracks than usual, although Sundance seemed to have spent more time than Butch riding the Northern Plains. The outlaw who carved his feared reputation in these parts was Butch's right-hand man, the volatile and homicidal Harvey Logan.

It is probably late 1892 or early 1893 when Harvey Logan, his two brothers and their associate Jim Thornhill stake a claim south of the mountains on Rock Creek. It is open range, tall grass country, ideal for a horse ranch.

Less than a year later, a notable bareknuckle fighter named Powell "Pike" Landusky strikes gold with two other prospectors just six miles away at Alder Creek, between Indian Creek and Sugarloaf Butte.

Thus, the small, typical gold rush township of Landusky is born, with its characteristic main street, duckboard sidewalks and false-fronted log buildings.

Before long, there is a feud simmering between Pike Landusky and the Curry brothers (as the Logans are known in those parts). This comes to a head during the 1894 Christmas festivities, in Jew Jake's saloon on December 27, when Harvey walks up to Landusky and smashes him ferociously on the jaw, decking him in the process. Pike comes off the floor groggy but fighting. As is usual in bar-room brawls, guns are drawn to prevent intervention.

Landusky's massive frame and fearsome reputation stack the odds in his favour, but they are greatly offset by age, drink and that first killer punch, so Harvey gives him a relentless pounding until he foolishly goes for his gun – which misfires. Whereupon Harvey draws, shoots Pike dead and, with his brother Lonny and Thornhill, heads at speed for Hole-in-the-Wall.

Some say Sundance is a witness to that killing – there is no vestige of proof, but we know he is in the area breaking broncos for John T Adams's Bar U ranch, and he certainly knows Harvey and Lonny.

It has to be local knowledge dating from this time that prompts Harvey Logan to establish Hideaway Coulee, likely a line cabin originally, in remote country around eighteen miles from Landusky, hidden deep in the Missouri Breaks. Used by Butch Cassidy on more than one occasion, and almost certainly Sundance too, it is perfectly sited. Though only a few hundred yards from the dirt road, if you stand at the edge of the bluff and look down for a hundred feet, you see nothing.

SIMON:

Sadly, the logs of this historic hideout site have long since been used for firewood. Careful inspection amongst the undergrowth yields only a stone chimney and a few wooden posts, almost lost in the brush.

Studying the maps, I reckoned that Bull Creek Road is probably the original track Butch and Sundance used to meet up with Harvey Logan before riding into Landusky.

Zortman had hardly changed since my visit in 1997. The outpost hamlet lay fifty-five miles from Malta and over a hundred and fifty miles north from Billings. It boasted a general store, post office and also a bar, which we noted for later. A white wooden structure ten feet square stood alone on the green – it was the old jail. There was a laundry, motel and garage, and along Main Street, which suddenly became a track, houses led towards a canyon. That was it.

Later that evening, we hooked up for dinner in a local restaurant with the Rummel family, whom I knew from my previous visit.

"So, how's it really gone?" Dave asked as we tucked in.

"Early on, it was brutal on the horses. Excessive heat, scant feed and little water," I replied.

"So what happened to Barbara?" was Brenda's blunt question.

"She quit at Hole-in-the-Wall. Hated us, the ride – everything. Can't blame her really," I answered impassively.

RICHARD:

The next day we scooted off to the general store in a borrowed pickup to re-supply. Simon was nervous about the size of our tab with Joe and hence our purchasing power. Suddenly, he noticed a white flash in the rear-view mirror.

"Stop! Stop!"

"What for?"

"The horses are on the roadside."

"Can't be. There's a cattle grid."

"Back up – they're out. I'm certain."

"Bullshit!"

"Seriously!"

I reversed the truck. Sunday and Ditch were grazing contentedly *outside* the field. Ditch had jumped a cattle grid for the second time and Sunday had followed suit. Shit!

"You can't turn your back for ten minutes. That damned Buckskin's a pain in the arse!" I said, fearing the gelding would run off and take Sunday with him. We caught the guilty pair and secured them by roping off the entrance. Ditch was incredibly cunning and still couldn't be trusted.

We were hanging loose and were almost glad when it was time to leave for Malta. I think it was anticipation, now that matters were coming to a climax.

From Bear Gulch, the land flattened considerably. Later, I turned, glimpsing the Little Rockies, the last range south of the Canadian line. A pale blue, cloudless sky formed a splendid wash behind the green and black mountains. Burnt yellow grass rolled like a glorious thick pile carpet to Coburn Buttes, and it soon got very hot.

Simon's knowledge of the outlaws had been building added value. In the early days, it was not important to me. I had no time to think. There was no teamwork then, only pressure. The enjoyment really began when we rode out on our own. Now, I was soaking up the atmosphere, holding on to my latest adventure. We rode on through scrubby grass in span formation, marvelling at the space and feeling elated.

"This is how it should've been from day one," said Simon. "Why we put up with all that shit earlier, I'll never know."

I agreed heartily, then after a pause switched to subject normal: Butch and Sundance.

"Do you think they really were popular in their time?" I asked, "Are we sure it's not just dime novels, movies and TV?"

"They're part of it, of course," said Simon, "but not the most important part. You have to remember these guys brought colour and excitement into pretty humdrum lives. In a sense, they were the movies. Also, people had to choose sides. If you were a hard-worked citizen with little or no security, never far from the breadline, who would *you* identify with – the rich, remote, greedy cattle and railroad magnates with their millions, or your more daredevil friends who put a lot of that money back into the community, spending it freely and often generously?

"They didn't do this because they were Robin Hoods (though I'm sure that like Robin – if he existed – they knew the value of good local PR), but because they were travelling on a short ride one-way ticket, and deep down they knew it. Eat, drink and be merry – tomorrow we die bloody."

"But didn't they spend mostly on booze, prostitutes and gambling?"

"Sure, in the sense of most often, but that was not all. You have to recognise how much spending power they had – the tens of thousands they stole were worth hundreds of thousands in today's money. They spent lavishly on food, clothes, travel, holidays, hotels, guns, horses, saddlery, you name it. Of the local stores, only the bank manager didn't welcome them with open arms.

"And perhaps their biggest trick was that, unlike the barons, they had never pulled up their roots. As well as the money angle, their ties with the ordinary folk guaranteed active help for them and zero help for the lawmen who hunted them. Even in the jury stand, 'dismissed for lack of evidence' cropped up surprisingly often."

I had one more question, while Simon was in relaxed platform mode:

"Were Butch and Sundance always together, really inseparable?"

"Most people think so, especially after the movie. But the celluloid version of Sundance was a composite of the real Sundance, Harry Longabaugh, and Elzy Lay, one of Butch's best friends and something of an underrated figure, especially where planning was concerned. Elzy had the best educated brain of all of them, even including Butch."

Simon's knowledge of the history was immense. Born in the wrong century, he constantly strove to touch, feel and breathe the past. As I began to learn more myself, I did dare to take issue with the maestro on one issue (for which I should have been Mentioned in Dispatches!). I could not help questioning the notion that these affluent, extravagant outlaws were forever astride a horse. It didn't make sense, crossing vast tracts of inhospitable land when they could have travelled in comfort by train, especially before the Fort Worth photo got circulated.

Knowing they frequented the sporting districts of a number of cities to spend stolen loot, my assumption is that the really long rides occurred directly after the robberies. I suspect these out-of-the-way and rather primitive hideouts acted as layovers and supply camps just until the coast was clear, and no longer.

SIMON:

Two riding days remained, with one more night under the stars – then Canada. A couple of press interviews, then we shot pool and reflected. Our feelings were mixed. We had retrieved from the dead pages of the history books the incredible freedoms of a vanished way of life. It was not going to be easy to give it up. Yes, homes and families beckoned very strongly, but the accompanying return to normality did not appeal.

The wind blew with ferocity, and the cold was biting. According to Dave Rummel, within a few weeks, the first snows were expected. Richard led across a vast pasture, and we took the DX Trail on a northwest bearing.

We jogged through rolling hills, Richard pushing hard on Sunday, me following on Ditch. Our horses rose to the challenge, and after a thrilling walk and fast trot combination, almost a chase, we reined in in downtown Malta at just fifteen minutes past eleven. It had been the fastest section completed on the trail; the horses were tremendously fit and demonstrated greathearted willingness.

Nate Murphy, palaeontologist and Western buff, invited us to inspect a superb Kid Curry display proudly housed in two glass cases in Phillips County Museum. Amongst newspaper cuttings and books lies an amazing item of "Americana" – Kid Curry's revolver. It was a nickel-plated Colt .45 with a short barrel. We inspected the piece, still in remarkably good order, and asked its current value.

"Oh, around $100,000," Nate replied.

Wow! I handled the pistol and felt I was touching history.

We exited town on the 242 for Assiniboine Creek, tuning in a donated ghetto blaster on cue to enjoy our fifteen minutes of local radio fame. When we got there, we had directions to our final rendezvous – Freddy Messerly's house, tucked back from the road. Freddy, short and stocky, in his early sixties, was a friend of a friend of the Rummels – we had been passed like parcels from friend to friend ever since Hole-in-the-Wall. Freddy bustled with energy and directed us to put the horses up.

"I want to show you a shortcut for tomorrow."

We leapt into the truck and drove for ten minutes. Turning off at the ten-mile marker Freddy took a dirt track up through the rolling green foothills, climbing over a huge bluff. At the high point, Richard scanned the horizon for a usable landmark. Miles distant an enormous grain bin looked about as big as a lolly stick. It would suffice. Satisfied with our recce, we returned to Malta, a town that featured at both ends of the train-robber era.

November 29, 1892. Sundance carries out his first train robbery. At 3 a.m., the Great Northern Number 23, an express and mail from St Paul, Minnesota on its way to Butte, Montana, is pulled up just outside Malta. Three masked men order the train to stop, then instruct the mail clerk to open the mail car. Finding nothing, two bandits proceed to the express car and tell the messenger to open the safes. Nineteen dollars and twenty cents in cash is removed. Harry Bass and Bill Madden are later arrested at Black's saloon in Malta, and Sundance is collared boarding an eastbound train. The trio stand trial. Bass is given ten years, Madden fourteen. Sundance escapes, but the others implicate him as the third outlaw.

The Wild Bunch's last successful express robbery in the United States takes place on the Great Northern Railroad near Wagner, Montana on July 3, 1901, also just down the road from Malta. Express Number 3, the Coast Flyer, is the victim. This raid may be Kid Curry's idea – it is on his home patch, and the country is ideal for bandits: rugged foothills and trackless mountains, never far from the railway lines.

EH Harriman, Union Pacific's Railroad baron is convinced that more depredations are a certainty. Following the Wilcox robbery, Union Pacific posts "dead or alive" rewards, broadcasting to the world that Wyoming is now unsafe territory for bandits. A year later, after Tipton, Harriman nearly puts the gang out of business by utilising man-hunters properly supported by lightning fast "posse cars."

Despite the increasing danger, between four and six robbers take part in the Wagner hold up. Butch is listed as present; so too are Harvey Logan, Ben Kilpatrick and OC Hanks.

After the train pulls out of Malta, one of the bandits climbs into the cab and takes control of the crew, instructing the engineer to stop at the designated hold-up site. A group armed with Winchesters waits at Exeter Switch. The trainmen fear a collision is imminent if the train is stopped on the tracks and run to put warning flares on the line. The robbers are taken by surprise and fire; both men are hit, and one of them later dies from his injuries.

The robbers open up the baggage-express car and dynamite the safe – at the fourth attempt. Running to their horses already staked near the tracks, they ride south towards the Milk River, turning as they ride to fire on the train. This robbery does not bear Butch Cassidy's hallmark. At the time, he is believed to be present, but he and Sundance are already in South America.

Despite sightings in all directions, the outlaws are never caught. They head for the safety of Hideaway Coulee, buy twenty-four hours of time, change their horses and divide a massive $40,000 before splitting ranks, a remarkable coup.

RICHARD:

We decided to investigate where the Wagner train was stopped: five miles outside Malta near the river bend, by a tiny bridge fording a creek. We walked along the tracks trying to imagine the events of ninety-eight years ago and again felt the brush of history's wings.

On September 2, we set off for our final ranch stopover, with Alan Wasson at Port of Morgan. We rode out to Little Cottonwood Creek, about eleven easy miles, and turned off for the shortcut into the low hills. I was keen to reach a high point to re-check the bearing I took yesterday. Riding through breaks, draws and coulees was hard on the horses and slowed us considerably.

We topped a ridge and decided to let them graze while I sighted up the grain bin. Simon glassed the region with his binoculars, commenting that the range seemed to spread for an eternity – looking back to Malta, the horizon literally fell away. Yellow grass was broken by greenish-black hills, and a circle of trees denoted the Milk River and town. Temperature had also sunk to the forties, dropping fifty degrees in two days.

"I don't see the grain bin," Simon sounded worried.

"We're still in low ground and need to top that rise," I replied, pointing ahead.

The land was confusing. We had made the halfway point, leaving the road hours earlier. Cutting across country always provided a few surprises, and now we couldn't find the landmark. We pressed on. Suddenly, the rolling hills stopped dead, leaving us on the edge of a bluff. I led Sunday down the steep slope to the bottom, across the valley and began negotiating the climb on the opposite side.

"So which way did the outlaws head for Canada?" I queried, trying to lighten a tense moment.

"If they were smart, not this way," Simon replied tersely.

Canada wasn't a solid option for hosting a Wild Bunch sanctuary. Law enforcement there was equally tough on banditry and the North West Mounted Police had an enviable reputation – not dissimilar to the Texas Rangers – for employing small numbers of skilled, dedicated Mounties who proverbially "always get their man."

Over Cottonwood Bench, I could just see the road. Vehicles tracked on the horizon, but no grain bin! What made the task difficult was the continual uphill haul. We cut through an enormous ploughed pasture hundreds of acres in size, and I spied cattle milling near a windmill. Stopping briefly while Sunday and Ditch filled up, I re-checked my compass. We were on the right heading. Within five minutes, we had topped a small hill and the "lost" grain bin towered. Looking back, I realised we'd been riding for miles in a long hole!

A noisy quad bike raced to meet us and Rancher Alan Wasson invited us in. Here was the last post before Canada. Just twenty-three miles remained. We sat for coffee, which led into dinner. Connie and Alan were great and treated us like royalty.

SIMON:

We had intended to finish the trail in Climax, Saskatchewan, just because of its highly appropriate name. But riding horses over the International line wasn't possible without ridiculous quantities of paperwork and delays. Officially, we had to import the horses from America to Canada and back again. Ridiculous. Also, our firearms were not allowed in Canada. Rules and paperwork – more bullshit we didn't need.

If we were caught breaking strict International laws the horse would be impounded. We decided reluctantly that we would ride past the obelisk that marks the International line, then turn back. To banish our disappointment, we rationalised: technically, getting a hoof or a toenail over it would count!

September 2 – our final day in the saddle. We left late, walking and jogging the horses along a wide barrow pit. It was noticeably cool and overcast. The last tiny outpost before the border was Loring, which comprised a church, a café and half a dozen houses.

"Fancy a last coffee before Canada?" I asked.

"We'll make it a quick one – I want to cross the line by one," Richard replied, very English.

We were taking the piss. Tying our horses to a hitching post, we stepped onto the wooden boardwalk and clumped inside. We ordered and drank our coffee and were riding again within fifteen minutes. The road ran straight as an arrow for sixteen miles. Montana here was wide-open spaces, seemingly limitless.

As Richard kicked Sunday into a trot, I urged Ditch, and we both leaned over the saddle horns like jockeys, keeping our weight off the horses' backs. Both horses were fit, Sunday supremely so. Richard remained ahead and I tried desperately to ride abreast, but Ditch would have none of it.

To finish in style, we took the last stretch at a full gallop, whooping and yelling. As we thundered towards the border, the horses clearly caught our excitement. The border patrolman in Montana was fast asleep as we raced over the International Line pell-mell, to rein in hard at the Canadian checkpoint.

Freddy, waiting with his camera, rushed to capture the golden moment.

"Did you cross over?" a voice barked.

A border patrolman had quit his comfortable domain and stood disapprovingly in front of us.

"We stopped right here," I replied truthfully.

"Where've you guys come from?"

"Mexico," I replied cockily.

"Okay." Either half-asleep or just totally unimpressed, the official read our passports then waved us away. We turned and rode back into Montana.

Richard and I were very happy men and made the most of milling round the concrete obelisk which denoted the International line. We had done it. I admit to feeling quite strange.

No media circus, though. Our witnesses numbered only three.

One border patrolman each for USA and Canada, and Freddie with his camera.

Richard:

We unsaddled and loaded up for our return. I leaned back in my seat in the pickup and watched the green flats and dull landscape slide past. The realization dawned that we wouldn't be riding horses for a long time. The freedom we had was suddenly lost, and like Simon, I had nothing on my agenda. Thoughts returned, as they had done so often, to Butch and Sundance. We felt much empathy with them. We had ridden their outlaw trail and seen their legendary hideouts, and we had done so the hard way, as they did: on horseback.

"How d'you feel now?" Freddy asked brightly.

I left it to Simon to answer. He thought for a moment.

"Pretty much like the outlaws must have felt at Fort Worth in 1900."

"How's that?"

"Mixed feelings, and a bit rudderless. We've immersed ourselves totally in a very special way of life – its rewards, some of its hazards, its thrills and spills. In a kind of way, we've been the very last of the bandit riders. And now, suddenly, the party is over."

After the final rendezvous in Texas, the Wild Bunch splits up. Butch and Sundance take Etta Place to South America in 1901. Will Carver and Ben (Tall Texan) Kilpatrick stay in Texas; Harvey Logan goes back to Montana. Elzy Lay is sentenced to life imprisonment in 1899. He actually dies with his boots off in Los Angeles in 1934.

Of the fringe members, the McCartys are wiped out escaping a bank job in Delta, Colorado in September 1893. Matt Warner is freed in 1900 following a five year sentence for murder; he later becomes a successful lawman and he too dies with his boots off in 1937. Bub Meeks is sent to the pen for thirty-two years. After an escape attempt, he is shot in the leg, shattering it below the knee – it has to be amputated. He ends his days in an asylum, dying in 1912. Tom O'Day is killed in a wagon accident in South Dakota in 1930, and Flat Nose George Currie is of course killed on the Book Cliffs in April 1900.

Kid Curry, Will Carver and Ben and George Kilpatrick get together again to pull a bank job in Sonora, Texas. Ben and the Kid wait on the edge of town while the lesser known Will and George go in to make the hit but are recognised. Lawmen order them to surrender, they go for their guns and they are cut down in a hail of bullets. George survives multiple wounds, but Carver dies, apparently game to the end, within a few hours.

Curry and the Tall Texan live to fight and die another day. Camillo Hanks joins them later for the Wagner, Montana job in 1901, then is shot dead in a saloon in San Antonio, Texas in April 1902. After a dramatic capture and escape at Nashville, Tennessee in 1901, Kid Curry is badly wounded in a shoot-out after trying to rob the Denver & Rio Grande Number 5 at Parachute, Colorado in June 1904. Rather than surrender, he takes his own life.

Ben Kilpatrick is apprehended in St Louis, Missouri in November 1901. Detectives have traced a paper trail of stolen bills from Wagner. He gets fifteen years hard labour at the Columbus, Ohio penitentiary. In 1911, he is released, claiming to have turned over a new leaf, but then in 1912, he attempts the last ever old-style horseback train robbery at Dryden, Texas and is clubbed to death by the express car messenger.

As for Butch Cassidy and the Sundance Kid, in South America they manage to stop the clock for a few years and carry on in the old style as los bandidos Yanquis. For decades afterwards, the date, location and manner of their deaths are hotly debated, but eventually, most people come to accept that the closest to the truth is the Bolivian shootout version, which has passed into legend.

A burst of gunfire. Freeze frame. The party is over.

EPILOGUE

"I got a great idea where we should go next."
BUTCH CASSIDY

"You just keep thinking, Butch. That's what you're good at."
THE SUNDANCE KID

SIMON:

Our return journey was like rewinding a holiday movie – we rode quite a chunk of the Outlaw Trail all over again, this time north to south and most importantly, riding wheels and not four legs. We lost out on romance and nostalgia, but we were very happy to trade those in for comfort and amazing speed.

We arrived at Assiniboine Creek in under an hour. Tomorrow, the trail would lead us south for Zortman, Sand Springs, Miles City (scooping up as we went various scattered horses and equipment) and eventually Hole-in-the-Wall, where we urgently needed to be for a rendezvous with Gene Vieh and the Armstrongs on September 6. Hopefully, Joe would accept our horses and gear in part payment of his enormous bill, after which we hoped to catch a lift with the Armstrongs back to La Mesa, New Mexico where it all began. It was a logistical nightmare and a financial tightrope. One slip in either department and we were in deep shit.

Freddy Messerly kindly returned us to Zortman. Back at the Storli place, I made anxious phone calls. Luckily, Dave Rummel had borrowed a small two-horse trailer and agreed to ship us to Bill

Brown's in Sand Springs the following morning. Bill was away in Colorado, so he was not available to haul us to Artie Larson's. I called and left a message for Artie reporting our impending arrival at the Browns' within twenty-four hours.

At six a.m., Dave arrived with his small trailer. Now, ranch horses load into massive contraptions capable of taking six horses. Sunday and Ditch eyed the tiny trailer with deep suspicion and stood stock still in the driving rain. Then Sunday stepped gingerly onto the ramp. I proffered some grain in a nosebag. She came for it, and hey presto; she was in, securing bar in place. This was a piece of cake.

I was far too optimistic. Ditch smelt trouble and baulked. He hauled back sharply. More grain in the nosebag and repeat the process, gently pulling and increasing pressure. One hoof, then two on the ramp, head craning forward. Nearly. The rain continued to pelt down and it was bitterly cold. Ditch wasn't budging. Heaving and pulling achieved zero. We backed Sunday out and ran her in again, then tried it on Ditch. Zilch! We were already soaked and pissed off.

"Who's got Monty Roberts' phone number, then?" I snapped. "Where are the fucking horse professors when you need them!"

We made three, four, five attempts, but Ditch wouldn't play. In his defence, the space inside was dark and miniscule; he had no idea what he was getting into.

"What next?" I asked Dave, a little tersely.

"Keep the mare as she is. You take the rope, Richard, and I'll heave him from behind."

I shook the nosebag. Predictably, Ditch stepped up and anchored. I tugged the rope. He moved a fraction closer to snatch a bigger mouthful of the bribe. Dave and Richard locked hands and made a sudden rush, taking Ditch by surprise, and in one massive heave, lifted his hind legs and bundled him bodily into the horse box. I slammed shut the retaining bar. We had done the business, and it had only taken an hour in the freezing rain. Brilliant!

We jumped into the truck and retraced our tracks along Route 191 towards the tiny settlement of Grassrange. Thick, grey clouds smothered the daylight and chucked squalls of rain against the truck. We turned left to Teigan and tracked a hundred and twenty-five miles through Montana's prime cattle country. Just like that.

At nine-thirty, we pulled in at the Brown's LO Bar Ranch. Reliable Artie Larson was waiting with an enormous trailer. I glanced towards the barn and saw Bones, grazing contentedly and looking fine, with no visible bandages. She walked over, giving no indication of lameness, and promptly snapped at Sunday, stared down Ditch and instantly re-established the pecking order. Unprompted, the horses leapt inside the cavernous trailer.

"You get trouble loading earlier?" Artie queried, pointing at the two-horse rig.

"Big time."

"Yeah, they don't like those small sons of bitches."

We gathered our packs and bade goodbye to Dave Rummel who had done a sterling job for us, both ways. The V8 engine rumbled into life.

"When you guys get back, call Marilyn," said Artie. "You can hitch a ride back to south Miles but you won't get a trailer out over the weekend – it's a public holiday."

"Shit!" I replied. "We've got to get back to Hole-in-the-Wall on Monday."

"You're gonna have to haul ass to make it!"

At Jordan, we turned south to Miles City on Route 59 past Cohagen. Despite whizzing along in a beefy truck at a steady fifty-five, Montana was still huge. It was bloody miles through undulating grassy hills and past remote ranches.

RICHARD:

Simon called Gene Vieh at Hole-in-the-Wall. Central Wyoming had been heavily hit by storms and was flooded out. Access in and out of the ranch was at a standstill, even for four-wheel drives. Nobody was going anywhere. I rang Sue Means in Buffalo to learn that her friend Bonnie Osmundsen wanted to meet up with us in Miles City tomorrow.

"Simon, get onto Gene. See if we can borrow a truck and trailer. We could hitch back to Buffalo."

It was our only hope. We were clean out of dollars, and the cost of organising a hauler to return us would wipe out the proceeds from the horse sale. Then Marilyn Fortune offered to collect us from Artie's and drive us to the Triple T Ranch. If we could get Gene to leave a rig in Buffalo, I was certain a ride with Bonnie was on.

Satisfied, I decided to look Bones over and check the small swelling. It had gone, and there was no heat in either leg – the mare was sound. Buoyantly, I returned to Simon.

"It's on for tomorrow," he said. "We'll meet at Marilyn's. She's bringing a stiff up to Miles."

"A what?"

I thought Simon had popped too many beers in Artie's office.

Apparently, Bonnie was delivering a body in Miles for an undertaker and wanted to see us. We rang Gene Vieh assuring him of our arrival in Buffalo. The arrangement was that Joe's rig was to be left there and we would collect the horses ourselves. I still felt it unlikely that we would arrive in time to catch a ride to New Mexico.

The roar of a truck announced the arrival of Marilyn Fortune. Thirty minutes later, we were heading to the Triangle T Ranch; sixty-five miles through yellow-gold fields got us back within the hour. Heavy rain turned the drive into a quagmire, suggesting it might be safer to re-route via Broadus to Wyoming. We broke for coffee and waited. An hour later, a smart-looking people carrier pulled up outside. In Simon's reverential phrase, Bonnie had dumped the stiff.

We trundled into Broadus. A few old brick buildings gave it the feel of a frontier township. I opted for shuteye, reminding Simon to take the right fork south to Gillette, Wyoming. Route 212 splits for the Wyoming and South Dakota line and leads to Belle Fourche, scene of the $97 bank bust.

As I drifted off, I wondered if the Wild Bunch went in for "unit enquiries": what went wrong, why, and what can we learn?

SIMON:

Richard kipped, and we rolled the hundred miles to Gillette. The expanse was breathtaking. An occasional hawk wheeled majestically over the deserted plains as I marvelled to see our days of riding turned into hours and our hours to minutes.

Sunday morning. At six the diesel in the big GMC clattered into life and we crept out of Buffalo, trying not to wake the neighbourhood.

Following our original route, we made good time to Decker, Montana. The tarmac road narrowed to one gravelled lane. Bumping along at forty-five mph was fast enough.

Landmarks flooded past until Birney, where we had started night riding, and thereafter, it was virgin territory. Lost in memories, we nearly drove right past the Triangle T. Bones, Sunday and Ditch were happily munching hay in the corrals. Yazz was with the ranch horses two miles away. I rode out to bring him back. He looked content, and had put on a little weight. The four were re-united. Bones and Yazz were still in love; Sunday nipped at Ditch; they kept well clear of my two – nothing had changed. We loaded.

RICHARD:

"You drive first," suggested Simon. "I've never hauled horses."

The miles racked by effortlessly. I nearly forgot the horses were aboard. Four hours later, we bumped down the winding dirt track to the Willow Creek. After unloading, we catalogued the gear and presented the inventory to Gene Vieh. In the bunkhouse Joe tendered a scrappy piece of A4 paper. The total read $18,706.07. We had sent $13,434.43 before arrival. A balance of $5,271.64 was owed and paid. Ouch.

Yazz, Sunday, Ditch and the equipment would stay at Hole-in-the-Wall. Rocket, still at Tom Klumker's in Alma, was an insurance payment for the hay bill Dube and Miss-Ap were currently running up at La Mesa. Tomorrow, we would take Rusty's Jeep and return to La Mesa at leisure.

September 6. We took photos and said farewells to Gene and Sammye Vieh, the Buckinghams and the other guests. I visited the corral one last time to make much of the horses, as they say in the Household Cavalry. They were content. Hole-in-the-Wall was a fitting place for them to end up. They would be excellent mounts for visiting tourists – with a good story attached.

We drove for Cheyenne, Wyoming's State capital. We found a cheap, soulless hotel and left for Denver first thing in the morning. We drove a hundred miles south on Interstate 25 and climbed over the high Pass before descending into Raton, New Mexico. Three miles south, using what had once been the Santa Fé Trail, the road forked to Cimarron.

The Interstate plunged through Socorro following the Rio Grande, and paralleled a desolate landscape called Jornada del Muerto, which means roughly "Dead Man's Journey." And all the time we drove, it got hotter, from the thirties near the Canadian border to the nineties in New Mexico.

With the San Andres Mountains away to our left, we cruised through Hatch, New Mexico, the chili capital of the world, and stopped in the little town of Mesilla, southwest of Las Cruces, where Billy The Kid was sentenced to hang but escaped. We strolled round the beautiful plaza and shopped for gifts.

Our last few days were spent tying up loose ends. Dube and Miss-Ap, now fattened, we wrote off against payment and vet bills. Simon dutifully wrote hundreds of postcards, and we got our two guns engraved as a surprise presentation to Joe and Rusty. A grand barbecue was held in our honour celebrating the completion of the ride, and we spent a very happy evening indeed. Then we returned to the sprawling border town of El Paso, Texas where the older buildings gave us our last glimpse of the Old West, the bygone era we had explored together.

I am very proud of what we achieved – especially as we started off in the worst possible way by breaking the golden rule; namely, that you don't do a major expedition with a scratch team. Go with people you know well – tried, tested and compatible. We were virtual strangers and bloody lucky not to come apart at the seams a hundred times. It was our greatest weakness. And when we finally became a real – albeit depleted – team in the closing stages, it was our greatest strength.

SIMON:

Joe Armstrong's words when we left Mexico on April 17, 1999 were: "They rode off side by side – but I never ever saw two people so far apart." When Richard and I said adios in El Paso, the opposite was true. Different as we were in almost every way, we had achieved friendship founded not only on a great shared experience, but on mutual respect; mine for Richard's brilliant ground leadership, navigation, horse management and survival skills, while he in turn had come to understand and value the years of solid research and planning I had put into this expedition, and also my unswerving, bloody-minded commitment to seeing it through.

So here we are, two guys who know they make a very good team – and who maybe will be ready for another great adventure before too long. When our role models Butch and Sundance felt the need to move on, they went off and continued their work in a far country. Now there is an idea: to retrace the final footsteps of Butch Cassidy and the Sundance Kid in South America. No one has ever done that. It would be a lot of research, and a helluva ride. Maybe the party isn't over yet.

"Next time I say let's go somewhere like Bolivia,
let's go somewhere like Bolivia."
BUTCH CASSIDY

BIBLIOGRAPHY

BOOKS

Adams, Ramon F. (1993) *The Cowboy Dictionary*, Perigree Books.

Baker, Pearl (1965) *The Wild Bunch At Robbers Roost*, Abelard – Schuman.

Baker, Pearl (1976) *Robbers Roost Recollections*, Utah State University Press.

Bartholomew, Ed (1955) *Black Jack Ketchum*, The Frontier Press.

Benton, Jesse James (1944) *Cow By The Tail*, Houghton Mifflin Co.

Betenson, Lula and Flack, Dora (1975) *Butch Cassidy, My Brother*, Brigham Young U.P.

Brecke, Alan Lee (1989) *Kid Curry – Train Robber*, Harlem News/Chinook Opinion.

Brock, J. Elmer (1944) *Powder River Country*, privately printed.

Burroughs, John Rolfe (1962) *Where The Old West Stayed Young*, Bonanza.

Burton, Doris Karren (1996) *History of Uintah County*, State Historical Society.

Burton, Jeff (1970) *Dynamite And Six Shooter*, Palomino Press.

Churchill, Richard E. (1972) *They Rode With Butch Cassidy*, Timberline Books.

Coburn, Walt (1968) *Pioneer Cattleman in Montana*, Norman University of Oklahoma Press.

DeArment, Robert K (1996) *Alias Frank Canton*, Norman University of Oklahoma Press.

DeJournette, Dick and DeJournette, Daun (1996) *One Hundred Years of Brown's Park and Diamond Mountain*, DeJournette Enterprises.

Drago, Gail (1996) *Etta Place: Her Life and Times With Butch Cassidy & the Sundance Kid*, Republic of Texas Press.

Dunham, Dick and Vivian (1947) *Our Strip of Land*, Daggett County Lions Club.

Eaton, John (1972) *Will Carver, Outlaw*, Anchor Publishing.

Edgar, Bob and Turnell, Jack (1978) *Brand of a Legend*, Stockade Publishing.

Elser, Smoke and Brown, Bill (1980) *Packin' In On Mules And Horses*, Mountain Press Publishing Co.

Ernst, Donna B (1992) *Sundance – My Uncle*, Creative Publishing.

Ernst, Donna B (1995) *The True Story of Will Carver*, Sutton County Historical Society.

Foster, Robert L. *The Duschesne Strip, Part 2: A Lawless Land*, Outlaw Trail Paper

French, Captain William (1965) *Some Recollections of A Western Ranchman: New Mexico, 1883-1899*, Argosy-Antiquarian Ltd.

French, Captain William (1965) *Further Recollections of A Western Ranchman: New Mexico: 1883 – 1899*, Argosy-Antiquarian Ltd.

Frye, Elnora L. (1990) *Atlas of Wyoming Outlaws at the Territorial Penitentiary*, Jelm Mountain Press.

Ganci, Dave and Wick, Devon (1981) *The Basic Essentials of Desert Survival*, ICS Books, Inc.

Garman, Mary (1978) *Harry Longabaugh – The Sundance Kid: The Early Years, 1867-1889*, Crook County Museum.

Goldman, William (1969) *Butch Cassidy & The Sundance Kid*, Bantam.

Heck, Larry (1996) *Pass Patrol: In Search of the Outlaw Trail Vol 1*, Pass Patrol Publications.

Heck, Larry (1993) *Adventures of Pass Patrol Vol 2*, Pass Patrol Publications.

Horan, James D. (1949) *Desperate Men*, Doubleday.

Horan, James D. (1970) *The Wild Bunch*, Signet.

Horan, James D. And Sann, Paul (1972) *Pictoral History of the Wild West*, Spring Books.

Kelly, Charles(1959) *The Outlaw Trail: A History of Butch Cassidy and His Wild Bunch*, Devin-Adair Company.

Kelsey, Michael (1990) *Hiking and Exploring Utah's Henry Mountains & Robbers Roost*, Kelsey Publishing.

Kenworth, Jesse Cole (1990) *Storms Of Life – The Outlaw Trail & Kid Curry*, 1/4 Circle Enterprises.

Kirby, Edward M. (1977) *The Saga of Butch Cassidy and the Wild Bunch*, Filter Press.

Kirby, Edward M. (1983) *The Rise and Fall of the Sundance Kid*, Western Publications.

Kouris, Diana Allen (1988) *The Romantic and Notorious History of Brown's Park*, Wolverine Gallery.

Krakel, Dean F. (1988) *The Saga of Tom Horn – The Story of a Cattleman's War*, University of Nebraska Press.

Lake, Carolyn (Ed) (1969) *Under Cover For Wells, Fargo*, Houghton Mifflin Co.

Lamb, F. Bruce (1991) *Kid Curry – The Life and Times of Harvey Logan and the Wild Bunch*, Johnson Books.

Lamb, F. Bruce (1860) *The Wild Bunch – A Selected Critical Annotated Bibliography*, High Plains Publishing Co, Inc.

LeFors, Joe (1953) *Wyoming Peace Officer*, Laramie Printing Co.

McCarty, Tom (1986) *Tom McCarty's Own Story – Autobiography of an Outlaw*, Rocky Mountain HousePress.

McClure, Grace (1985) *The Bassett Women*, Swallow Press/Ohio University press.

Meadows, Anne and Buck, Daniel (1994) *Digging Up Butch and Sundance*, St Martins Press.

Metz, Leon Claire (1987) *Pat Garrett – Story of a Western Lawman*, University of Oklahoma Press.

Mokler, Alfred James (1923) *History of Natrona County, Wyoming, 1888- 1922*, Donnelly & Sons.

Moulton, Candy (1995) *Roadside History of Wyoming*, Mountain Press Publishing.

O'Neal, Bill (1979) *Encyclopaedia of Western Gunfighters*, University of Oklahoma Press.

Patterson, Richard (1998) *Butch Cassidy, a Biography*, University of Nebraska Press.

Patterson, Richard (1991) *The Train Robbery Era: An Encyclopaedic History*, Pruett Publishing.

Pfaff, Betty Carpenter (1978) *Atlantic City Nuggets*, Privately Printed.

Pointer, Larry (1977) *In Search of Butch Cassidy*, University of Oklahoma Press.

Rakocy, Bill (1988) *The Mogollon Diary Number 2*, Bravo Printing.

Redford, Robert (1978) *The Outlaw Trail: A Journey Through Time*, Hamish Hamilton.

Rusho, W.L. and Crampton, Gregory C. (1992) *Lee's Ferry: Desert River Crossing*, Cricket Productions.

Selcer, Richard F (1991) *Hell's Half Acre: The Life and Legend of a Red-Light District*, Texas Christian University Press.

Siringo, Charles A. (1912) *A Cowboy Detective: True Story of Twenty-Two Years with a World-Famous Detective Agency*, W.B. Conkey.

Siringo, Charles A. (1927) *Riata and Spurs; The Story of a Lifetime Spent in the Saddle as Cowboy and Detective*, Houghton Mifflin.

Smith, Helena Huntington (1966) *War on Powder River*, McGraw-Hill.

Soule, Arthur (1995) *The Tall Texan The Story of Ben Kilpatrick*, Trail Dust Publishing.

Swallow, Alan (1966) *The Wild Bunch*, Sage Books.

Waller, Brown (1968) *Last of the Great Western Train Robbers*, A.S. Barnes & Co.

Warner, Matt (1959) *The Last of the Bandit Riders*, Bonanza Books.

MAGAZINES

Elks Magazine; Frontier Magazine; Frontier Times; Idaho Yesterdays; Journal of the Western Outlaw-Lawman History Association; Old West; The Outlaw Trail Journal; Quarterly of the National Association and Center for Outlaw and Lawman History; Tally Sheet – The English Westerners' Society; True West; Wild West.

NEWSPAPERS

Billings Gazette, June 15 1897
Billings Times, September 30 1897
Buffalo Bulletin, January 18 1900
Carbon County Journal, June 3 1899
Cheyenne Leader, August 31 1900
The Clipper, March 6 1896
The Clipper, August 6 1897
Craig Courier, January 9 1897
Craig Courier, January 16 1897
Daily Pottstown Ledger, August 31 1900
Denver News, March 6 1898
Denver Republican, September 2 1900
Denver Republican, July 4 1901
Fremont Clipper, April 1892
Fremont Clipper, June 23 1893
Idaho Daily Statesman, August 14 1896
Idaho Daily Statesman, July 5 1901
Kaycee Times, March 01 1900
Kaycee Times, September 22 1900
Natrona County Tribune, June 8 1899
New York Times, July 10 1899
Ogden Standard, September 9 & 11, 1896
Pioneer Times, June 29 1897
Rawlins Republican, September 5 1900
Rocky Mountain News, June 27 1889
The Silver State, September 20 1900
Sundance Gazette, March 18 1887
Vernal Express, May 14 1896
Vernal Express, May 28 1896
Vernal Express, September 24 1896
Wyoming State Tribune, June 16 1939
Wyoming State Tribune, July 2 1897
Wyoming State Tribune, February 8 1889
Wyoming State Tribune, September 27 1900

ACKNOWLEDGEMENTS

Two notable past events provided the first vital spark which led eventually to our mammoth project. The first was the brilliant George Roy Hill/William Goldman film *Butch Cassidy and the Sundance Kid* (1969); the second was the *National Geographic Magazine*/Elm Tree Books' handsome photographic record (1975) of Robert Redford's three week ride along part of the Outlaw Trail. Both have continued to inspire us, and we owe them a great debt – especially the Goldman Screenplay, a brief, apt quote from which prefaces (and decorates) our every chapter.

Heartfelt thanks are also due to so many other people and institutions without whom our ride would not have happened, been completed, or been such a rich experience.

To historians past, for precious research on Butch Cassidy, the Sundance Kid and the Wild Bunch, and especially to Charles Kelly, Pearl Baker and James D. Horan.

To historians present, especially Jim Dullenty, for steering us via many key books and manuscripts through the outlaw world; Dan Buck and Anne Meadows for supplying essential contacts along the trail, and much else; Donna Ernst for great research on her uncle, the Sundance Kid; Richard Patterson for his definitive Butch Cassidy biography; also Arthur Soule ('The Tall Texan'); John Eaton & Jo-Ann Palmer (Will Carver); F. Bruce Lamb & Brown Waller (Harvey Logan).

To those who gave vital help prior to as well as during the expedition: the late A.C. Ekker, Glori Ekker; the Dickinson clan: Dick, Polly, T. Wright, Jeanne, Dee-Dee, Marc & Girda; Gene & Sammye Vieh & family; Tom & Jane Klumker & family; Dave & Brenda Rummel; Hugh B. II and Margie McKeen & family, and most especially to Dr Joe and Rusty Armstrong and family, who were so much more than our outfitters.

To Doris Burton for liaising with ranchers around Brown's Park; Mike Bell of Birmingham, for direction in northern Wyoming; Western Outlaw-Lawman History Association (WOLA); National Association and Center for Outlaw/Lawman History (NOLA); Outlaw Trail History Association & Center; English Westerners Society; Larry Walker's Magazine House, La Pine, Oregon.

To the equine explorers who alerted us wisely and kindly to the 'demons' of horseback expeditions: Robin Hanbury-Tenison OBE, Dylan Winter, James Greenwood, Benedict Allen, Johanna Cooke, Jeremy James and John Labouchere.

To Bill Goldman, Robert Redford, Hugh Sidey of *Time Magazine*, Peter Miller of *National Geographic Magazine*, broadcaster Alan Whicker and Paul Morrison of *Wanderlust*, for their good wishes and encouragement. To all those who, in addition to those named above, helped us to keep going during the ride itself:

In Texas: Don Lucero – U.S. Border Patrol, Horse Division.

In New Mexico: Joby Priest, Herb Greathouse, Kent Thomas, Jim Connolly, Wes Dixon; Buck Mullins (farrier); Skip Pritchard (vet); Marvin Tessneer of *Las Cruces Sun*; Henry Elliott & David Jones – Burris Bar on Interstate 10; Brent & Ida Houser; Sonny Diaz; Leonard & Ethel Goad; Jim Hyatt, Sid Savage; the David & Joe Miller families; Oscar & Sue Davis.

In Arizona: Bill & Barbara Marks, Jim Joy (farrier), Dink & Suzanne Robarts, Terry Wagner, Dean Berkey, Joel & Donna Quisenberry, Richard Ayres – High Country Feeds, Rick & Robin Cummings, Reidheads Feed & Corrals, J.R. De Spain, Charlie & Jeanie Clark, Navajo Tribal Police, Navajo Tribal Resource Control, Jerry Tso, Lavern White, Greg Anderson & Steve Donlan – Wupatki National Monument Rangers, Kee & Dewayne Robbins, Jean Seagroves & Mary, George & Belinda Begaye & family, Charlie Dandy, Royce Maloney, David Sharndi, Don Polich, James Cly and Leroy & Tori Teeasayatoh.

In Utah: Dennis Ekker, Suzie Burch, Stormy Red Door; Cynthia Beyer & Gary Cox – Hans Flat BLM, Chris Ramsay; Jay, Joanne & Stephen Ekker; Ted & Iona Ekker; Bruce Nelson, Jim Wilcox, Duane Riches, Kurt Olsen, Gary Dye, Percy Jenks, Joe & Dianne Batty & family, Mr & Mrs Gene Brown, Craig & Beth Kossoff, Ray & Marilyn Hunting, Doris & Troy Burton, Liz King, Stan McMickel, Bob & Lawella Nielson, Steve Wallis of *Vernal Express*.

In Colorado: Bernt Kuhlman; Jack Cox of *Denver Post*.

In Wyoming: John & Debbie Eversole, Ray & Jacci Barber; Leonard & Mary Hay, Steve Green, J.D. & Patti Green, Gary, Lori & Brooke Barney, Rich & Fawn Venzer, Tim & Dawn Thompson, Bill & Fran Thoren, Zane & Ginger Fross, the Sheppersons, Ord & Carol Buckingham, Jim & Carrie Richendifer, Mitch & Jean Johnson, Brock & Paula Hanson, Wally & Sally Ramsbottom, Earl & Barbara Madsen, Glen & Sue Means, Bonnie Osmundsen, the Goodwins, Dr John Wilson (vet) & staff, Steve Kobold (farrier), Robert Waggener of *Buffalo Bulletin*, Steve Miller of *Sheridan Press*, Charlie & Kathy Larsen.

In Montana: Irv & Clara Alderson, Don Bixby, Marilyn Fortune, Robyn Baker, Alane Stabler & families, Bruce & Sandie Lockie; Dr Cal Davidson (vet) & staff – Miles City Veterinary Center, Gary Anderson; Denise Hartse of *Miles City Star*, Grant Miller, Artie & Nancy Larson, Diane Brooks; Jim & Carol Williams; Tom & Nancy Horn, Gus & Karen Glasscock, Bill & Phyllis Brown, Joe Gibson, Chuck Pohney, Ed & Art Rich, Bill & Vicky Harris, K.C., Teri, Bob & Pat Weingart, Per & Winnie Storli, Willie & Cheri Doll, Curtis Star of *Phillips County News*, Nate Murphy – Phillips County Museum; Sonia Young – KMMR Radio, Freddy Messerly, Alan & Connie Wasson and Dave Hirsch.

In England: Mark & Thomas Kempster – CTT Group Ltd, Tunbridge Wells; Nigel Harvey & Ruth Taggart – Ride World Wide; North Tawton, Devon; Hamilton-Barr Insurance; John Farmer – Lloyds of London; Tina Banerjee of *Travel Trade Gazette*; Sharon Casson; Freddie Horton; Patrick Lynn; Mike Easton – Just America (map sponsorship); Peter Faunch – Peter Faunch Design, Crawley (map design); Dave & Chris Newton – Enhanced Images, East Grinstead (slides) and Barry Wilcox – A.C. S., Horley (PC).

To our publisher Dan Hiscocks and Eye Books for going with our story, for Dan's unfailing support and encouragement; and especially to our wise editor Gordon Metcalf, whose enthusiasm for the book, feeling for the subject matter and empathy with the authors would be very hard to match.

Above all, to our patient, loving families, for their strong support before, during and after the long ride, and also the long write which followed. And a special final mention to Greg Bates for refreshing Simon's interest in the American Frontier and sharpening him for this adventure of a lifetime.

eyeSight

Our greatest fear is not that we are inadequate, our greatest fear is that we are powerful beyond measure. By shining your light, you subconsciously give permission to others to shine theirs.
Nelson Mandela

Travel can be a liberating experience, as it was for me in 1990, when I was just one hundred yards from Nelson Mandela as he was released from prison. I watched this monumental occasion from on top of a traffic light, amidst a sea of enthralled onlookers.

This was the 'green light' moment that inspired the creation of Eye Books. From the chaos of that day arose an appreciation of the opportunities that the world around us offers, and the desire within me to shine a light for those whose reaction to opportunity is 'can't and don't'.

Our world has been built on dreams, but the drive is often diluted by the corporate and commercial interests offering to live those dreams for us, through celebrity culture and the increasing mechanisation and automation of our lives. Inspiration comes now from those who live outside our daily routines, from those who *challenge the way we see things*.

Eye Books was born to tell the stories of *'ordinary' people doing 'extraordinary' things*. With no experience of publishing, or the constraints that the book 'industry' imposes, Eye Books created a genre of publishing to champion those who live out their dreams.

Twelve years on, and sixty plus stories later, Eye Books has the same ethos. We believe that ethical publishing matters. It is not about just trying to make a quick hit, it is about publishing the stories that affect our lives and the lives of others positively. We publish the books we believe will shine a light on the lives of some and enlighten the lives of many for years to come.

Join us in the Eye Books community, and share the power these stories evoke.

Dan Hiscocks
Founder and Publisher
Eye Books

www.eye-books.com

eyeCommunity

At Eye Books we are constantly challenging the way we see things and do things. But we cannot do this alone. To that end we have created an online club, a community, where members can inspire and be inspired, share knowledge and exchange ideas. Membership is free, and you can join by visiting www.eye-books.com, where you will be able to find:

What we publish
Books that truly inspire, by people who have given their all, triumphed over adversity, lived their lives to the full. Visit the dedicated microsites we have for each of our books online.

Why we publish
To champion those 'ordinary' people doing extraordinary things. The real celebrities of our world who tell stories that celebrate life to the full, not just for 15 minutes. Books where fact is more compelling than fiction.

How we publish
Eye Books is committed to ethical publishing. Many of our books feature and campaign for various good causes and charities. We try to minimise our carbon footprint in the manufacturing and distribution of our books.

Who we publish
Many, indeed most of our authors have never written a book before. Many start as readers and club members. If you feel strongly that you have a book in you, and it is a book that is experience driven, inspirational and life affirming, visit the 'How to Become an Author' page on our website. We are always open to new authors.

Eye-Books.com Club is an ever-evolving community, as it should be, and benefits from all that our members contribute, with invitations to book launches, signings and author talks, plus special offers and discounts on the books we publish.

Eye Books membership is free, and it's easy to sign up. Visit our website. Registration takes less than a minute.

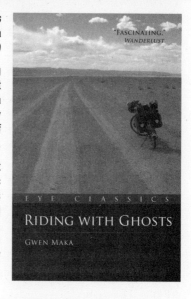

Jasmine & Arnica
Nicola Naylor
£7.99

Nicola Naylor had always been enthralled by India, but her travel fantasies dissolved when she lost her sight. Overcoming her own private fears and disregarding the warnings, Naylor set out to experience India alone.

This is the inspiring account of her unique journey. Told with a vivid and evocative insight, *Jasmine & Arnica* is a story of a young woman's determination, a celebration of the power of vision, beyond sight, to reveal what's closest to the heart, and to uncover life's most precious, unseen joys.

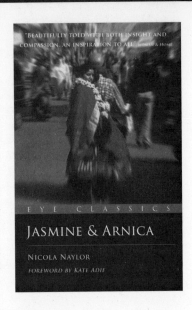

"BEAUTIFULLY TOLD WITH BOTH INSIGHT AND COMPASSION. AN INSPIRATION TO ALL" *Woman & Home*

EYE CLASSICS

JASMINE & ARNICA

NICOLA NAYLOR

FOREWORD BY KATE ADIE

"MESMERISING" *THE SUNDAY TIMES*

EYE CLASSICS

TOUCHING TIBET

NIEMA ASH

FOREWORD BY THE DALAI LAMA

Touching Tibet
Niema Ash
£7.99

Niema Ash was one of the first people to enter Tibet when its borders were briefly opened to Westerners in 1986. In this highly absorbing and personal account, she relates with wit, compassion and sensitivity her encounters with people whose humour, spirituality and sheer enthusiasm for life have carried them through years of oppression and suffering.

Touching Tibet takes the reader on a unique journey into the heart of this intriguing forbidden kingdom.

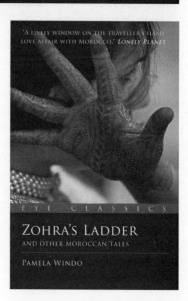

eyeAuthors

Simon Casson

Simon Casson is a freelance sales, business development and marketing professional, who also doubles as a sales and personal development trainer. He is founding partner of Outlaw Trails and a recognized authority on Butch Cassidy and The Sundance Kid.

Simon organizes bespoke horse pack trips, long rides and expeditions in the Americas, for adventure travelers, Old West students, private groups, corporate, charitable fund-raisers and the military. He has ridden deep in Utah's Canyonlands, cowboyed on historic cattle ranges in Brown's Park, Colorado and Hole-in-the-Wall country of Wyoming and tracked Butch & Sundance's Wild Bunch across the Western States of America. Quite possibly no one, since the original bandit riders themselves, has explored the remote outlaw hide-outs and hidden back trails of America's Wild West as extensively as he.

Richard Adamson

Richard Adamson was a former special forces Royal Marine warrant officer with over 20 years' service, who also had a wealth of experience working with humanitarian agencies in Africa. After he left the Armed Forces, Richard owned and operated a centre for leadership, adventure and survival training in Devon, England. One of his disciplines was horse riding and equine management.

Richard worked globally and in the 1990s, he was held hostage in Somalia. He had been working for a cargo company in Hargeysa, when rebels kidnapped him. Up until 2007, he used his great experience in logistics, crisis and disaster management, working for various International corporations, latterly a leading British security company. Sadly, Richard was murdered in a robbery in Kabul, Afghanistan on August 16, 2007.